ATTAINABLE
SUSTAINABLE

Kris Bordessa

ATTAINABLE SUSTAINABLE

THE LOST ART OF SELF-RELIANT LIVING

WASHINGTON, D.C.

CONTENTS

Previous pages: *New seedlings wait to be planted.*
Opposite: *Marshmallows are a campfire staple, but try roasting fruit over open coals for a sweet treat.*

INTRODUCTION

Before the days of pizza delivery, ready-made meals, and self-checkout lines, people were do-it-yourselfers by default. What couldn't be had at the dry goods store was made at home from simple ingredients or materials out of pure necessity: There just wasn't another alternative.

People knew how to make food. They knew how to raise food. They sewed and weaved and brewed. They understood the pull of the seasons, and what those seasons meant for their family.

Times certainly have changed. The dry goods store is now a superstore packed to the rafters with items that Ma Ingalls couldn't have dreamed up. And although there's certainly a place for some of the convenience items we've come to depend on, we as consumers seem to be yearning for simplicity. Canning jars and pectin are once again readily available at many supermarkets, and cast-iron pans and butter churns are making a comeback. In a high-tech, somewhat disconnected society, it seems that handwork and home cooking provide a much needed touchstone.

My own meandering path of simple living has ebbed and flowed through a modern-era landscape. As I was growing up, my mom taught me to make (and preserve) homemade jam that was frequently slathered on slices of Wonder Bread. My parents and grandparents were gardeners, so I learned how to grow vegetables from them. (But I shudder to remember my seven-year-old self in charge of the fun shaker can full of diazinon, an insecticide that was banned for residential use decades later.) While I snacked on miner's lettuce—an edible wild green—after school every spring, at the dinner table we consumed more conventional alternatives like a head of iceberg lettuce. ("Who eats *weeds?*" my mom might have asked.)

My efforts at self-reliant living are founded in the simple fact that I learned to cook (mostly) from scratch at my mother's elbow. I gardened, sewed, camped, used power tools, and preserved food. And although in hindsight the execution appears somewhat flawed, I nevertheless had a base of knowledge to build on as I shifted my lifestyle to include healthier, less toxic options for both my family and the world around us.

I started reading labels in earnest when my children were little; one of my sons was having what the pros might call "behavioral issues." After months of experimenting with his diet, I realized that food dyes in particular were wreaking havoc. If we avoided food with dye, his behavior was that of a normal preschooler—but with it, he became a wild child. These experiments were purely anecdotal, but as they say, the proof is in the pudding. Comparing his behavior with and without food dyes on many occasions, we soon had a very clear visual of how what he ate impacted him.

And I wondered: If food dyes are problematic, what about all those other unpronounceable ingredients in commercially prepared foods? Thus began my swing toward the other end of the pendulum.

Although I'd never ceased my routine of canning seasonal produce, I redoubled my efforts to clean up our diet. Out went the convenient boxes of flavored rice. Bottled salad dressing became a thing of the past. And we switched from yogurt tinted with red dye number 40 to homemade. The toxic cleaners got the boot, too, as we substituted with vinegar.

Dip sprigs of lavender into a jar of honey to infuse with gourmet flavor (recipe on page 229).

As I focused on the quality of our food, I learned more about transgenically modified crops (also known as genetically modified organisms or GMOs). These crops are developed in a laboratory to survive being doused with herbicides so that farmers can easily kill weeds growing in fields of corn or soy. Those same herbicides are sprayed on crops like wheat and oats to hasten the drying process right before harvest. Although these tactics cut labor costs in the field and are touted as safe, I'm not really comfortable with the idea of eating food that's been sprayed with poison.

And then there's the packaging. We're not only talking about Lunchables and ready-to-eat cereal in plastic cups, but also tomatoes sold in plastic clamshells, bananas packaged on plastic-foam trays, and individually plastic-wrapped potatoes. Single-use disposable plastic like this unnecessarily contributes to the waste stream—and oftentimes, we don't even think twice about it because it's become the norm.

Enough of this, I decided.

If only it was that easy. The prevalence of fast-food joints, instant supermarket food, synthetic additives, and of course, packaging, is insidious. Couple that with the fact that we all lead busy lives and time-saving shortcuts can be very appealing, even when we know they're not the most environment-friendly options.

A potent folk remedy to clear the sinuses (see page 132)

The changes came slowly, but they came. I began to notice that improving the quality of our food was not only good for our health, it was also good for our budget. Fewer packaged goods in the shopping cart and food scraps tossed into the compost meant we were making fewer trips to the landfill, too.

I began fermenting; I dabbled with alternative personal care products. Some of the changes stuck—I still make all my salad dressing from scratch; others, like the no-poo system of cleaning my hair, didn't.

Today, I continuously strive to improve the quality of food we consume, as well as my family's ecological footprint. We're a work in progress, and that's okay. Trying to change everything at once would result in burnout (and perhaps mutiny from the other members of my household).

As it turns out, shifting to a predominantly home-cooked lifestyle wasn't hard, because I understood the basics of cooking; it just required breaking habits. Growing more of the produce my family consumed didn't require a whole new skill set, just a larger garden area. Because I had that background, I did not have to learn everything.

Others are not so lucky, however. I hear regularly from readers of the Attainable Sustainable blog who lament the fact that they never learned basic cooking skills. Or how to sew. Or garden. Or use power tools.

The past several decades have really done a number on "normal." We're so accustomed to convenience products and the "faster, better, easier" mentality that the idea of switching to a slower, handmade way of living can seem daunting, no matter how desirable it may be.

Just for reference, here are some things I did not learn while I was growing up:

1. How to raise chickens
2. How to butcher chickens
3. How to make soap
4. How to ferment foods

These things came to me later, one project at a time. And although they're easy for me now, *learning*

Felted soap is a creative project that also makes the bars last longer (see page 94).

was the sticking point—or, more accurately, the *idea* of learning, the effort of trying something new. Whereas cooking from scratch is something I can do by feel, thanks to lessons learned while growing up, these new skills required that I take one step at a time. These were not difficult tasks, though—just unfamiliar. Once I committed to doing it, learning was pretty easy. If you, too, desire a change in your lifestyle, I hope you'll join me in making it happen, one small step at a time from where you are now.

This book offers the basics on a variety of simple living skills that can help you achieve a more self-reliant, hands-on, homemade way of living. Consider these projects an appetizer course: tidbits to pique your interest in tackling certain projects. You'll walk away from each chapter with new skills and knowledge to apply in your own home and garden, opening up a world of opportunities as you build on those lessons. The kimchi recipe on page 37, for instance, is just a starting point. Once you discover how easy (and tasty!) fermented food is, you'll be inspired to use this method for preserving other items as well. Your own fermented sour pickles? Giardiniera? Sauerkraut? That new skill—fermenting—just expanded the possibilities of what you can produce in your kitchen. The six pages in this book about fermenting are a mere overview—but one that I hope will inspire you to experiment a bit. Ditto with sections on quilting, foraging, and beekeeping.

Although it's easy enough for me to give you a recipe for mayonnaise and send you on your way, "how to raise rabbits" really requires more than the scope of this book can cover. For instance, Bill Mollison, father of the permaculture movement, wrote an entire book on this subject, whereas I only have several pages in which to introduce you to this concept. But I hope this broad survey will inspire you to try projects you'll learn to love. If you find yourself enjoying them, dig deeper for more detailed information by seeking out some of the books listed in the resource section.

Making the choice to live a simpler, healthier, more environment-friendly lifestyle in the 21st century requires a certain awareness. But altering our habits slowly makes for change.

One step, one skill at a time, I hope you'll join me in striving for a more connected, DIY lifestyle.

—Kris Bordessa

PART I

INDOORS

EAT | MAKE | CLEAN

• chapter one •
EAT

EAT

We live in a time that allows us to dash to the supermarket for just about anything we might want to eat: ready-made meals, bottles of salad dressing, and precut fruits and vegetables. But this is a new kind of normal.

Not all that long ago, a trip to the store meant stocking up on staples—flour, sugar, rice—to cook meals from scratch. But today, you'll have a more difficult time figuring out the healthy options, and boxed shortcuts have a certain appeal when the workday is done and everyone is hungry. Advertisers, of course, have capitalized on this desire, slapping labels like "natural" and "fresh" on products that still have additives and preservatives for extended shelf life.

There is also the worrisome issue of packaging. A package of ready-to-microwave potatoes promises a cook time of just five minutes. But these magical potatoes come with a disposable plastic tray (plus a cardboard box). Buying potatoes in bulk and carrying them home in a reusable bag eliminates that unnecessary packaging. Sourcing whole food from a farmers market, a butcher, or your own garden is a great way to improve the quality of your food and take control of your kitchen.

Honing your cooking skills will net dividends for the rest of your life. Savoring meals that incorporate your favorite flavors and ingredients and are prepared with your own hands is so much more satisfying than takeout. Breaking bread with a friend becomes more meaningful when it's a homemade loaf fresh out of the oven. Special occasions are much more so when toasted with a cocktail made of fruit from your backyard.

You may not be ready to start churning your own butter—yet! But learning to re-create your favorite foods will get you a little closer to a homemade kitchen, one recipe at a time. Experiment with the offerings here and you'll be serving meals Grandma would be proud of in no time!

• CONTENTS •

Previous pages: *Soft flour tortillas fresh off the skillet (see page 47)*
Opposite: *Fresh-squeezed grapefruit juice (see page 34)*

FOOD PRESERVATION 101

If you grow a large garden, take advantage of local farmers markets, or belong to a community-supported agriculture (CSA) program that delivers produce on a regular basis, you might find yourself with more fresh fruits and vegetables than you know what to do with. Take a cue from the old-timers who "put by" food and preserve the abundance to last through the winter. Although root cellaring and freezing are pretty straightforward, we'll dig deeper into other methods for extending the shelf life of fresh produce in the coming pages.

Root Cellaring

This is really the easiest method of storing food; a cool, dark place is all you need. Root vegetables like potatoes, carrots, beets, and winter squash, along with hard fruit like apples and pears, will keep for months in a root cellar. Generally speaking, fruits and vegetables should be stored in separate containers; most fruits emit ethylene gas, which can hasten ripening (and thus, spoilage) in many vegetables.

Freezing

Another easy method, freezing requires a bit of prep work—slicing vegetables or perhaps blanching them—but little in the way of special equipment. There are a couple of drawbacks to freezing, though. Storing your vegetable harvest in the freezer takes up precious space, and a long-term power outage could mean a fair amount of loss.

Dehydration

If you intend to do a lot of dehydrating, it's probably worth investing in a dehydrator, though you can dry fruits and veggies in the oven or even outside on a hot, dry day. No matter the method you use, once foods are thoroughly dehydrated, they're shelf stable as long as they're stored in airtight containers without any moisture.

Fermentation

Fermenting produce extends the shelf life of food and has the added bonus of probiotics.

Water Bath Canning

Preserving food in jars creates a shelf-stable product that's essentially a stand-in for canned goods you'd purchase at the grocery store. Water bath canning is a safe way to process high-acid foods. Jams, jellies, pickles, many fruits, and most tomato products are all good candidates for this method.

Pressure Canning

Lower-acid foods—vegetables and meats—require a different sort of process to be shelf stable. They are canned under pressure to kill potential botulism spores. Although that may sound scary, pressure canning, done properly, is a safe way to fill your pantry with things like broth, ready-to-eat soup, and beans.

Freeze-Drying

Although commercial processors have been freeze-drying foods for some time, this method has only been introduced on a home scale recently. The process is similar to that of dehydration, but it does require a specialized piece of equipment that is not cheap. A home freeze-dryer would be a great candidate for a co-op or a shared purchase between several like-minded individuals.

Learn the tricks of fermenting, pickling, and canning to make long-lasting food with specialty flavors.

DEHYDRATING

The process of dehydrating removes much of the moisture from produce, making fruits and vegetables more shelf stable. As fruits and vegetables dry, their water content is reduced. This intensifies the flavor and makes them much lighter in weight—and thus perfect snacks for hiking and backpacking. Dehydrated foods take up less storage room than canned goods, making this a good option if you're tight on pantry space.

Dehydrating can be as simple or as elaborate as you like. Setting a bunch of fresh grapes outside in the hot summer air will result in raisins if conditions are right. Regions with hot, dry summer days offer plenty of opportunity for natural dehydration; all it takes is placing sliced fruits or veggies on a clean window screen covered with a light cloth to keep bugs off. In cooler areas or those with humid climates, you'll have better results using your oven on a low setting or investing in an electric dehydrator. These run about a hundred dollars, give or take, depending on size.

Preserving Dehydrated Foods

The most important thing when dehydrating food is to achieve sufficient moisture reduction. If too much moisture remains in dried foods, they'll mold during storage. Fruit dried at home should have a moisture content of about 20 percent.

Due to inconsistent thickness, some pieces of fruit may retain a bit more moisture than others. As a result, moisture levels can vary within a single slice of fruit. Conditioning the dried fruit will help redistribute the moisture evenly. Cool fruit thoroughly and place loosely packed pieces in a large jar. Seal the jar and let stand for a week, shaking it daily to break up the fruit. The excess moisture in some pieces will be reabsorbed by drier pieces. If any condensation appears on the inside of the jar itself, there's still too much moisture in the fruit. Return it to the dehydrator to remove more moisture.

Unlike fruit, vegetables should be dehydrated to the point of being crisp or crunchy.

Store dried foods in a cool, dark place in airtight containers.

RECIPE

Chewy Dried Bananas

Makes 4 cups dried bananas

When fresh bananas are on discount because they've started to get spotty, pick them up for a song and dehydrate them so they'll be shelf stable; people will clamor for these healthy, chewy banana chips. This recipe calls for five pounds of ripe but firm bananas (mushy ones are better for banana bread), but you can easily scale the recipe up or down. Stored in a sealed container at room temperature, they'll keep for months.

You'll Need:
5 pounds ripe but firm bananas, sliced ¼ inch thick
½ cup fresh lemon juice
Special equipment: dehydrator

1. Place the banana slices and lemon juice into a baking pan. Gently turn the banana slices in the juice to coat.
2. Spread the banana slices on dehydrator trays in one layer, touching slightly if at all.
3. Dehydrate at 135°F until dry to the touch but pliable, 8 to 10 hours, depending on humidity and the dehydrator; plan to be around to check them during those last couple hours.

RECIPE

Beef Jerky

Makes about 1 pound

Packaged beef jerky will set you back about $16 a pound for a budget brand; organic and gourmet options can cost double that. Save your hard-earned cash and make

Bananas processed in a dehydrator result in a soft, chewy snack.

your own protein-packed on-the-go snack. You'll find that slicing beef extra-thin is easier if you place it in the freezer for 15 to 20 minutes beforehand. Or save time and ask the butcher to slice it for you.

NOTE: This recipe requires the beef to marinate for eight hours or overnight before dehydrating it. Store beef jerky in a sealed container for three or more months.

You'll Need:
½ cup soy sauce
½ cup Worcestershire sauce
1 garlic clove, crushed
1 teaspoon onion salt
1 teaspoon black pepper
2 pounds lean round or flank steak, sliced as thin as possible
Special equipment: dehydrator

Perfect for road trips or backpacking, beef jerky is easy (and less expensive!) to make at home.

1. In a bowl, mix together the soy sauce, Worcestershire sauce, garlic, onion salt, and pepper.
2. Add the beef and toss to thoroughly coat with the marinade.
3. Cover and refrigerate for 8 hours or overnight.
4. Drain the beef in a colander.
5. Arrange the beef strips on dehydrator trays so that they're close but not touching.
6. Dehydrate at 160°F until dry but still pliable, 5 to 8 hours depending on the thickness of the slices and your dehydrator.

DIY

Moisture Absorbers

Store-bought foods that need to stay dry sometimes come with little desiccant packets. You can make your own to help extend the shelf life of dried foods (and stored grains). Best of all, these desiccant packs are reusable. Dust off the fabric and place them in an oven set to low (250°F) for four to five hours and they'll be good as new.

You'll Need:
Cotton fabric, 4 × 24-inch
About 1 cup silica gel beads
Pinking shears
Wooden chopsticks (don't break them apart)
Sewing machine

1. Fold fabric in half lengthwise, wrong sides together. Using a basic straight stitch, sew up the long side and across one end. You now have a long, skinny tube with a closed end.
2. Spoon one tablespoon full of silica gel beads into the tube. Hold the tube upright so the beads fall to the bottom. Use the chopsticks as a clamp of sorts, sliding them down the tube to hold the beads in place. Sew across the tube near the chopsticks.
3. Sew a second seam across the tube about ¾ inch from the previous seam. The two seams you made will keep the beads secure and start a new "pocket."
4. Spoon another tablespoon of beads into the tube. Again, use the chopsticks to hold the beads in place, and sew as above.
5. Continue in this manner, adding beads and double seams, until you reach the end of the tube.
6. Use pinking shears to cut between each double set of seams. This will create about 12 individual desiccant packs.
7. Trim all sewn edges with pinking shears to reduce fraying.
8. Place your homemade desiccant packs in containers of dry goods to absorb wayward moisture.

Dehydrated Vegetables

If your garden is churning out piles of fresh vegetables, it's a perfect time to preserve the bounty. As garden vegetables ripen, slice and dry them at 135°F for 8 to 10 hours or until crispy. This will vary based on their moisture content and size; if you dry several kinds of veggies at once, some may be done before others.

Dried vegetables make healthy chips for snacking (sprinkle a little salt on them if you like) and can be used in a variety of ways in your kitchen. Grind them up in a blender to make a vegetable powder that can be added to smoothies or gravy. Chop them roughly and mix them into meat loaf.

A medley of dehydrated veggies makes an easy vegetable soup starter. Fill a quart-size jar with a variety of soup vegetables such as potatoes, tomatoes, zucchini, carrots, celery, and onions. This dehydrated mix will help you get dinner on the table in no time. It's also great to take camping. One jar of dried vegetables is sufficient for about a gallon of liquid. The dried vegetables will absorb liquid and rehydrate. It might not look like enough when you first add them, but they'll grow in size as the soup simmers.

Sweltering Summer?

Believe it or not, your car or truck can be an excellent stand-in for a dehydrator.

It's a bit unconventional, but it works: The heat that accumulates inside a closed vehicle on a hot day will dry your produce in no time. Cover a cookie sheet with a kitchen towel and place sliced fruits and vegetables close together on the tray. Place the trays inside your vehicle and close the windows and doors. Check the trays every couple of hours, turning the sliced produce each time. Because the temperature inside the car will vary, it's hard to say exactly how long the drying process will take with this method.

DRYING HERBS

It's easy enough to grab dried herbs off the spice rack at the supermarket, but drying your own at home has a number of benefits. Of course, you'll avoid buying one more jar that will end up in the recycle can. But herbs dried fresh from your yard or garden will cost less, taste better, and give you bragging rights. The time it takes for herbs to dry will depend entirely on the temperature, humidity, and method used. Once leaves are crispy, rub them between your fingers to remove the stems. Store dried herbs in an airtight container.

Air-Drying

Herbs hanging from rafters to dry evoke a simpler time, don't they? And truthfully, if you've got the right space for it, that's still one of the easiest methods. Simply cut stems of herbs and bundle them together using a twist tie or rubber band. If you're concerned about dust, you can wrap the bundles loosely with muslin to keep off the dust, though it's not necessary.

Hang bundles in a warm, dry space that gets plenty of airflow. Use an S hook to hang herbs on a pretty shelf or if you're lucky enough to have high rafters, string them up there until they're thoroughly dried. Because heat rises, the air is warmer near the ceiling and will help speed drying.

Outdoor Sun Drying

You can use the heat of the sun to dry herbs, too. Create an inexpensive drying rack at home using an upcycled picture frame from a thrift store. Cut window screen material so it's just a bit larger than the frame and attach using a staple gun. Set the rack on blocks so air will flow all around the herbs. In a pinch, you could even borrow a window screen from an unused window of your house. Avoid setting the herbs in the direct sun.

When to Harvest

Harvesting herbs at the right time ensures superior flavor. The best time to harvest herbs is in the cool morning, just after the dew has evaporated. Look for stems that have plump flower buds that have yet to open.

Dry fresh herbs for a flavorful pantry.

Oven Drying

To dry herbs in your oven, place leaves and stems on a cookie sheet in a single layer. Turn the oven on low, and prop open the oven door. Temperature capabilities vary by oven manufacturer. If yours is a newer oven with a bread proofing setting, use that; otherwise, aim for a temperature no higher than 180°F. It will take two to four hours for herbs to completely dry.

Dehydrating

Although you don't need anything fancy to dry most herbs, those with a high moisture content like basil, mint, oregano, and tarragon will mold if the drying process takes too long. If you're concerned about it, a food dehydrator offers a more controlled environment.

Hanging bundles of herbs where they receive plenty of airflow is an easy way to preserve them (plus, it's pretty!).

CANNING AT HOME

A pantry lined with shiny jars full of golden peaches, bright red strawberry jam, and pickled goodness offers an incredible sense of accomplishment for home canners—and that burst of summertime flavor in the dead of winter is priceless. Home canning is the most time-intensive method for preserving food, but quite possibly the most rewarding. There's nothing like the *tink!* of a jar lid as it successfully seals!

The Science of Canning Safety

Canning preserves food by removing oxygen, destroying the enzymes normally present in fresh food, and preventing growth of bacteria, yeast, and mold. The vacuum seal created by processing foods keeps food isolated from contamination. Producing safe, shelf-stable food at home is a skill that's within reach if you follow simple instructions. It's important to keep your cooking utensils and hands clean to avoid contaminating ingredients. And it's really important that low-acid items such as meat or vegetables are processed with a pressure canner. *Clostridium botulinum* spores, also known as botulism, can survive a water bath process and can grow inside sealed jars of low-acid foods. This rare and severe form of food poisoning can be fatal. Don't let that scare you off, though; I've been canning my own food safely for years. As long as you use proper canning methods, equipment, and processing times, you'll have a finished product worthy of a state fair blue ribbon (or at the very least, one that won't make you sick).

Canning Jars

One thing is crucial in canning: It needs to be done in specialized jars. Canning jars come in a variety of sizes and can have wide or narrow mouths. Once you've made the initial investment, you'll be able to store food in those same jars for years and years. Canning jars are generally embossed with a brand name (for example, Ball or Kerr) and are easily recognizable. Although they're not a huge expense new, you can often find them at garage sales for a less expensive way to get started.

Canning at Altitude

If you live above an altitude of 1,000 feet, you'll need to adjust the cooking time and/or pressure accordingly. Check with your local county extension agent for details on canning in your region.

A rack prevents jars from rattling together during processing.

Canning jars are sealed with a two-part system that consists of a flat lid (called "flats") and a ring or band that holds the flat in place during processing. Like the jars, rings can be reused repeatedly, though you'll want to replace them if they begin to rust. Flats though, cannot be reused for sterile canning purposes. They have a sealing compound on the perim-

With its nonslip coating, a jar lifter makes it easy to remove hot containers from a water bath canner.

eter of one side. Positioned to sit atop a jar's rim and secured in place with a ring, the flat is what actually seals the jar as it's processed.

Sterilizing Canning Jars

Start with sterilized jars for any product that will be processed for less than 10 minutes in a water bath canner (see the following). Products with a longer processing time or those that are pressure-canned do not need to be put in sterilized jars; just wash them thoroughly. To sterilize, put empty jars on the rack in your water bath canner. Fill canner with hot water to an inch above the jar rims. Heat to a boil. Boil for 10 minutes, plus an additional minute for every thousand feet elevation above a thousand. Remove, drain, and fill jars one at a time.

Water Bath Canning

Specialized water bath canners are large pots that come with a wire rack to keep jars from rattling together. A standard water bath canner holds seven jars at a time.

Fresh grapes create a flavorful juice—perfect for making homemade jelly.

1. Fill canner with enough water that jars will be covered by 1 to 2 inches of water. How much water is required will vary depending on the size of your jars.
2. Bring water to a boil.
3. Heat water to 140°F for raw-packed foods or 180°F for hot-packed foods.
4. Use a jar lifter to place full jars in the water. Cover and bring water to a full boil over high heat.
5. Start timing when the water begins to boil.
6. Once processing time has elapsed, turn off heat and remove jars, placing them on a towel-covered surface. Allow jars to cool.
7. Check for a seal: The flat should feel solid and a bit indented. If it flexes, the product is not shelf stable. Store it in the refrigerator and use it soon.
8. Remove bands from sealed jars and wash the outside of the jars before storing.

Pressure Canning

Like water bath canning, this method requires heating jars in water. Pressure canning essentially creates superheated water, with temperatures reaching substantially higher than the 212°F achieved by simply boiling water. A specialized pressure canner is required; these come in a variety of makes and models. (All-American is the best of the best, but Presto makes a good product as well.) This is the only safe way to can vegetables, meats, and other low-acid foods.

To process jars in a pressure canner:

1. Add about 3 inches of hot water to the canner.
2. Lift filled jars onto the rack.
3. Fasten the canner lid securely and heat on high with vent open, watching for steam to escape.
4. Let steam escape for 10 minutes, then close vent, allowing canner to begin pressurizing.
5. Start timing when the dial indicates that the desired pressure has been reached. Maintain steady pressure for the recommended amount of time.
6. If pressure drops below the recommended amount at any time, return the canner to pressure and start the timing process over.

Venting Pressure

Pressure canners vent steam in a couple different ways. Some have a small valve called a petcock. Others use a weighted gauge. Read the manufacturer's instructions to familiarize yourself with how your model works.

7. When time is up, allow the canner to depressurize naturally, then open the vent.
8. Wait 10 minutes, remove the lid, and lift jars onto a towel-covered surface to cool.

RECIPE

Grape Jelly

Makes 4 to 5 pints

When I was a girl, a family friend invited my mom to harvest grapes from her yard. I still remember the intoxicating aroma of the ripe Concord grapes hanging from that arbor.

If you're lucky enough to know someone with an abundance of grapes—or if you're growing your own—you can juice them as discussed on page 34. You can also use 100 percent grape juice from the store. It's a shortcut that will net jelly without the added high-fructose corn syrup in most processed jams and jellies. Store sealed jars of jelly at room temperature for up to two years; refrigerate upon opening.

You'll Need:
1 box Pomona's Universal Pectin
4 cups grape juice
¼ cup lemon juice
½ to 1 cup honey
Special equipment: 4 to 5 pint-size jars, water bath canner

1. Prepare the calcium water: Put ½ teaspoon of the calcium powder (the small packet) from Pomona's Universal Pectin package and ½ cup water in a small jar with a lid. Shake well before using.
2. In a large stockpot, combine the grape juice, lemon juice, and 4 teaspoons of the calcium water. (Refrigerate the remaining calcium water for a future batch of jelly.)
3. In a small bowl, combine the honey and 4 teaspoons Pomona's Universal Pectin.
4. Bring the pot of fruit juice to a boil over high heat, stirring frequently. Add the honey mixture

and stir vigorously to dissolve the pectin. Return the juice mixture to a boil, then remove it from the heat.

5. Ladle the hot mixture into the jars to within ¼ inch of the rim. Wipe the rims clean with a damp cloth. Set the flats in place on the jars and add the rings. Use your fingertips to screw each ring on firmly tight—but not too tight.
6. Process in a water bath canner for 10 minutes.

RECIPE

Chow Chow (Green Tomato Relish)

Makes 10 pints

This piquant relish recipe adapted from the *Ball Complete Book of Home Preserving* is a bit old-fashioned; I remember helping my mom make it when I was growing up. We used a hand-crank grinder, though. Spread chow chow on sandwiches or serve it with roasted meats. Sealed jars will keep at room temperature for up to two years; refrigerate upon opening.

You'll Need:
12 pounds green tomatoes
8 large yellow onions
10 green bell peppers
6 hot peppers
3 tablespoons salt
1 quart apple cider vinegar
3 tablespoons dry mustard
1¾ cups sugar
Special equipment: 10 pint-size canning jars, water bath canner

1. In a food processor, working in batches, pulse the tomatoes, onions, bell peppers, and hot peppers into ⅛- to ¼-inch dice (or cut them by hand).
2. Combine the diced vegetables in a large bowl, sprinkle with salt, cover with a loose towel or lid, and refrigerate overnight.
3. Drain off the liquid from the bowl, then transfer the vegetables to a large stockpot. Stir in vinegar, mustard, and sugar.
4. Bring to a slow boil over medium-high heat, then turn down the heat and simmer until the vegetables are tender, about 15 minutes.
5. Ladle the hot relish into pint-size canning jars. Set the flats in place on the jars and add the rings. Use your fingertips to screw each ring on firmly tight, but not too tight.
6. Process in a water bath canner for 10 minutes.

RECIPE

Salsa

Makes 7 to 9 pints

I've experimented with salsa recipes a lot, and this continues to be a family favorite. We enjoy this salsa with chips, of course, but if I have an abundance of jars in the pantry, I use it as an ingredient in making homemade chili and soup. Store sealed jars at room temperature for up to two years; refrigerate upon opening.

You'll Need:
14 cups chopped tomatoes
3 large red or yellow onions, chopped
6 jalapeño peppers, diced and seeds removed (use gloves)
4 banana peppers or other mild pepper, diced and seeds removed
4 garlic cloves
2 cups fresh lemon juice
1 tablespoon salt
1 tablespoon sugar
1 teaspoon black pepper
Optional, for thicker salsa: 1 to 2 (12-ounce) jars tomato paste
Special equipment: 7 to 9 pint-size canning jars, water bath canner

1. If the tomatoes are extra juicy, drain off some juice until they're the texture you want your salsa to be; the juiciness going in the pot is the same as what will end up in the jar.
2. Combine all ingredients in a large stockpot. Bring the mixture to a boil over high heat, reduce heat, and let simmer for 30 minutes, stirring occasionally.
3. Ladle the hot salsa into 7 to 9 jars, depending on how much salsa you have, leaving a ½-inch headspace.
4. Set the flats in place on the jars and add the rings. Use your fingertips to screw each ring on firmly tight—but not too tight.
5. Process in a water bath canner for 15 minutes.

Soup Broth

Canned broth at the supermarket is expensive, but it's a valuable ingredient to have on hand for cooking. Making broth at home is like finding free food. Instead of tossing the bones from a roasted turkey or chicken, you can use them to make a rich broth. For beef broth, I roast soup bones in the oven first for a richer flavor.

A slow cooker is a great tool for making broth, but you can also make this on the stove top. It's simple, either way. Put the roasted bones or carcass into a pot. Cover with water and cook on low for 24 to 48 hours. Strain broth and add salt, if desired.

To process broth:

1. Ladle hot broth into jars, leaving a one-inch headspace.
2. Wipe the rims with a damp cloth, set flats in place on the jars and add rings. Use your finger-tips to screw the rings on firmly tight—but not too tight.
3. Process in a pressure canner using 10 pounds of pressure. If you're using pint-size canning jars, process for 20 minutes. For quarts, process for 25 minutes.

Processing homemade broth in a pressure canner results in a shelf-stable product ready for use in your favorite recipes.

PICKLING

Pickles are vegetables and fruits (and sometimes eggs or meat!) that have been preserved by immersing them in a vinegar brine. Pickling whole or sliced veggies imparts a tangy, sour flavor and is another great way to preserve the garden harvest. We're not talking just cucumbers, though. Vegetables like okra, zucchini, carrots, onions, cauliflower, and green beans are all fair game, but you can expand on those by diving into pickling fruits, too. Pineapple, watermelon rind, peaches, and pears all respond well to pickling.

Using a water bath process (see pages 25–27) creates shelf-stable pickles that you can tuck into the pantry. If you don't want to bother with those extra steps, refrigerator pickles might be the answer. Covered with an acidic vinegar brine, vegetables will keep for months (and months) in cold storage. Another reason to love refrigerator pickles? They're easy to make in small batches as your garden vegetables ripen.

RECIPE

Refrigerator Bread and Butter Pickles

Makes 2 quarts

If you find yourself with an abundance of cucumbers, make pickles! They're easy to make, and their sweet tang is great on sandwiches or in potato salad. Homemade pickles in their juices can be stored in the fridge for six months or more.

You'll Need:

6 cups sliced cucumber rounds
2 cups thinly sliced white onions
2 tablespoons salt
2 cups sugar
1 cup apple cider vinegar
1 teaspoon celery seed
1 teaspoon mustard seed
½ teaspoon ground turmeric

1. Combine the cucumber, onion, and salt in a large bowl. Cover completely with cold water and let sit for 3 to 6 hours at room temperature.
2. Drain the cucumbers and divide them between 2 quart-size jars with lids.
3. In a saucepan, combine the sugar, vinegar, celery seed, mustard seed, and turmeric, then simmer over medium heat, stirring occasionally, until the sugar dissolves. Let the mixture cool to lukewarm, then pour it over the cucumbers to fully submerge them.
4. Seal the jars tightly with lids. Refrigerate for 2 to 3 weeks before sampling.

Pickle Me This

A crunchy pickle is a sure way to perk up a simple sandwich or add zing to a potato salad—but what flavor will you choose?

Dill: These pickles can be made with a vinegar brine or fermented, but the prominent dill flavor is their trademark.

Sour/half sour: Submerged in a salt brine instead of vinegar, these pickles are only partially fermented and somewhat mild. They're sometimes referred to as "new dills."

Sweet or candied: Packed in a heavy syrup or brine, the sugar to vinegar ratio is about 2:1. These are pickles for those with a sweet tooth.

Bread and butter: These sweet and sour pickles are flavored with mustard seeds and turmeric, giving the finished product a slightly yellow color.

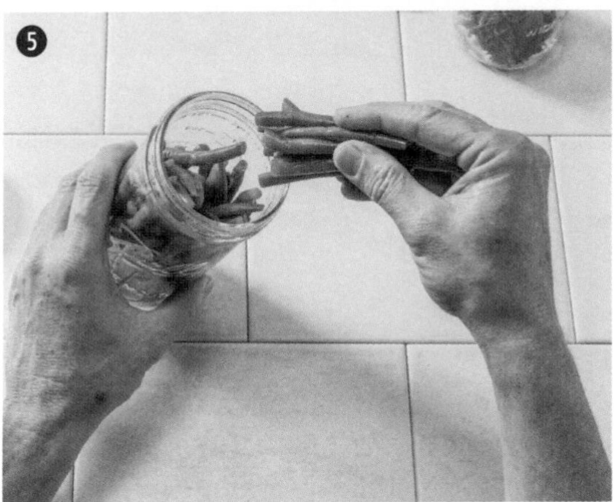

RECIPE

Dilly Green Beans

Makes 2 to 3 pints

Adapted from a recipe I found many years ago in *Kids and Grandparents: An Activity Book,* these crunchy pickled green beans have a bit of a kick to them. They're great for snacking or adding to Bloody Mary cocktails. You'll need two or three pint-size jars, depending on how tightly you pack the beans. Store unopened pickled green beans in the refrigerator; they'll last six months or more.

You'll Need:

3 pounds green beans, ends trimmed
1 cup chopped fresh dill
4 garlic cloves, sliced
3 whole jalapeño peppers
2 cups white wine vinegar
4 teaspoons sugar
2 tablespoons salt

1. Bring a large pot of water to boil.
2. Add the green beans and boil until crisp but tender, 8 to 10 minutes. Meanwhile, fill a large bowl with ice water.
3. Drain the beans, then immediately submerge in ice water to halt the cooking process.
4. Divide the dill, garlic, and jalapeño peppers between the jars.
5. Pack the beans into the jars, holding the jars at an angle so you can stack them as you fill. When the jars are full, squeeze in more beans until they're fairly tightly packed.
6. In a medium saucepan, combine the white wine vinegar, sugar, salt, and 2 cups water; bring to a boil over high heat, stirring occasionally.
7. Remove the pan from the heat, then pour the hot liquid over the beans into the jars, ensuring the beans are completely submerged.

8. Slide a butter knife between the packed beans and the side of the jar to release any air bubbles trapped between the beans.
9. Seal the jars with the lids, then refrigerate for at least a week before serving.

RECIPE

Easy Pickled Veggies

Makes 2 quarts

Use whatever fresh, unblemished vegetables you have on hand for these perky pickled veggies. Carrots, cauliflower, green beans, and sweet peppers are a good start. If you like a bit of kick, add a whole hot pepper to each jar. This recipe calls for two quart-size jars, but you can use four pint-size jars or any other similar-size, tightly sealing jars. Refrigerated pickled veggies will keep for six months or more.

You'll Need:
2 tablespoons black peppercorns
6 to 8 garlic cloves, smashed
2 tablespoons pickling spice (available at well-stocked grocers)
8 to 10 cups raw vegetables, washed then sliced or chopped into similar-size pieces
2 cups apple cider vinegar
2 tablespoons salt
2 tablespoons sugar

1. Divide the peppercorns, garlic, and pickling spice between 2 quart-size jars.
2. Fill the jars with the vegetables.
3. In a saucepan, combine the vinegar, salt, and sugar with 2 cups water. Bring to a boil, lower the heat, and let simmer for 5 minutes.
4. Pour the hot liquid into the jars, covering the vegetables completely.
5. Seal the jars with their lids, then let cool to room temperature.
6. Store in the refrigerator for a week before sampling.

A Note on Jars

When making refrigerator pickles, you're not processing the jars in hot water or trying to create a fully sealed product, so any jar with a good lid will work. And when trying to pack vegetables snugly—as in the case of the dilly green beans—a wide-mouth jar is easier to work with.

RECIPE

Watermelon Rind Pickles

Makes 6 pints

My *Ball Blue Book Guide to Preserving* is tattered and stained from years of use. This recipe is adapted from that well-worn guide and is an excellent example of "waste not"; these sweet-and-sour pickles divert watermelon rinds from the compost pile. Serve them as a side dish or make a unique appetizer by wrapping them in bacon and baking them on a rimmed baking sheet at 400°F until the bacon is crispy. Store sealed jars of watermelon rind pickles at room temperature for up to two years; refrigerate upon opening.

You'll Need:
Rind of 1 large watermelon
1 cup salt
4 teaspoons whole cloves
15 cinnamon sticks
1 tablespoon mustard seed
8 cups sugar
4 cups apple cider vinegar
Special equipment: cheesecloth and butcher's twine or 1 spice bag, canning funnel, water bath canner

1. Remove and discard all pink and green parts from the watermelon rind.
2. Cut the remaining white part of the rind into 1-inch pieces.
3. In a very large bowl, combine 1 gallon water with the salt, stirring to dissolve. Add the rind, then let soak overnight.
4. Fill a water bath canner and bring to a boil while completing the next steps.
5. Drain the watermelon, transfer it to a large stockpot, top it with enough water to cover, then bring to a boil over medium-high heat. Reduce the heat and let simmer until the watermelon rinds are almost tender, 30 to 40 minutes. Drain.
6. Place the cloves, cinnamon, and mustard seed into the center of the cheesecloth; tie it tightly into a sachet with the twine. Add the sachet to the now empty stockpot along with the sugar and vinegar.

7. Bring the vinegar mixture to a boil over high heat. Turn down the heat and let simmer for 15 minutes. Add the watermelon rinds, raise the heat, bring the mixture to a boil, and cook until the rinds are transparent, about 20 minutes.
8. Using a canning funnel, transfer the hot rinds into the canning jars. Ladle the hot pickling liquid into jars to cover the rinds within ½ inch of the top.
9. Wipe the jar rims with a damp cloth, set the flats in place on the jars and add the rings. Use your fingertips to screw the rings on firmly tight, but not too tight.
10. Process the jars in a water bath canner as described on pages 25–27 for 10 minutes.

RECIPE

Pickled Ginger

Makes about 1 pint

If you're a sushi fan, you're probably familiar with the paper-thin pickled ginger slices served as a condiment. But you might not realize how easy they are to make at home for use as a condiment or marinade addition. This recipe calls for a pint-size jar, but any small, tightly sealing container will do. Store pickled ginger in the refrigerator for up to six months.

You'll Need:

½ pound fresh, peeled ginger, sliced as thin as possible, preferably with a mandoline slicer
1 cup rice vinegar
¼ cup sugar
1 teaspoon salt

1. In a saucepan, bring 1 quart of water to boil. Add the ginger. Cook until just tender, 2 to 3 minutes, depending on the thickness of the ginger slices.
2. Drain the ginger well; let cool.
3. Place the ginger in a pint-size jar.
4. In a saucepan, combine the vinegar, sugar, and salt, and bring to a boil.
5. Pour the hot liquid over the ginger in the jar.
6. Seal the jar with its lid, then invert several times to mix.
7. Refrigerate for 3 days before eating.

Make zingy pickled ginger at home for a dye-free version of this sushi staple.

EXTRACTING FRUIT JUICE

Mechanical juicers grind fruits and vegetables, separating the solids from the liquid. A juicer like this can make quick work of fresh summertime fruits, transforming them into pure fruit juice in a hurry. The juice that comes from a mechanical juicer like this is raw juice. If you've ever seen an apple cider press in action, it also creates raw juice by grinding the fruit and pressing the juice from the solids.

There are other ways to extract juice from fruit, and not all require special equipment. The following methods all use heat to soften the fruit and help extract the juice more easily. What remains—the peels and seeds—can be tossed into the compost pile.

Manual Extraction

With this method, you'll fill a stockpot with fruit and cook it until the fruit is soft (see chart). Once the fruit is cooked, you can strain the juice in a couple ways. The least expensive and most rudimentary uses gravity and the weight of the fruit itself:

1. Line a bowl with several layers of cheesecloth or a thin flour sack towel.
2. Pour cooked fruit into the bowl, and gather the towel or cheesecloth above the fruit.
3. Tie securely with kitchen twine and suspend this bag of cooked fruit over the bowl.

The hardest part with this method is often finding a reasonable place to hang the bag. A sturdy cupboard handle or hook will work, but what's available will depend upon your kitchen.

Another way to manually extract juice is with a sieve. You can pour cooked fruit into a standard kitchen sieve and let the juice drain off, or you can use a special cone-shaped sieve meant for just this sort of thing. These come with a specially shaped wooden pestle to help press the juice through its tiny holes.

Preparing Fruit for Manual Extraction and Preservation

Fruit	Size	Water	Cook	Processing time for juice
Apples	Cut into quarters	Barely cover with water	20–25 minutes	5 minutes
Apricots	Halve	3 cups fruit to 2 cups water	Heat to simmer	15 minutes
Blackberries	Whole	No cooking required	Mash clean fruit	5 minutes
Grapes	Whole (remove from stem)	Barely cover with water	Heat to simmer	5 minutes
Grapefruit	Halve	No cooking required	Ream juice from fruit	10 minutes
Peaches	Crushed fruit	Equal parts water and fruit	Heat to simmer	15 minutes
Plums	Whole	1 inch in pan	10 minutes	5 minutes
Tomatoes	Small pieces	No water	Simmer until soft	35 minutes/pints, 40 minutes/quarts

Hanging fruit in layers of cheesecloth allows gravity to do most of the extraction work for you.

Steam Extractor

Another specialized piece of equipment, a three-tiered steam extractor, is a worthwhile investment if you harvest bushels of fresh fruit every summer. (They're available online for less than a hundred bucks.) The bottom is a large pot that's filled with water. The top tier is a strainer, much like a colander. This is where the fruit goes. The middle tier is the juice collector. It's solid except for a raised hole that allows the steam from the lower tier to move up to the top tier. (It looks a bit like a Bundt pan.) As the steam softens the fruit, the juice drains through the holes and into the juice collector. The juice-collecting tier is equipped with a drain tube for collecting the juice while it's cooking.

Preserving Fruit Juice

Extracted fruit juice is tasty; fresh out of the fridge, it will last about a week. If you want it to last longer, process it in a water bath canner to create a shelf-stable juice that can replace store-bought jugs. It can also be boiled down to make jelly. See page 24 for more on canning.

FERMENTATION

People have been using fermentation to preserve or improve food for thousands of years. A metabolic process requiring an absence of oxygen, fermentation produces organic acids (commonly lactic acid), gases, or alcohol. I've incorporated it into my repertoire for another reason: probiotics. These live microorganisms develop readily in fermented foods and have been shown to improve gut flora and digestion.

Sauerkraut and kefir are two familiar ferments, but fermentation offers so many possibilities that the art of this method is experiencing a revival. Microbreweries offer a modern spin on ale making that dates to the Middle Ages. Probiotic-rich, fizzy kombucha sits alongside sodas in refrigerated sections at the supermarket. And producers of small-batch ferments are becoming a common sight at many farmers markets.

Understanding Fermentation

Vegetables, grains, and raw dairy products are home to beneficial organisms in their natural state. Providing conditions in which these bacteria flourish causes them to multiply, producing lactic acid. This process of lacto-fermentation extends the shelf life of fresh foods and also adds enzymes, vitamins, and probiotics to the final product.

If you've spent any time at all in the kitchen, you know that leaving perishable foods out on the counter will eventually result in rotting food. Although you do leave foods at room temperature when fermenting, providing certain conditions prevents that decomposition and instead preserves the food.

French chemist Louis Pasteur described fermentation as respiration without air. An anaerobic environment is required when preserving most vegetables. This means that the vegetables cannot be exposed to oxygen; make sure the vegetables are entirely covered with a saltwater brine. Use a weight to hold the vegetables under the liquid, ensuring they won't be in contact with air. Under these conditions, lactic acid grows quickly, decreasing the pH to a point at which competing organisms cannot grow.

Get the Lingo

The science behind fermentation and the action of enzymes is known as zymology.

Good Ferments Gone Bad

By providing ideal fermentation conditions, you set nature up to do the work of preserving for you. But the results may look a bit different than the pickled products with which you're familiar.

It's rare that a ferment needs to be tossed. The few times I've experienced problems have been when the contents became exposed to air, due to loss of brine. Bubbly, active ferments can overflow—that's normal!—but if too much is lost, you need to replace some of the liquid so the vegetables remain submerged. At some point, you may see a thin layer of white yeast on top of the liquid. That's normal; simply scrape it off.

You should make a few observations before you serve your homemade kraut. Although white yeast is normal, if the layer of yeast sitting on the surface is more colorful—green, pink, yellow, or blue—toss it into the compost bucket.

Looks good? Give the jar a sniff. A successful ferment has a pleasant sour or yeasty odor. If your jar of vegetables looks and smells good, try a little nibble. A strong taste is okay. The flavor of a ferment will change some as time passes, but it should never taste objectionable.

Placing a fermented food product in the refrigerator drastically slows the fermentation process. Refrigeration, however, is not necessary. Most ferments can last as long as a year stored in a cool, dry pantry or cellar.

Top a rice bowl with crunchy kimchi—or add it to a Reuben or grilled cheese for a sandwich with a twist.

What You Need for Fermentation

A lot of tools are on the market for use in fermentation. Many are useful, but not at all mandatory. Glass weights are helpful in holding ingredients below the liquid, but some people make their own by simply filling a plastic bag with water and settling that on top of the liquid. Air locks seal jars while allowing gases to release as food ferments. If you don't have an air lock, you'll need to open the lid of your ferment daily to release the pressure that builds up, or else you might wind up with fermenting liquid all over your floor.

Ancestral Fermentation

The current popularity of fermenting foods and beverages has roots that trace back thousands of years. Kombucha seems to have originated in China, then spread along the famed Silk Road. Kefir made its entrance onto the world stage in the late 19th century from the Caucasus Mountains. It's hard to pinpoint who we can thank for the invention of beer, but it's likely that fermented, beerlike beverages developed alongside the early production of cereal crops.

RECIPE

Kimchi

Makes 6 to 8 cups

Kimchi is a traditional Korean side dish commonly made with napa cabbage and daikon radish, but there are countless variations. My garden-fresh version isn't authentic, but it is spicy, crunchy, and a great introduction to fermenting at home. You'll need a half-gallon jar or other large tight-sealing container for this recipe. Store kimchi in the refrigerator for up to three months.

You'll Need:

- 1 head napa cabbage
- 3 small bunches (about 4 cups) bok choy, coarsely chopped
- 3 green onions, sliced
- 1 cup shredded daikon radish
- 1 cup carrots, thinly sliced or shredded
- 1½ tablespoons sea salt
- 10 garlic cloves, minced
- 1 (1-inch) piece fresh ginger, peeled and minced
- 1 to 2 tablespoons red pepper flakes, depending on spice preference

Special equipment: 1 glass fermenting weight

1. Reserve one outer leaf of the cabbage, then coarsely chop the rest.
2. In a large bowl, combine the chopped cabbage with the bok choy, green onions, daikon, carrots, and salt.
3. Press and smash the ingredients with a pounding tool or the back of a sturdy wooden spoon until the vegetables reduce in volume by about half.
4. Stir in the garlic, ginger, and red pepper flakes.
5. Transfer the mixture to a half-gallon jar. Push down the greens until they're covered by their juices. It won't look like there's much at first, but when you smash down the ingredients in the jar, you'll be surprised at how much liquid comes out.
6. Top the kimchi with the reserved cabbage leaf to help keep the smaller bits submerged, then weigh the vegetables down with a glass fermenting weight so they remain submerged. Completely submerging the ingredients is essential, so if they aren't entirely covered by juices, top off the jar with a bit of filtered water.
7. Seal the jar. If you have one with an air lock, use that. Otherwise, loosen the lid daily to release built-up gases.
8. Let the kimchi sit at room temperature for a week. Sample it as it sits. When you're happy with the flavor, enjoy!

Versatile Vinegar

Vinegar is an essential kitchen staple. Added to oil, it becomes a simple salad dressing. It adds pizzazz to potato or macaroni salad. In marinades, it can help tenderize and flavor meat. And, of course, it's critical for pickling vegetables.

Making your own fruit vinegar is easy. It's also a way to use every last bit of the fruit that passes through your kitchen. You can use the peels and cores left from baking or canning projects to create vinegar for use in cooking or in making natural cleaning solutions.

Save the Brine

Instead of draining the brine down the sink, stir it into various condiments, use it to flavor pasta and potato salads, or drink it neat for a health boost.

Just about any fruit can be fermented to make vinegar, but some are more palatable than others. You can also make your own wine vinegar with white or red wine, or create a malt vinegar with beer.

RECIPE

Apple Cider Vinegar

Makes 6 to 7 cups

If you've ever let unpasteurized apple cider sit too long, you know it can get a bit bubbly, becoming alcoholic hard cider. Let it sit a bit longer, and that alcohol turns to vinegar. You can replicate this process by making vinegar at home. Wash your apples well to remove any residue before you peel them. If you don't have enough apples to make a batch of vinegar all at once, freeze your apple scraps until you have the amount you need. When covering the apples with cloth, stick with fabric, not something airier. A napkin allows the vinegar to breathe yet keeps out bugs; fruit flies can get through cheesecloth. Finished vinegar can be stored at room temperature indefinitely.

You'll Need:

6 cups apple trimmings (cores, peels, and/or 1-inch apple chunks)
3 tablespoons sugar
½ gallon filtered water
Special equipment: 1 clean, wide-mouth half-gallon jar; 1 glass fermenting weight; sealable bottles for finished product

1. Fill the jar three-quarters of the way with the apple trimmings.
2. Sprinkle the sugar over the apples, then top with enough of the filtered water to cover.
3. Set the glass weight on top of the fruit to hold it under the liquid.
4. Cover the jar with a thin napkin or piece of cloth; secure it with a rubber band.
5. Place the jar in a cool, dark cupboard until the apples ferment and create vinegar, at least 4 weeks or longer if your storage area is cooler than 70°F. Don't worry if you notice a gooey layer floating on top. This is the "mother" and can be used as a starter for your next batch of vinegar. (Include it in your next batch and you won't need to add any sugar.) Just pull it off and store it, refrigerated, in a jar with a bit of the finished vinegar.

6. Check on the vinegar every 1 to 2 days to make sure the fruit remains submerged. Add more filtered water if necessary.
7. Strain the vinegar and return it to the jar. Cover it once again with the thin cloth and rubber band and let it ferment for another 2 to 3 weeks, stirring occasionally, until it begins to take on the color and flavor of your favorite store-bought apple cider vinegar.
8. Decant the vinegar into sealable bottles, and use as desired. Discard the apple trimmings into your compost bin.

Homemade apple cider vinegar utilizes apple scraps: waste reduction at its best.

FERMENTED DRINKS

Fermented beverages have a little extra zing. The process of fermentation transforms sugars into acids or alcohol. Although beer and wine have measurable levels of alcohol, the level of alcohol is negligible in other homemade ferments. Kombucha and water kefir are both made by fermentation, offering a probiotic punch in a refreshing fizzy drink. Jun is another fermented drink to look for; it's made with green tea and honey.

What's a SCOBY?

This symbiotic culture of bacteria and yeast (SCOBY) is the key to homemade kombucha.

A SCOBY is the "mother" that helps kick off fermentation. It's a kind of weird, leathery thing that floats on top of the liquid when making kombucha. Made of bacteria and yeast, a SCOBY helps to transform plain black tea and sugar into a slightly fizzy fermented drink, growing larger with each batch. This makes it possible to divide and share your SCOBY with friends who want to try their hand at brewing kombucha. In fact, if you've got a thriving SCOBY and make kombucha regularly, you'll likely find yourself with more SCOBY than you need.

Although it's possible to grow a SCOBY from store-bought kombucha, it's easier to start with one from a friend, or purchase one that's been dehydrated from sources such as *culturesforhealth.com*.

RECIPE

Kombucha

Makes about 3 quarts

Dating back thousands of years and brewed in home kitchens for centuries, kombucha was prized for its purported healing properties. But after finding a place in today's mainstream diets, the fermented probiotic tea is now available at grocery stores. Making your own costs pennies on the dollar and you can customize it with your favorite fruit flavors. But to make it, you will need to grow or borrow a SCOBY. You will also need to use bottles specifically made for fermentation to avoid potential fermentation-related explosions; Grolsch-style glass bottles (available at kitchen stores) are ideal, as are repurposed, clean, swing-top beer or other fermented-drink bottles. Swing-top bottles that are not round (such as maple syrup bottles) should NOT be used for making kombucha. (Ask me how I know.) Refrigerated, sealed bottles of homemade kombucha keep for several weeks. For continuous brewing, complete steps one through three on the day you begin the second ferment, starting another cycle.

You'll Need:
¾ cup sugar
1 tablespoon loose black tea
1 SCOBY
2 teaspoons honey, divided
¼ cup fresh soft fruit, such as blueberries, raisins, strawberries, or 4 tablespoons fruit juice of choice
Special equipment: 1 (1-gallon) wide-mouth glass container, 4 quart-size swing-top bottles (see headnote), funnel

1. Boil 3 quarts water in a stockpot.
2. Let it cool slightly, then stir in the sugar and tea. Let the tea steep until it's cool.
3. Strain the sweet tea into glass container. Add the SCOBY.
4. Secure a thin piece of fabric over the jar opening with a rubber band to allow airflow yet keep out bugs. Let sit at room temperature for a week.
5. Remove the SCOBY from the big jar and set it aside in a bowl with ½ cup of the liquid.
6. Begin the second ferment: To each quart-size swing-top bottle, add ½ teaspoon honey and several pieces of fruit or 1 tablespoon fruit juice.

Kombucha is easy to make at home.

7. Using a funnel, fill the swing-top bottles with the tea, leaving 2 to 3 inches of headspace. Securely close the lids and set the bottles in a cool, dark place at room temperature for a week.
8. Cool bottles in the refrigerator, then enjoy.

RECIPE

Water Kefir

Makes 1 quart

Water kefir starts with kefir grains, which are not traditional grains but rather are composed of a symbiotic culture of bacteria and yeasts. Find a friend who can share some or purchase them in dehydrated form (*culturesforhealth.com* is a good option) and rehydrate them before starting this recipe. Once you strain the kefir grains from the sugar water, you can drink it or give it a second ferment, which results in a more carbonated, soda-like drink. At that point, you can also begin making more water kefir by adding the strained grains to a new batch of sugar water. Keep bottled water kefir in the fridge; enjoy it within a few weeks.

An Alternative to Soda

The sugar that remains in each bottle of kombucha or water kefir after fermentation is negligible. Instead of a sugary soda, pop the top on a bottle of homemade goodness.

You'll Need:

¼ cup sugar
½ cup hot water
3 cups room-temperature water
1 packet or tablespoon water kefir grains, rehydrated in room-temperature water for several days, if starting with dry grains
½ cup fruit juice of choice (only needed for a secondary ferment)
Special equipment: 1 quart-size swing-top bottle (only for a secondary ferment)

1. Combine the sugar and hot water in a quart-size jar or container. Stir until the sugar is dissolved.
2. Add the 3 cups room-temperature water.
3. Add the water kefir grains.
4. Cover the jar with a thin cloth napkin and set in a warm place (70°F to 85°F) for 24 to 48 hours. (The sugar content is reduced by longer fermentation.)
5. Strain the kefir grains from the water kefir, keeping the liquid and also the grains. Retain the grains for making another batch of water kefir.
6. Drink the water kefir immediately, or bottle it for a second ferment, which makes a fizzy drink.
7. For a secondary ferment, pour the water kefir into the swing-top bottle and add the ½ cup fruit juice. Let sit at room temperature for at least 24 to 72 hours, less time if the room is warm or more time if it's chilly. Open the bottle daily to avoid pressure building up (especially if the weather is really warm). Refrigerate, and use caution when opening the bottles.

Seek out water kefir grains to make this DIY fizzy drink.

COCKTAIL HOUR

If you like to indulge in festive drinks, capture the flavors of summertime by making your own infused cocktail flavors or liqueurs. These recipes are just another fun way to preserve your garden (or orchard) bounty. Be sure to make plenty; these custom-flavored adult beverages make fantastic holiday gifts, too. Decant some into pretty bottles, tie on a ribbon, and print recipes for using the elixir in a variety of cocktails.

RECIPE

Flavor-Packed Vodka

Makes about 3 cups

It's fun and easy to infuse your own vodka, and flavor options are only limited by your imagination and access to produce. Choose a single fruit or opt for a more complex combination of fruit, vegetables, herbs, or spices. You can use 100-proof vodka, but it will be a bit more fiery. Infused vodka keeps indefinitely in the pantry.

You'll Need:

2 cups chopped fresh fruit or whole berries with skins gently broken by a wooden spoon

2 to 3 cups 80-proof vodka

Special equipment: cheesecloth or fine sieve, 1 narrow-necked 750-milliliter or other similar-size bottle with a tight-sealing lid

1. Put the fruit in a quart-size jar or other sealing container.
2. Pour the vodka over the fruit to cover, then seal the jar.
3. Place the jar in a cupboard and let the flavors infuse, tasting daily until it achieves your desired flavor, 2 to 5 days. (Don't let it go for too long or it will create a harsh flavor.)
4. Strain the vodka through the cheesecloth, perhaps twice, so no fruit bits remain. For a really clear infusion, follow by straining through a fine mesh coffee or tea strainer.
5. Pour into the narrow-necked bottle (to reduce contact with air) and seal.

Ten Flavor Combinations to Try

Combine fresh fruit with various spices and herbs for endlessly customizable flavors. Happy hour just got happier!

- Apple + cinnamon stick
- Peach + ginger
- Strawberry + basil
- Cucumber + mint
- Blackberry + thyme
- Strawberry + blueberry
- Pear + ginger
- Cranberry + orange
- Lime + mint
- Peach + vanilla

RECIPE

Limoncello

Makes about 5 cups

The Italians claim that drinking limoncello after a meal is good for digestion. I'll leave it at saying that limoncello after a meal is good. This Italian liqueur is made in two stages, so it takes a bit longer to make than a basic infusion, but the end result? *Delizioso!* Limoncello keeps in the refrigerator for up to a year.

You'll Need:

Zest of 10 lemons (reserve the fruit of the lemons for other use)

1 (750-milliliter) bottle vodka

2 cups sugar (or more, to taste)

Special equipment: cheesecloth or fine sieve

Savor the flavor of fresh strawberries—or other soft fruit—in drinks made with a refreshing shrub syrup.

1. Place the lemon zest in a quart-size jar or other container with a lid, add the vodka, and seal. Shake, then store in a cool, dry place for 2 weeks.
2. In a small pot, combine 1¾ cups water and the sugar, then bring to a boil over high heat. Remove from heat and let cool.
3. Pour the syrup into the jar of zest-infused vodka. Cover and let sit for 24 hours.
4. Strain the limoncello through a fine sieve twice to remove all the zest particles. Store in an airtight container.

RECIPE

Strawberry Shrub Syrup

Makes about 3 cups

An old-fashioned drink with a funny name, a refreshing shrub combines fresh fruit flavor with the tang of vinegar and effervescence of soda. It's become one of our favorite summertime drinks. This recipe for shrub syrup, which is essential for the drink, calls for strawberries, but other soft fruits work well, too. To make a strawberry shrub, mix a tablespoon of this syrup into a glass of sparkling water. You can also use this syrup as a cocktail mixer or to flavor salad dressings. Store syrup refrigerated for several months.

You'll Need:
2 cups strawberries, chopped fresh or frozen
2 cups apple cider vinegar
1½ cups sugar
Special equipment: cheesecloth or fine sieve

1. Place the strawberries in a quart-size jar or other sealing container.
2. In a small saucepan over medium heat, bring the vinegar just to a simmer. Remove from the heat and immediately pour the vinegar over the strawberries. Seal the jar.
3. Store the vinegar in a cool, dark place until the vinegar absorbs the flavor of the strawberries, 2 to 4 weeks.
4. Strain the vinegar through the cheesecloth, repeating until the vinegar is free of fruit particles.
5. Combine the strawberry-flavored vinegar and sugar in a saucepan and bring to a boil. When the sugar is dissolved, remove the saucepan from the heat and let the shrub syrup cool.
6. Pour the syrup into a clean container with a lid, and store in the refrigerator.

BAKING BREAD

Fragrant, freshly baked bread makes even the most mundane of meals feel special. Crafting loaves in your own oven also reduces both your grocery bill and the single-use plastic bags in your life. Before stepping into the kitchen, get to know the basic chemistry of bread baking.

❶ **Leavening:** This is what causes bread to rise; without it, bread would be a dense brick. If you've ever accidentally forgotten the baking soda or baking powder in a recipe, you're probably nodding your head. It's edible, certainly, but not terribly palatable.

❷ **Quick breads:** Typically leavened with quick-acting baking soda or baking powder, a loaf of quick bread popped in the oven will start to rise almost immediately.

❸ **Yeast bread:** These loaves require a fermentation process that begins when yeast is combined with warm water. When added to a bread dough recipe, the activated yeast consumes the sugars in the dough, excreting carbon dioxide and alcohols. This causes the bread to rise, leaving those perfect little air pockets that give yeast bread its texture. Generally speaking, yeast breads have a lower fat and sugar content than quick breads. And their ingredient list tends to be simple, often calling for just flour, water, yeast, and salt.

❹ **Sourdough:** Using a fermented sourdough culture imparts a tangy flavor to loaves. Sourdough breads use a "starter culture" that captures wild yeasts from the air. A sourdough starter is a fermented batter that can start with varied ingredients—often just flour and water—and live for years. Some starters have been passed from one generation to the next. Sourdough starter can stand in for yeast in bread recipes and also be used in making muffins, pancakes, and pizza dough.

Quick Bread
2
3
Yeast Bread

QUICK BREADS

Whether you're satisfying a sweet tooth craving or seeking a savory flavor to accompany a meal, quick breads are the way to go. They can be made start to finish in an hour or two—even less if you opt for smaller loaves. Quick breads have a tender texture, more cakey than the chewy, crusty mouthfeel that you get with yeast breads and sourdough. For ease and versatility, they cannot be beat.

Banana bread, corn bread, and Irish soda bread are all quick bread loaves. Muffins, scones, and biscuits may not be shaped in a loaf, but they're made with the same basic quick-rising method.

If you stock your pantry with prepackaged bread mixes, this is your chance to make an easy switch from ready-made to homemade. Many of those prepackaged mixes have "bonus" ingredients to make them last for extended periods of time on a store shelf. They often require you to add fresh ingredients like milk and egg. While you're doing that, you might as well measure out a few dry ingredients and wow your family with a freshly made version that you can call your own.

Freshly baked oat bread

Go Easy

When making quick breads, mix just until the ingredients are combined. Overmixing can cause the bread to be tough.

RECIPE

Buttermilk Oat Bread

Makes 1 loaf

Sometimes you want fresh bread to go with a meal but don't have time to let a yeast version rise. This savory quick bread is a great stand-in, and it's ready in under an hour. Serve it warm with butter, or use it for sandwiches.

You'll Need:

1 cup old-fashioned rolled oats (plus more for sprinkling on top)
2⅓ cups unbleached all-purpose flour
2¼ teaspoons baking powder
½ teaspoon baking soda
1 teaspoon salt
1 cup plain yogurt
1 large egg
¼ cup olive oil
¼ cup honey
1 cup buttermilk

1. Preheat oven to 375°F. Grease a 9 × 5-inch loaf pan.
2. In a mixing bowl, combine the oats, flour, baking powder, baking soda, and salt.
3. In a separate bowl, mix together the yogurt, egg, oil, and honey until combined. Stir in the buttermilk.

The flavor of freshly made tortillas makes the extra effort entirely worth your while.

4. Stir the yogurt mixture into the flour mixture.
5. Pour the batter into the prepared loaf pan, smoothing the top and sprinkling it with oats, if desired.
6. Bake until golden brown on top and a toothpick inserted into the center of the bread comes out clean, 60 to 70 minutes.
7. Place the pan on a wire rack to cool for an hour before slicing.

RECIPE

Easy Soft Flour Tortillas

Makes 10 tortillas

More flatbread than loaf, homemade tortillas are great for making tacos, quesadillas, or wraps. These are soft and chewy, with a fresh flavor that far surpasses the store-bought versions. It's not quite as fast as opening up a package, but they're so good that even my husband has delved into tortilla making. Wrap and refrigerate leftover tortillas for one to two weeks, or freeze them between sheets of waxed paper for up to three months.

You'll Need:

2½ cups unbleached all-purpose flour, plus more for dusting
2 teaspoons baking powder
1 teaspoon salt
½ cup lard or slightly softened butter
1 cup hot water

1. Lightly dust a clean countertop with flour.
2. In a large mixing bowl, combine the flour, baking powder, and salt.

> **Baker's Tip**
> A flour sack towel spread flat on a countertop and sprinkled with flour makes a great nonstick surface for rolling out dough.

3. Using a pastry cutter or fork, cut in the lard until it's thoroughly mixed in and the mixture is crumbly.
4. While stirring the crumbly mixture, gradually add just enough of the hot water that the dough sticks together and forms a ball.
5. Turn the dough out onto the floured countertop, and knead the dough into a smooth ball with your hands.
6. Divide the dough into 10 even pieces, then roll them into balls. Cover the balls of dough with a damp towel and let them rest for 30 minutes.
7. Preheat a large cast-iron or other heavy-bottomed skillet over medium-high heat.
8. Dust a clean surface with flour, then use a rolling pin to roll a ball into an 8-inch round.
9. Cook the tortilla in the hot skillet until golden and bubbly, about 30 seconds. Flip it and cook until golden on the second side. Wrap the tortilla in a clean towel.
10. Repeat with the remaining dough, stacking the tortillas in the towel until you're ready to eat them.

RECIPE

15-Minute Drop Biscuits

Makes 10

These drop biscuits have all the buttery flavor of rolled biscuits but are much faster to make. Feel free to vary the flavor: Add one or two pressed garlic cloves and a few tablespoons of Parmesan cheese to the dough, or sprinkle poppy seeds on top before baking. Store cooked biscuits in a sealed container at room temperature for two to three days; reheat to serve.

You'll Need:
2 cups unbleached all-purpose flour
1 tablespoon sugar
1 tablespoon baking powder
1 teaspoon salt
½ cup cold butter, cut into cubes
1 cup milk

1. Preheat oven to 450°F. In a bowl, mix together the flour, sugar, baking powder, and salt. Using a pastry blender or fork, cut in the butter until mixture is a fine crumble. Stir in the milk until it's just combined.
2. Spoon ¼-cup scoops of biscuit dough onto an ungreased cookie sheet about 1 inch apart for crusty sides or just barely touching for softer edges.
3. Bake until the biscuits begin to brown, about 10 minutes. Remove to a wire rack; serve warm.

Going Gluten Free

People with a gluten sensitivity need to avoid the wheat flour called for in most bread recipes. A gluten-free flour mix can work well for quick breads but will drastically change the texture of yeast breads because gluten is what gives them their chewiness.

Linen Bread Bags

If you struggle with homemade bread becoming moldy before you finish a loaf, storing it in a linen bread bag can extend its shelf life. Linen fabric absorbs moisture, wicking it away from the loaf. Most fabric stores carry linen cloth, but you can also keep your eyes open at thrift stores for linen napkins or tablecloths to upcycle. Use the instructions for making a produce bag on page 86 to make your own linen bread bags, changing the dimensions to fit your usual loaf size.

> **Using Whole Wheat**
> When baking quick breads, it's generally safe to substitute up to half the white flour with whole wheat flour. The texture of the bread shouldn't change much, though the bread will be darker in color. Bread products made with whole wheat tend to have a rich, somewhat earthy flavor.

Achieve the flavor of old-fashioned biscuits in less time with this easy method requiring no rolling.

YEAST & SOURDOUGH

Yeast breads are surprisingly simple to make, yet making bread is one of those skills that people often hesitate to tackle. The time required for rising, kneading, and a second rise can seem daunting, even though it's not all hands-on effort. For many people, it's a beautiful transformation—and that first taste of fresh homemade bread is often enough to change the minds of even the most hesitant bakers.

Kneading bread dough can be a kitchen meditation.

The Need to Knead

Kneading is crucial to a successful loaf of yeast bread. When first combined, yeast dough ingredients are quite lumpy and sticky. The act of kneading forms strands of gluten, a protein that gives bread its elasticity and structure. As gluten forms and kneading continues, air is trapped within the dough, creating air bubbles that give rise to the bread.

Kneading is a method of repeatedly folding and stretching dough until it's smooth. To achieve this by hand, sprinkle flour liberally over your work surface. Place a ball of dough on the flour and sprinkle on more flour. Use the heel of your hand to push the dough, making an indentation in its center. As you push, use your fingers to lift and pull the dough toward you, placing it back over the dough. Repeat with the opposite hand. Lift and turn the dough, adding more flour as necessary to prevent sticking.

Kneading bread dough requires about 10 minutes, give or take, but you'll get into a rhythm. You know you're done when the surface of the dough feels smooth and not sticky. If you look closely, you might be able to see tiny air bubbles starting to form under the surface.

Our ancestors didn't have the option of letting machines do the work for them, but we do. An electric stand mixer equipped with a dough hook can knead the dough for you, often in less time.

Commercial Yeast

Active dry yeast is sold in little envelopes and usually comes three to a pack at grocery stores, but you can purchase yeast in bulk at discount warehouse stores or online.

RECIPE

Honey Wheat Sandwich Bread

Makes 1 loaf

This sandwich bread recipe has been in my collection since my kids were toddlers. It makes a soft, tender loaf and is perfect for slicing. Try it; odds are you'll never go back to packaged sandwich bread. Store baked bread at room temperature in an airtight container for up to a week.

You'll Need:

½ cup milk
½ cup hot water
2¼ teaspoons (1 envelope) active dry yeast
1½ to 2 cups unbleached all-purpose flour
1 cup whole wheat flour
¼ cup melted butter or coconut oil, plus more for greasing
2 tablespoons honey
1 teaspoon salt

1. In a large bowl, combine the milk and hot water; add the yeast and stir until dissolved. Let the yeast sit until it begins to bubble, about 10 minutes. Add 1½ cups of the all-purpose flour, the whole wheat flour, and the melted butter, honey, and salt. Stir until the dough starts to form a ball; if the dough is too sticky, gradually mix in some of the remaining ½ cup all-purpose flour until the dough comes together in a loose ball and the surface is somewhat smooth.
2. Lightly grease a clean surface and a clean bowl with a bit of butter. With greased hands, transfer the dough to the prepared surface, then knead it until supple and tiny air bubbles begin to show just under the surface when you look closely.
3. Place the dough in the prepared bowl, then flip the dough over so both sides are coated with butter. Cover with a tea towel and let the dough rise in a warm spot until almost doubled in size, 1 to 2 hours.
4. Lightly grease a clean work surface and a 9 × 5-inch loaf pan. Gently punch down the dough with your fist, then transfer the dough to the prepared surface. Press the dough into a rectangle about the size of a sheet of paper. Fold the dough into thirds, then place it into the prepared loaf pan, seam side down.
5. Cover the pan with a clean, dampened tea towel and let the dough rise in a warm, draft-free place until it rises slightly above the pan edge, about 1 hour. Meanwhile, preheat the oven to 350°F.
6. Bake the bread until lightly browned, 30 to 35 minutes. Place the pan on a rack to cool for 40 minutes, then turn out the loaf onto the rack to continue cooling. Let cool thoroughly before slicing.

The aroma of freshly baked bread is second only to the flavor of a warm slice, liberally buttered.

RECIPE

Family Favorite Pizza Dough

Makes 2 (12-inch) pizzas

We parbake this pizza dough and freeze it for busy nights. But you can make, cook, and eat it on the same day, too. Topped with whatever's freshest from the garden or refrigerator, it's almost as convenient as takeout. If you don't have a stand mixer, prepare the dough by hand in a bowl. No pizza stone? An upside-down cast-iron skillet or griddle works, too.

You'll Need:

1½ cups warm water (120°F to 130°F)
2 tablespoons sugar
2¼ teaspoons (1 envelope) active dry yeast
1 teaspoon salt
2 tablespoons olive oil, plus more for greasing
2 teaspoons Italian seasoning
4 cups unbleached all-purpose flour (you can substitute whole wheat or spelt flour for up to 2 cups)
Cornmeal to coat a pizza peel
Pizza sauce and toppings of choice (only necessary if you're not freezing crusts for later use)
Special equipment: pizza stone, pizza peel

1. Make the pizza dough: In the bowl of a stand mixer fitted with the hook attachment, combine the warm water, sugar, yeast, salt, olive oil, and Italian seasoning. Let the mixture sit for 5 minutes to proof.
2. Using the stand mixer, mix the proofed ingredients on low, gradually adding just enough of the flour for the dough to come together in a smooth, nonsticky ball, about 7 minutes.
3. Grease a clean bowl with oil. Place the dough into the oiled bowl, flipping it once to coat. Cover the dough with a tea towel, then let it rise in a warm place for 45 minutes.
4. Sprinkle flour on a smooth rolling surface. Divide the dough in half, then using a rolling pin, roll one of the dough halves into a 12-inch round, flipping it frequently as you roll and adding more flour as needed to prevent sticking. Repeat with the other half. (If you prefer individual-size pizzas, divide the dough evenly into small, tennis ball-size rounds before rolling.)
5. Cook the dough: Preheat the oven and a pizza stone to 450°F. Liberally cover a pizza peel or a baking sheet with cornmeal. Transfer one of the dough rounds to the prepared pizza peel. To parbake the crust for future use, slide the dough onto the hot pizza stone and bake until the surface begins to bubble up, about 7 minutes, then let cool, wrap, and freeze. To cook and eat immediately, add sauce and toppings of choice to either uncooked dough or parbaked dough (this makes it easier to transfer). Slide the pizza onto the hot pizza stone, and bake until the edges are lightly browned and crispy, 10 to 12 minutes. Repeat with the following dough round.

Perfect pizza starts with freshly made homemade dough.

RECIPE

Sourdough Starter

Makes 1 cup

As a leavening agent, sourdough is the most traditional, and may date back to ancient Egypt. Using this traditional method, coupled with a well-stocked pantry, allows you to create a well-risen sourdough loaf without depending on commercial yeast. Maintaining a sourdough starter requires a bit of a commitment. To keep it thriving, you'll need to feed it and use it regularly. As wild yeast differs from region to region, the flavor of a sourdough starter will vary from place to place. This is why sourdough baked in Kansas doesn't taste the same as the famous San Francisco sourdough loaves.

You'll Need:
5½ cups unbleached all-purpose flour, plus more if needed
5½ cups room-temperature filtered water, plus more if needed

Day 1: Mix ½ cup flour and ½ cup of the filtered water in a quart-size jar. Stir well to combine. With a rubber band, secure a cloth napkin over the jar opening. Leave at room temperature for 24 hours.

Day 2: Stir in ½ cup each of the flour and filtered water, to "feed" the starter. Do this once in the morning and once at night.

Day 3: Repeat step 2.

Day 4: By now, you should see bubbles and notice a sour but not unpleasant odor from the starter. Stir the starter and pour off all but ½ cup each time you feed it from here on out; dispose of or reserve what you pour off for another use. Repeat step 2.

Days 5 and 6: Continue feeding as in step 4. By now, the starter should be bubbly and growing in size between each addition of flour and water. If it's not actively bubbling yet (likely due to the temperature), continue feeding for up to a week. Sometimes a brand-new starter takes longer, especially if your kitchen is cool.

Bubbly sourdough starter gives rise to homemade bread. The more bubbly, the better.

Once the starter is bubbling, it's ready to be used in various recipes. To keep it active and ready to use, continue feeding it daily and keep it at room temperature. You'll find that it gets more active in warmer conditions, making for a good rise. If you won't use it immediately, keep it refrigerated, then bring it to room temperature 24 hours before you plan to bake with it. Stir it, feed it, and then add the room-temperature starter to your recipe of choice.

RECIPE

Crunchy Sourdough Baguette

Makes 2 (12-inch) baguettes

Forming bread into a long, skinny loaf means more crust area, perfect for people who clamor for the crunchy ends. Slice your baguette thinly and toast it, then top it with spreads like homemade hummus (page 58).

You'll Need:
2 cups unbleached all-purpose flour, plus more for kneading
½ teaspoon sea salt
½ cup active sourdough starter
Oil, for greasing the pan

1. In a mixing bowl, combine all the ingredients and ½ cup water. Mix well.
2. Sprinkle ¼ cup flour onto a clean work surface. Knead the sticky, loose dough lightly, working in the flour until the dough just begins to hold its shape.
3. Grease a baking sheet. Divide the dough in half. Pat each half into a 12 × 4-inch rectangle, roll it up lengthwise, and pinch its seams closed. Each loaf should be about 2 inches in diameter and 12 inches long. Place the baguettes, seam sides down, onto the prepared baking sheet.
4. Cover the dough with a damp tea towel and set in a warm place to rise until the dough has doubled in size, 5 to 6 hours.
5. Preheat oven to 425°F.
6. Bake until nicely browned, about 15 minutes.
7. Cool on a rack for 30 minutes; slice and serve.

GRAINS & LEGUMES

These pantry essentials were the basis of a hearty diet for pioneers, often purchased at the local dry goods store in quantities to last for months to help ride out a rough winter. Just as they were then, whole grains and legumes are excellent—and inexpensive—staple ingredients. Vegetarians often use beans in lieu of meat in recipes, as they are excellent sources of dietary fiber and protein. If you're working to reduce animal protein in your diet, take a cue from them and embrace the simple goodness of legumes. They're a low-fat, budget-friendly way to bulk up a meal, as well as a good source of potassium.

RECIPE

Cooking Dry Beans

Cooking with dry beans is easy, but it requires some forethought. An overnight soak helps reduce the phytic acid, sometimes called an "anti-nutrient." Phytic acid can inhibit the body's absorption of minerals like iron, zinc, calcium, and magnesium. Soaking the beans also speeds cooking time and makes them easier to digest. Once the beans are cooked, stir them into chili, make burritos, or in the case of garbanzo beans, puree them into hummus. Store cooked beans covered and refrigerated for several days.

Plan ahead and soak dried beans for a faster-cooking meal.

Under Pressure

If putting dinner on the table fast is important to you, consider investing in an electric pressure cooker. With one of these, you can go from dry beans to chili in less than an hour. But it doesn't just make cooking grains and legumes fast; cooking meat under pressure results in fork-tender meals, even if you start with less expensive—often tough—cuts.

You'll Need:

Dried beans of choice, such as kidney beans, lentils, or pinto beans

1. Sort and rinse the beans, checking for small rocks.
2. Place the beans in a bowl, cover with at least 2 inches of water, then let the beans soak 6 hours or overnight.
3. Drain and rinse the beans, then place them in a stockpot and cover them with 2 inches of water.
4. Cover the pot with a lid. Bring the water to a boil over medium-high heat, reduce the heat to low, and let the beans simmer until tender, 45 minutes to 2 hours, depending on the type of bean you use. (Lentils are the fastest-cooking legume; kidney beans will take longer.)
5. Drain the beans.

Whole Grains

Many don't realize that whole grains are the raw form of flour. A household equipped with a grain grinder can transform whole grains into flour for use in baking. Freshly ground grains—try rye, barley, or oats—impart a flavor in baked goods that is unmatched by breads and sweets made from commercially milled flour. Whether you're growing your own grains or buying them in bulk, grinding your own grain results in a superior product.

Whole grains can also do double duty in the kitchen. Cooked in broth or water, rice, quinoa, and bulgur wheat absorb moisture to become plump little morsels. From breakfast porridge to hot dishes and salads, grains can be served up sweet or savory, depending upon how they're prepared.

Storing Grains and Legumes

Although flour tends to go "off" after a year or so (sooner in a humid climate), whole grains and dry legumes stockpiled properly can last for years, making them easy to keep on hand for frugal meals and hearty stews. (They're great for keeping in an emergency food stash, too.)

The key to long-term storage of grains and legumes is dryness. They need to be kept in an airtight container that will prevent any moisture from entering. If you keep only a small amount on hand, a canning jar will suffice. For larger quantities—I often purchase 25-pound bags—one of the best storage methods is a food-grade five-gallon bucket equipped with a gamma lid. A gamma lid comes in two pieces: a round ring that snaps onto standard buckets and a twist-off lid. These are far and away the easiest and most effective storage options. Adding a moisture absorber to the storage container can help, too (see directions for sewing your own on page 21).

Dried legumes in airtight containers will last for years, making them great emergency food to keep on hand.

PANTRY STAPLES

Want to start making simple fare you'll use every day? Pinpoint a couple packaged foods that you find yourself buying regularly and learn to make them yourself—maybe fresh salsa or salad dressing. Maybe you depend on those packets of seasoning for making tacos. Or gravy. These recipes will help you make quick work of replacing your favorite store-bought products with homemade versions, saving money at the checkout and eliminating unnecessary single-use plastics. Making them at home allows you to customize recipes to suit your taste buds, too. Make your hot sauce as fiery as you like, add extra garlic to your salad dressing, or experiment with a splash of white wine or ale in your grainy mustard.

RECIPE

Grainy Mustard

Makes about 2 cups

You'll Need:
1 cup mustard seeds (yellow, brown, or a combination)
¾ cup apple cider vinegar

1. Place the mustard seeds, vinegar, and ¼ cup water in a pint-size jar. Cover and let sit for 2 days to soften the seeds. (An extra couple of days won't hurt.) If the liquid is completely absorbed during soaking, add a bit more water. The absorption rate will vary depending upon the seeds. If you feel like you're adding a lot of extra water, add a splash of vinegar, too, to maintain the vinegary kick.

Deep Dive Into Homemade

When making these staples, you can use ingredients from the store or *really* make it homemade by adding a dash of homegrown dried herbs (page 22) to salsa or spices, fermented apple cider vinegar (page 38) to dressings, or other basics you've learned to make at home.

Grainy mustard can be made with countless flavor variations.

2. After 2 days, pour the contents of the jar into your blender and process until the mustard is of desired consistency (less if you like it grainy, more if you prefer it creamy).
3. Put the finished mustard back into the jar the seeds were in. (Not even a jar to wash!)
4. Store homemade mustard covered in the refrigerator for 4 months.

Variations: If you like the flavor of traditional yellow mustard, add ½ to 1 teaspoon turmeric. Or, for flavor variation, try using white wine or your favorite stout instead of water. You really do need some vinegar, but you can play around with the amounts and ingredients a fair bit once you've discovered how simple this is.

RECIPE

Smoky Hot Sauce

Makes about ½ pint

You'll Need:
15 hot peppers, such as jalapeño, serrano, or if you're brave, ghost peppers
Juice of ½ lemon
2 tablespoons apple cider vinegar
1 teaspoon salt
1 teaspoon sugar
Special equipment: disposable gloves

1. Preheat the broiler. Wearing gloves to prevent burning your skin, remove and discard the stems from the peppers, then slice the peppers in half.
2. Remove the seeds and membranes, reserving them if you want a hotter sauce; they're the hottest part of the pepper.
3. Place the pepper halves, skin side up, in a cast-iron skillet or on a metal baking sheet. Broil until the skins begin to blister and brown, about 5 minutes.
4. Use tongs to move peppers into the bowl of your blender.
5. Add to the blender ½ cup water and the lemon juice, apple cider vinegar, salt, and sugar, plus the reserved pepper seeds if you like. Puree.
6. Pour the hot sauce into a jar with a lid.
7. Covered hot sauce can be refrigerated up to 6 months.

This hot sauce will take on the color of peppers you use.

RECIPE

Caesar Ranch Dressing

Makes about 2 cups

You'll Need:
1 egg, at room temperature (about 75°F; this is critical)
1¼ cup extra-light olive oil
1 garlic clove
1 tablespoon mustard
1 tablespoon lemon juice
2 teaspoons apple cider vinegar
1 tablespoon anchovy paste
1 teaspoon Worcestershire sauce
½ teaspoon salt
½ teaspoon pepper
¼ cup buttermilk
¾ cup grated Parmesan cheese
Special equipment: immersion blender

1. In a wide-mouth quart-size jar or other container, combine the egg, oil, and garlic.
2. Place the blade of an immersion blender at the bottom of the jar and pulse on and off 5 or 6 times, then hold the power on, moving the blender up and down until ingredients are well blended and emulsified, 30 to 60 seconds.
3. Add the mustard, lemon juice, vinegar, anchovy paste, Worcestershire sauce, salt, and pepper; blend to combine.
4. Stir in the buttermilk and the cheese.
5. Cover and refrigerate leftover dressing for up to 3 days; if it thickens after refrigeration, stir in a few tablespoons of buttermilk before serving.

RECIPE

Fresh Garden Salsa

Makes about 2 cups

You'll Need:
5 to 6 fresh tomatoes, chopped into ¼-inch pieces
1 small onion, diced
1 garlic clove, crushed
1 jalapeño pepper, diced
Juice of ½ lime
1 to 2 tablespoons cilantro, chopped (optional)

1. In a bowl, stir together the tomatoes, onion, garlic, jalapeño, lime juice, and cilantro.
2. In a closed or covered container, salsa keeps for several days in the refrigerator.

RECIPE

Hummus

Makes about 4 cups

You'll Need:
2 (15-ounce) cans garbanzo beans or 4 cups cooked garbanzo beans (see "Cooking Dry Beans" on page 54)
3 tablespoons tahini
½ to ⅔ cup lemon juice
4 large garlic cloves
1 teaspoon cumin powder
½ teaspoon salt

1. Drain the beans, reserving some liquid.
2. In a food processor, combine the drained beans, tahini, ½ cup of the lemon juice, and the garlic, cumin, and salt. Process until smooth, adding a little more lemon juice, some of the reserved liquid, or water if necessary for a good consistency.
3. Covered hummus keeps in the refrigerator for up to a week.

Made from garbanzo beans, hummus makes a hearty snack.

RECIPE

Vanilla Extract

Makes 2 cups

You'll Need:
2 vanilla beans
2 cups vodka

1. Split the vanilla beans down the center with a knife or scissors and slip the beans into a pint-size jar.
2. Fill the jar with vodka, screw on the lid, and let the mixture sit for 3 weeks while the vanilla infuses the alcohol. It will continue to darken as it ages.
3. Store at room temperature for up to 2 years.

RECIPE

All-Purpose Baking Mix

Makes about 7 cups

You'll Need:
6 cups unbleached all-purpose flour (you can substitute whole wheat flour for up to 2 cups)
3 tablespoons baking powder
1 tablespoon salt
2 tablespoons sugar
1 cup butter

1. In a large mixing bowl, mix together the flour, baking powder, salt, and sugar.
2. Cut in the butter using a fork or pastry blender until the mix has a fine texture. (If you have a food processor, it will make quick work of this step.)
3. Refrigerate the baking mix in an airtight container for up to 3 months.

RECIPE

Mayonnaise

Makes about 1 cup

You'll Need:
1 cup extra-light olive oil or avocado oil
1 egg, at room temperature (about 75°F; this is critical)
2 teaspoons apple cider vinegar
2 teaspoons grainy mustard
Pinch of salt
Special equipment: immersion blender

1. Pour the oil directly into a quart-size, wide-mouth canning jar to the 1-cup mark.
2. Add the egg.

Skip the EVOO

Although extra-virgin olive oil is good for many things, with its strong flavor, it's not the best option for making mayonnaise.

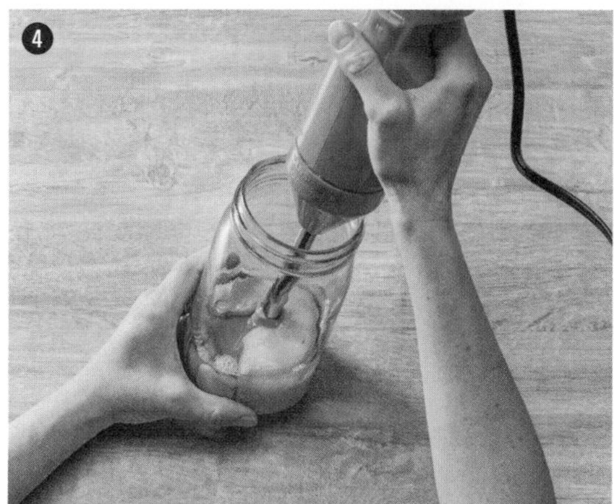

3. Using an immersion blender with its blade sitting at the bottom of the jar, pulse 10 times.
4. Now hold the power on while moving the blender up and down to emulsify the egg and oil to a thick consistency, about 30 seconds.
5. Add 1 teaspoon water and the vinegar, mustard, and salt, and process briefly with the blender just to combine.
6. Homemade mayo keeps covered in the refrigerator for a week.

INFUSED OIL & VINEGAR

Oil and vinegar are pantry staples in most kitchens, but it's easy to rev things up by infusing them with herbs, spices, flowers, or fruit. They make great gifts, too; you'll see them at gourmet or specialty shops. Making your own at home will result in a high-end product without the high-end cost. Just decant the oil or vinegar into pretty glass bottles; you can pick these up at places like Target and HomeGoods, or even at thrift stores.

Making Oil Infusions

When making infused oils, I generally recommend using dried herbs or flowers, because any moisture introduced can cause the oil to go rancid. If you're growing your own herbal garden, take the time to thoroughly dry anything you plan to add in. (See page 22 for drying instructions.)

Begin with a neutral oil like safflower, sunflower, or macadamia nut. Olive oil isn't a great base, because it tends to have a short shelf life when infused. How much dried material to add depends on what you're infusing. For most herbs, though, a good rule of thumb is to use about one cup dried leaves per quart of oil. More potent herbs, such as rosemary, require less plant material; several sprigs might be enough for a whole jar.

There are two ways to make an infusion, one much faster than another:

- **Solar-infused oils:** With this method, the heat of the sun does the work for you, as the name implies. Place your jar of oil and herbs in a place that is warmed by the sun but out of direct sunlight. Let the oil steep for four to six weeks, inverting it every few days.

- **Heat-infused oils:** If waiting a month for your oil isn't in the cards, you can infuse this version right on the stove top. To do so, place the oil and herbs in a double boiler and bring to a low simmer. Heat for 30 to 60 minutes.

When the infusion is complete, remove the plant materials from the oil for storage. Strain the oil through cheesecloth, making sure to squeeze out as much of it as you can. Store in a tightly sealed glass bottle in the refrigerator. Be sure to label the finished oil (including the date) so that you know what is in the jar. Infused oils should last for about six months.

Infused oils are good for imparting flavor to various dishes, but don't use them on the stove; heating the oil will ruin the flavor. Instead, use them as a finishing drizzle over cooked foods like sautéed vegetables, soups, and pizza, or simply dip a crusty baguette straight into the oil.

RECIPE

Savory, Flavory Rosemary Oil

Makes 2 cups

Drizzle this oil over roasted vegetables, or use it in your favorite pasta salad for a vibrant punch. Flavored oils are excellent additions to salad dressing, too. This oil keeps, covered and refrigerated, for six months. For a fun serving option, combine a fresh sprig of rosemary and infused oil in a pretty bottle, though note that the shelf life will be shorter.

You'll Need:
2 cups safflower or sunflower oil
6 dried sprigs rosemary

1. Combine the oil and rosemary in a jar.
2. Seal the jar and place in a warm spot away from direct sunlight.
3. Invert the jar every 2 to 3 days for 4 to 6 weeks.
4. Remove the rosemary from the oil, straining if necessary.

For a fun serving option, combine a fresh sprig of rosemary and infused oil in a pretty bottle.

RECIPE

Hot Chili Oil

Makes 2 cups

If you like to heat things up in the kitchen, keep a bottle of this spicy oil on hand for sprinkling on any meal that needs a boost. You can use it to kick up the flavor of kale chips, or toss it with stale bread cubes to make homemade croutons. Keep the jar of oil from sitting directly on the heat by placing it on a wire rack or three canning rings on the bottom of the pan. This oil keeps, covered and refrigerated, for six months.

You'll Need:

2 cups safflower or sunflower oil
2 tablespoons dried red pepper flakes, plus more if you like it really hot

1. Combine ingredients in a glass canning jar.
2. Place the rack on the bottom of a saucepan.
3. Put 2 to 3 inches of water in the saucepan and set the jar on the rack.
4. Over medium heat, bring the water to a low simmer. Adjust heat to maintain simmer until it begins to darken in color and takes on the flavor of the peppers, 30 to 60 minutes.
5. Cool the oil, then strain it into sealing bottles or jars.

RECIPE

Marinade for Chicken or Grilled Vegetables

Makes about ½ cup

This is a versatile marinade you can keep covered in the refrigerator for up to a week. Pour it over chicken and refrigerate for several hours or overnight before cooking. Or toss it with four to five cups of sliced vegetables, such as summer squash, peppers, and onions, about a half hour before grilling them.

You'll Need:

3 tablespoons balsamic vinegar
3 tablespoons Savory, Flavory Rosemary Oil (page 60)
6 garlic cloves, crushed
1 teaspoon dried oregano
½ teaspoon salt
½ teaspoon pepper

1. Combine all ingredients in a small jar.
2. Shake to combine.

Flavor Combinations

The flavor possibilities for infusing vinegar are almost endless, but these are a good start:

- Lemon + thyme
- Peppercorns + garlic
- Lemongrass + mint
- Rosemary + garlic
- Ginger + garlic
- Italian seasoning + dried tomatoes
- Lime + cilantro

Infused Vinegar

Creating infused vinegar is a good way to preserve the essence of the garden when you have only small amounts of fruit. Adding extra flavor to vinegar can turn salad dressing, sauces, and marinades into something really special. Use blueberry-infused vinegar to drizzle on pork chops, add a little peppercorn vinegar to spice up a homemade barbecue sauce, or make a vinaigrette with a raspberry infusion to create an innovative salad. The possibilities are endless!

You can infuse any kind of vinegar: apple cider, white wine, or even balsamic—all are fair game. Generally speaking, use about a one-to-one ratio, flavoring to vinegar. Less is more with stronger herbs and spices like rosemary or jalapeño peppers. And if you're using dried herbs, a one-to-two ratio is better. This is one of those projects that can be endlessly fiddled with to suit your taste.

RECIPE

Refreshing Strawberry Switchel

Makes 6 to 7 cups

Also known as Haymaker's Punch because it was used as a hydrating drink during haying season, a switchel is a refreshing drink made with vinegar. Infusing the vinegar gives it a deeper flavor profile. This drink packs a punch—enjoy it straight or dilute it with water. Store leftover switchel covered in the refrigerator for three weeks.

You'll Need:

4 cups raw apple cider vinegar
4 cups fresh or frozen strawberries
½ cup fresh basil leaves
2 tablespoons fresh ginger, grated
Zest of 1 lemon
1 to 2 cups honey
Special equipment: sieve or cheesecloth

1. Pour the vinegar into a half-gallon jar or other large, sealing container. Add the strawberries, basil, ginger, and lemon zest. Use a slotted spoon or a fork to smash the berries and herbs against the side of the jar, releasing their flavor.
2. Seal the jar and store in a cool, dry place for 2 weeks.
3. Strain the vinegar through a sieve or several layers of cheesecloth to remove the fruit and herbs.
4. Thoroughly stir enough honey into the infused vinegar to achieve your desired sweetness.
5. Serve over ice.

RECIPE

Blueberry Lemon-Infused Vinegar

Makes about 1½ cups

Capture the flavor of summer-fresh berries in this fruity vinegar; it's a tasty addition to salad dressings. Or stir some into cream cheese for an unexpected pop of flavor on your next everything bagel. Store the vinegar in a cool, dark cupboard or in the refrigerator for up to six months.

You'll Need:
1 cup fresh blueberries
Zest of 1 lemon
1 cup balsamic vinegar
Special equipment: cheesecloth or coffee filter

Blueberries and lemon pack a flavor punch in infused vinegar.

1. In a jar, muddle the blueberries and lemon.
2. In a small saucepan, warm the vinegar over low heat; don't boil, as this can degrade it.
3. Pour the warm vinegar over the blueberries. Let the sealed jar sit at room temperature for 2 days.
4. Strain the vinegar through cheesecloth or coffee filter, squeezing as much liquid from the berries as you can. Keep the berries for another use.
5. Fill a bottle or other sealing container with the strained vinegar.

RECIPE

Garlic Tarragon Vinegar

Makes 2 cups

This savory vinegar is good for salad dressing recipes and marinades, or you can add a splash to soups or stews. Store the vinegar in a cool, dark cupboard or in the refrigerator for up to six months.

You'll Need:
6 garlic cloves
8 sprigs fresh tarragon
2 cups white wine vinegar

1. In a jar, combine the garlic and tarragon.
2. In a small saucepan, warm the vinegar over low heat; don't boil, as this can degrade it.
3. Pour the warm vinegar over the tarragon and garlic. Seal the jar, and let it sit at room temperature for 2 days.
4. Remove and discard the tarragon and garlic from the vinegar. Strain to eliminate remaining bits, if necessary.
5. Fill a bottle or other sealing container with the strained vinegar.

Reading Labels

Some major vinegar brands are offering products that aren't exactly what they seem. Take a closer look at what you think is apple cider vinegar; you may see the word "flavored" tucked in there. Although the flavor may be similar, it's not actually made of apple cider. Along those same lines, white vinegar is not white *wine* vinegar; these somewhat deceptive versions are actually made from grains like corn. And corn is one of America's prominent genetically altered crops.

SOURCING QUALITY MEAT

There are some real issues to consider when putting meat on the dinner table. From chicken to beef and pork, cuts of meat are readily available at the supermarket. Problem number one: Meat usually comes packaged on foam trays, which are themselves an environmental disaster. Problem number two: That steak most likely came from a concentrated animal feeding operation (CAFO). These feedlots house a multitude of animals in a confined space free of any vegetation. The animals are wholly dependent upon the importation of feed. They could also be noshing on candy or any number of "waste" products to round out their diet.

Problem number three: The feed provided in CAFOs is often supplemented with prophylactic doses of antibiotics. These antibiotics are given whether or not an animal is sick. This casual use of antibiotics is under scrutiny as a possible cause for the antibiotic resistance we're starting to see in humans.

All that is to say: Omnivores, it's time to figure out a better source for your meat than the supermarket.

■ **Find a good butcher:** A butcher shop is a great way to access quality meat in smaller quantities. You'll want to find out where the shop sources its meat and ask questions about how it was raised. Alternatively, check out FreshDirect.com grocery delivery to see if it serves your area.

Fresh meat hangs in an old-fashioned butcher shop.

■ **Support the Grand Champion:** Every summer, 4-H and FFA (Future Farmers of America) members from across the nation bring their market animals to the county fair for judging and to be auctioned off to the highest bidder. Before the auction, take time to visit the animal barns and seek out members who have raised their animals in a manner that you support. Take note of several of these animals, decide how much you're willing to spend per pound, and get bidding.

■ **Buy the whole cow:** If you have the freezer space, consider purchasing beef, pork, or lamb in bulk. Farmers who raise just a few head of cattle (or pigs or sheep) will often make those available to buyers in quarters, halves, or whole. When you buy it this way, you'll pay a flat per-pound rate and get a variety of cuts; hamburger and prime rib all cost the same.

Finding the Farmer for You

Ask at your farmers market or cooperative extension office for referrals to locate a farm that's raising animals ethically. The following are some questions to ask to be sure you're happy with the conditions under which the meat has been raised.

■ **What do you feed your animals?**

You don't want to buy an animal that has been fed junk. With cows, a diet of grass, hay, and silage is ideal. Cows have not evolved to eat corn, but many growers "finish" their cattle by feeding corn prior to butchering to fatten them up.

If your farmer feeds grains, find out what kinds. Much of the corn and soy in America contains genetically modified organisms (GMO). Cottonseed meal is

A knowledgeable butcher can guide you in choosing the right cut for meals—and perhaps even wrap it in paper.

On the Hunt

Consider wild meat as another option. Although you may not be ready to embrace your inner Elmer Fudd, find out if your state or county has a program that offers meat (usually the whole animal) from animal eradication programs or those that have recently met their demise on a roadway.

another feed product that has a high risk of GMO contamination. If you want to skip the genetically modified feed, find a farmer who opts for organically grown grains. Just know that organic feed will increase the price of the meat. Conventionally grown crops like oats, barley, and wheat are good compromises, as no GMO versions are on the market yet.

- **Where do your animals spend most of their time?** Terms like "free-range" sound good, but if that just means a thousand chickens fighting for a chance to spend a moment in a small outdoor enclosure, they're not really free-range, are they? Animals that have access to green pasture and sunshine will have a more diverse and natural diet than those that have been confined.

- **Are your animals given antibiotics or steroids?** Sometimes it's necessary to medicate a herd or flock for an illness. But you might want to avoid a farmer who gives growth hormones or uses antibiotics as a preventative measure.

Once you've heard the answers to these questions, you can decide for yourself if this is the right source for you.

CHARCUTERIE

Loosely translated, the word "charcuterie" can mean "pork butcher's shop," or refers to the products created there. Those definitions don't do the term justice, though. Visit a charcuterie and you'll find a mind-boggling assortment of cured sausage, bacon, ham, and other delectable cured meats, oftentimes suspended tantalizingly from the ceiling. And although pork may predominate, it's not used exclusively.

Originally developed as a way to preserve meat before refrigeration, the art of charcuterie these days has been embraced purely for the flavor. Let's face it: A perfectly cured slab of bacon or slice of Italian prosciutto involves an artistry.

Using charcuterie techniques that hark back to the medieval era can turn a mediocre cut of meat into a flavorful addition to mealtime. There are so many options, from whole cuts to cased sausages, but homemade bacon is a great starting place for those just starting to experiment with curing and smoking.

RECIPE

Blissful Homemade Bacon

Makes about 5 pounds

Bacon, that sweet, smoky breakfast meat so many love, starts out as a bland slab of pork belly. When I was a girl, bacon came from the butcher as a slab, and we cut slices off the smoked bacon as needed. You can replicate that old-fashioned goodness right in your home oven. Although it takes several days to cure, the transformation in flavor may be enough to convince you to make your own all the time. It's far superior to the packaged variety sold at the supermarket, it's less expensive to make at home, and you'll have the option to cut out nasty nitrites. Bacon can be wrapped and refrigerated for two weeks or frozen for three months.

Flavoring Your Bacon

You'll want to stick to the base mixture provided in the recipe, but you have a little room to experiment with different herbs and spices to change up the flavor.

If you like your bacon sweet, you can add another ½ cup brown sugar and maybe some nutmeg. For more savory bacon, add some crushed fresh garlic, bay leaves, or maybe cayenne pepper. You can also add ½ teaspoon liquid smoke to give the bacon a smoked flavor.

You'll Need:

½ cup coarse kosher salt
½ cup brown sugar
1 tablespoon coarsely ground peppercorns
2 teaspoons pink curing salt (optional)
5 pounds pork belly, roughly equal parts lean and fat, skin (rind) removed

1. Make a dry rub: in a small bowl, thoroughly mix the salt, brown sugar, peppercorns, and optional curing salt.
2. Pour half the dry rub into a casserole dish large enough to accommodate the pork belly.
3. Set the pork belly into the dish and sprinkle it with the remaining dry rub.
4. With clean hands, spread the dry rub onto the meat, ensuring every part of the pork belly is covered, including the cracks and crevices.
5. Refrigerate the pork belly in a sealed container for a week, turning it daily. The salty rub will draw the moisture out of the meat.
6. Preheat the oven to 200°F. Thoroughly rinse the dry rub from the pork belly, then pat it dry.

Making bacon and sausage at home allows you to customize the flavor with herbs and spices to suit your palate.

7. Set a rack on a rimmed baking sheet. Place the pork belly on the rack, then bake until the internal temperature is 150°F, about 90 minutes. (The goal is to heat but not fully cook the bacon.)
8. Cool to room temperature, then transfer the bacon to a sealed container.
9. Slice the bacon thick or thin as you like it. Now it's ready to use any way you wish.

An old-fashioned hand grinder turns cuts of meat into a mince for making sausage or your own ground beef.

Sausage

Sausage making essentially entails mixing chopped or ground meat with seasonings to create a flavorful blend. It's a great way to utilize inexpensive cuts of meat or butchering by-products. Blood sausage, for instance, is made from blood, seasonings, fat, and other fillers.

Bulk sausage is generally made into patties or cooked and crumbled (hello, pizza!). It's the easiest kind of sausage to make. **Link sausage** takes a bit more work, requiring ground meat to be fed into a casing. Natural sausage casings are made from animal intestine and are edible. Artificial casing can be made from a variety of materials—including plastic! Hot dogs, salami, bratwurst, kielbasa, and Spanish chorizo are all link sausages; their flavor varies based on ingredients and method of curing. Fresh sausage links are soft and must be cooked prior to eating. These are different than cured and dried sausages—the kind you'd see hanging in a delicatessen—which are hard and ready to be sliced. Without many special tools, a real meat-lover will find it worth their while to make sausages by hand—at a fraction of the cost for store-bought.

Grinding Meat for Sausage Making

An old-fashioned hand-crank grinder—available at many hardware stores for about $25—works fine for small batches. If you're processing a lot of meat, consider investing in an electric meat grinder. Grinding attachments are available for stand mixers, too. You can also use a food processor, but that method can be a bit finicky to get right.

Cut meat into chunks that will fit through your grinder. Spread meat chunks in a single layer on a baking sheet and freeze for about 15 minutes. This will make it a bit easier to grind, but if you don't have room in your freezer, you can certainly skip this step.

You'll have the option to choose the coarseness of the grind. Some sausage is generally finer than others, but in the end, it's a matter of preference. Experiment to see what you like.

Note on Curing Salt

Most commercially produced bacon has sodium nitrite listed among its ingredients. It's antimicrobial, and it prevents incidents of botulism when cured meats are not held at the appropriate temperature. In high doses, sodium nitrite is toxic. In smaller doses, it can cause migraines. You can avoid this additive: Just be sure to use extremely clean hands and implements when working with the meat, and maintain proper temperatures as it cures. It's listed as an optional ingredient here. Only you can decide if you're more comfortable adding it or avoiding it.

RECIPE

Italian Sausage

Makes about 5 pounds

We started making homemade sausage years ago, on kind of a whim, when my Italian husband decided it would be fun to give it a try. The ability to choose good-quality meat and fine-tune the spices to make our taste buds happy sold us on doing it again and again. The fact that we could leave out the anise commonly found in prepared sausage—which we both loathe—was a bonus. If you don't have a meat grinder, ask the butcher or meat department to grind the pork butt for you. Wrapped raw sausage keeps in the refrigerator for two to three days and in the freezer for up to six months.

You'll Need:

5 pounds pork butt, cut into 2-inch chunks
½ pound pork fat (optional)
½ cup red wine
2 tablespoons Italian seasoning
5 teaspoons salt
10 garlic cloves, minced
1 tablespoon black pepper
2 teaspoons red pepper flakes
5 tablespoons smoked paprika

1. Run the pork chunks through a meat grinder. If the meat is lean, you'll want to add some extra fat; grind it just as you do the pork butt. (Aim for about 80 percent lean, 20 percent visible fat.)
2. In a large bowl, thoroughly combine the ground meat, enough pork fat to create an 80-20 percent ratio of lean meat to fat, the red wine, Italian seasoning, salt, garlic, pepper, red pepper flakes, and smoked paprika.
3. Heat a small frying pan and cook a small bit of sausage to check its flavor. Although the flavors will meld more as the sausage ages, this gives you a chance to adjust seasonings to suit your taste.
4. Wrap the sausage in a couple layers of freezer paper, and freeze it in portions or cook it immediately.

• chapter two •

MAKE

MAKE

Long ago, people's survival depended on their ability to make what they needed to get through life. Men and women of the house created the items required to build and maintain a household, from clothing to furniture, right on site.

With the advent of the industrial age, handmade items were replaced by machine-manufactured versions. This new way of outfitting a home and family—purchasing rather than making what was necessary—was embraced first by the wealthy, but eventually worked its way into all walks of life. Although these advancements saved much work in a busy household, this also meant, of course, a loss of expertise in artisan handicrafts and endeavors that supported a self-sufficient lifestyle. But it also meant that we were no longer using our creativity to produce necessary—but beautiful—household items that doubled as works of art.

Although working with our hands is not as crucial now as it was for our ancestors, there's still a lot to be said for it. Making a quilt may no longer be necessary for winter warmth; candles may no longer be a household's sole source of lighting. But crafting a beautiful and functional project from scratch provides immeasurable value. Crafting can help calm the nerves, reduce stress, and provide a much needed social outlet if performed with friends and family.

This chapter is filled with projects for crafting at home: some practical and some purely artistic. Many utilize upcycled materials to create something new and fabulous. Others call for natural materials, some of which may be found right in your own backyard. Most will result in a functional item that you can proudly use in your own home or give as gifts.

No matter which projects you choose to tackle, the simple act of creating something with your own hands is a tremendous step toward self-reliance and reducing consumerist tendencies.

· CONTENTS ·

Previous pages: *A rainbow of naturally dyed cotton yarn*
Opposite: *Cloth napkins make for festive place settings.*

CANDLEMAKING

In medieval times, candlemakers—or chandlers as they were known then—supplied the light sources for homes, churches, and businesses. These days, thanks to the electric lightbulb, few people depend solely on candles to light the way. But candles are nevertheless a valuable resource for power outages, and they're must-haves for quiet, romantic evenings at home or for a relaxing soak in the tub after a hard day.

Choosing Materials

Traditionally, candles were made from beeswax or tallow. **Tallow** candles have a tendency to smoke, so they've largely fallen out of fashion. In addition to beeswax, modern-day candlemakers often use paraffin or soy wax. (**Paraffin wax** is a petroleum byproduct, so I choose to avoid it; the fumes from paraffin wax irritate the eyes and respiratory tract.) **Soy wax** is made from soy oil but is sometimes blended with other materials including paraffin or palm oil. **Beeswax,** the most natural option, is available from beekeepers or online. It's a more expensive option than other common waxes, running about $10 a pound—but there's nothing quite like its rich, light scent.

Melt wax in a double boiler to prevent scorching.

Wax Melting Basics

Wax can be melted using a traditional double boil technique, but you'll need to make a special receptacle for your wax called a **melt-and-pour container.** It's much cleaner than ruining a kitchen stockpot with wax.

1. Make a melt-and-pour container from a recycled tin can. Firmly pinch one edge of the can's open end between pliers and give them a twist to create a pour spout. Place the wax inside.
2. Add water to a stockpot so that the water level comes halfway up the can.
3. Heat on high, but don't let the water temperature exceed 200°F. Use a candy thermometer to monitor this.
4. Keep an eye on the wax; it needs to liquefy, but don't let it exceed 165°F.

DIY

Taper Candles

Hand-dipping candles is done today much like it was in the days of the chandlers. Making your own candles—for yourself or for gifts—is a bit meditative and helps perpetuate a simple traditional skill.

You'll Need:
A tall container for melting wax
Beeswax pellets
Wicking
Metal washers (for weight)
Ice water
Dyes for color (optional)

Easy Cleanup

Cover your work area with newspaper or a drop cloth to prevent wax drips everywhere. If you have an outdoor burner, this might be the time to use it.

1. Determine the length of your candles. You'll be limited by the height of the container in which you melt the wax; use a taller container for candles you want to use at the dining table, a shorter one for birthday candles.
2. While wax is melting (as described on page 74), cut a length of wicking twice as long as the candle height, plus about 5 inches. Tie weights to each end of the wicking, then fold in half.
3. Hold wicking at its midpoint, dip both ends into melted wax, lift, and allow to air dry for a few seconds.
4. Dip candles again, then plunge into ice water. Repeat this process (twice in wax, then once in water) until the candles reach the desired thickness.
5. Hang candles to dry for 24 hours, making sure they don't touch. A laundry drying rack works well for this, or in a pinch, you can set a broom handle over the back of two chairs.
6. Use a knife to cut off the weights. Snip the wick to separate the pair of candles.
7. If you want a really pretty finished product for gift giving, you can dip the cut ends again to finish them. If desired, get creative by dying your wax or adding a partial topcoat of a different color.

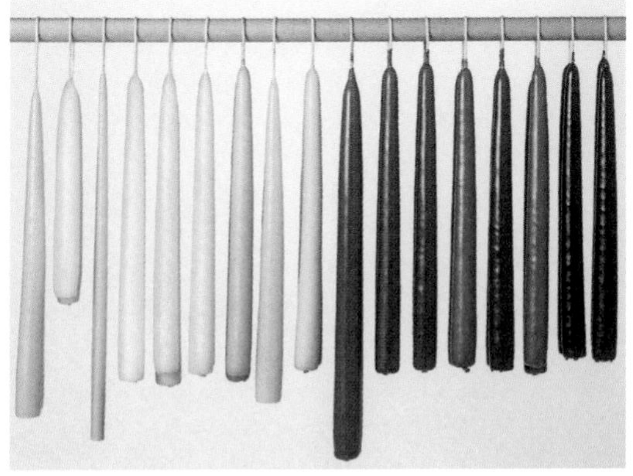

Hand-dipping taper candles means no two are alike.

DIY

Easy Melt-and-Pour Candles

Create one-of-a-kind candles from a variety of containers with this easy candlemaking method. Upcycled teacups from the thrift store, decorative tins, or even terra-cotta pots are all good options.

Vintage teacups are perfect for upcycling into candles.

You'll Need:
Heat-resistant containers
Chopsticks or twigs
Beeswax pellets
Wicking
Essential oils for fragrance (optional)

1. Place containers on a flat surface. Cut wick to length, so that the end will sit on the bottom of the container and extend 4 inches past its top. Tie a chopstick or twig to one end of the wicking. Set the chopstick across the top of the container with the wick extending into the vessel.
2. Melt wax (as described on page 74). Add essential oils to melted wax for fragrance, if desired—use 20 to 30 drops per cup of wax.
3. Carefully pour wax into the container, almost to the rim.
4. Allow to set. If you notice that the wax pulled away from the side of the container or sunk as it dried, melt a bit more wax and top it off for a clean finish.

OIL LAMPS

Before the power grid made lighting a room as easy as flicking a switch, oil lamps were the go-to sources for light after the sun went down. Lamps are still great to have on hand for emergencies. The gentle light from an oil lamp can be easier on the eyes than harsh overhead lighting, too. Light one of these easy-to-make oil lamps, turn off the overheads, and feel the stress of the day melt away.

You can use any sort—and any size—of glass jar for this project. A canning jar works, but so will an upcycled jar. Just make sure the lid is tight fitting. Hint: To remove residual label glue from an upcycled jar, rub it with a bit of vegetable oil until it dissolves, then rinse with soap and water. Dry thoroughly before filling the jar with oil.

DIY

How to Make an Oil Lamp

The bigger the wick, the brighter the flame. Flat, wide braided wicks—like you'd use in a kerosene lantern—provide enough light to comfortably read by, and they last much longer. Small, round wicks create light similar to a candle and burn faster.

You'll Need:

Jar with lid (for safety's sake, avoid tall bottles that could easily tip over)
3d nail
Hammer
Round wicking, 5 inches longer than the jar you'll be using
Nut or washer for weight
Vegetable or olive oil (in a pinch, you could use kitchen grease)

Citrus Lamps

In a pinch, you can make an oil lamp out of an orange, lemon, or grapefruit cut in half. Hollow out the fruit to make a cup while leaving the soft white core intact. Pour in some vegetable oil and light the core like a wick!

Glass jars become oil lamps with a few easy modifications.

1. Use the nail and hammer to punch a single hole in the underside of the jar lid.
2. Push one end of the wick through the hole. Use the nail to help push it through, if necessary.
3. Tie a nut or washer to the opposite end of the wick.
4. Fill the jar with oil.
5. Drop the weighted end of the wick into the jar and screw on the lid. Allow the wick to thoroughly soak up the oil before you attempt to light it.
6. Once soaked, use a lighter or match to light the wick. The flame may burn slowly at first, but it should grow in intensity as it begins to draw the oil up the wick.

1

2

3

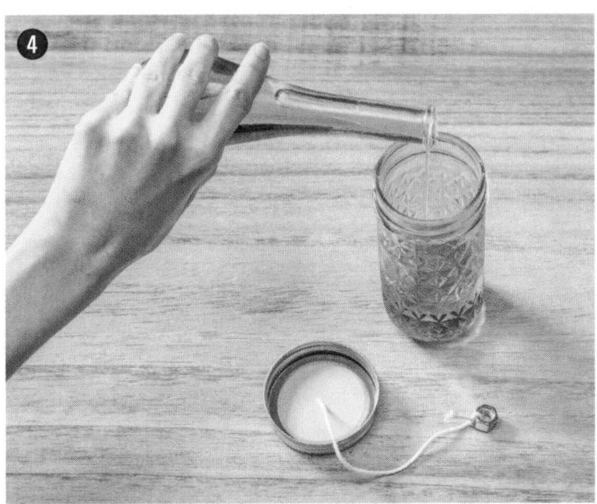
4

5

6

7. To trim the wick, use pliers to pull fresh wick about ¼ inch above the level of the lid. Cut off the burned part. Do this each time you extinguish the flame so that it's ready to use next time. When the wick is used up, replace with a new length of wicking.

NOTE: For an oil lamp with a wider—brighter—braided wick, make two holes in the lid spaced as wide as the wick itself. Use wire cutters to snip the space between the holes. Use caution, as the cut edges will be sharp. Follow the previous instructions.

DYEING

Long before tie-dye became part of the cultural zeitgeist, the process of coloring cloth was more natural. Dyed materials more than 4,000 years old have been found in Egyptian tombs. Blue was one of the most difficult and sought-after colors. During the 1700s, indigo was cultivated on plantations in the American colonies and exported to Europe for its vivid blue dye. It was so valuable that cakes of indigo were used as currency.

But by 1900, 90 percent of dyes were synthetic. Commercially produced dyes and fixatives (treatments that help the color stick) made it easier to keep up with the increased demand that followed the industrial revolution. Synthetic dyes are often derived from coal tar and petroleum and are "fixed" with heavy metal mordants that help color adhere to cloth, such as cadmium, mercury, or lead. These compounds can be harmful to humans and pose environmental problems. Dyeing fabric with plants and berries is a much less toxic project from start to finish, and choosing plant materials locally brings your unique dye batch even closer to home.

Dyed in indigo, natural yarn becomes a deep blue.

There are a couple of options when it comes to using natural dye. You can buy powdered and prepared natural dyes (I like Dharma Trading Company), or you can use the natural materials themselves.

Dyeing With Plant Materials

Dyeing is one of those projects that never turns out the same way twice. This is especially true when using plant-based dyes. Each batch of dye will vary in color and intensity and will react differently to various types of fabric; that is both the beauty and frustration of dyeing. As you delve more deeply into this hobby, experiment a bit to find what works best with the plant materials available in your region.

A mordant (or fixative) is not absolutely necessary, but your color will generally come out stronger and more vibrant if you use one, and it won't wash out. There are a number of different options for mordant. Some are made from toxic metals like copper; safer options include alum, cream of tartar, and tannins (a natural substance derived from bark and other plant materials). If you want to be really authentic, you can use stale urine, as dyers in the Middle Ages did. The yarn or fabric presoaks in the mordant before moving on to the dyeing stage.

Colorful Pilgrims

We often think of early American settlers wearing all black, all the time. But in fact, brown, brick red, blue, and yellow were more common, because black was a hard color to achieve.

A variety of natural dyes will net a wide range of colors, from pastels to vibrant hues.

DIY

Basic Dyeing

Rather than using a powdered pigment or liquid dye to color your fabric, try creating a plant-based dye that starts from scratch with raw, natural material. Depending on the desired color, this may be leaves, roots, bark, flower heads, or even parts of fruits or vegetables. The process takes several stages, so be prepared for this to take a couple days. What a fun way to capture the colors of your local flora! Flour sack towels, made of absorbent, lint-free cotton, are great first-time projects, and you'll use them again and again.

You'll Need:
Cotton fabric
Plant materials for color (to start, try nettle for green, walnut husks for brown, or red cabbage for purple)
4 tablespoons alum
2 tablespoons cream of tartar
8-quart stockpot

Prepare the fabric:

1. Soak fabric in cold water for an hour, making sure there are no dry pockets of fabric, which could cause streaks.
2. Meanwhile, fill the stockpot with water and bring to a boil. Add alum and cream of tartar; stir to dissolve. Remove from heat; cool to room temperature.
3. Add wet fabric to the stockpot; bring to a simmer over medium heat. Allow to simmer for an hour (do not boil). Turn off heat, leaving fabric in the pot until cooled. Rinse well and set aside. (If you're not using the fabric right away, hang to dry.)

Make the dye:

1. Fill a clean stockpot almost to the top with plant material. The more plant material you add, the richer color you will achieve. Don't be skimpy! Add enough water to cover.
2. With a lid on the stockpot, bring the water to a boil, then turn down the heat to a simmer. Simmer for a minimum of an hour. Remove pot from heat and let sit overnight.
3. Strain out plant materials and return the dye to the stockpot.
4. If your fabric has dried, soak in water until it's saturated.

5. Add wet fabric to the dye, making sure that the fabric is entirely submerged. Add more water if necessary.
6. Cook on low heat for 2 hours, stirring occasionally to distribute the dye. Remove from heat, and let the fabric sit in the dye overnight.
7. Rinse and wring out the fabric thoroughly; hang to dry. You can retain the remaining dye for future projects, though the color may lose intensity over time.

DIY

Flower Pounding

Need a bit of colorful instant gratification? Instead of cooking up a dye, the flower-pounding method allows you to transfer the color of a flower or leaf directly to fabric (or paper), leaving behind a

Using fresh or ground turmeric roots to dye fabric results in a pleasing deep yellow hue.

Pounding fresh plant material results in a variety of colors and endless opportunities to get creative.

watercolor-like imprint. Keep in mind that the color from flowers can fade with regular washing.

You'll Need:
Light-colored fabric; muslin is a good option
Towel
Flowers and leaves
Rubber mallet
Tweezers
Hot iron

1. Mordant your fabric with alum as directed in steps one to three on the previous page. Wring out the fabric.
2. Lay a towel down on a sturdy surface. Place the fabric on top of the towel.
3. Set flowers and leaves on one half of the fabric in a pattern. When using a flower with a prominent center, such as a coneflower, you may need to cut it so the petals lay flat. Fold fabric in half.
4. Use a rubber mallet to repeatedly pound each piece of plant material. Color from the flowers or leaves will transfer to both sides of the fabric.
5. Unfold and remove remaining bits of plant material with tweezers. Smaller bits can be brushed away with a dry rag.
6. Once dry, use a hot iron to set the color.

What to Dye

When it comes to successfully dyeing fabric, the most important thing to consider is the fabric itself. Synthetic fabric doesn't accept color well. Instead, choose natural fibers like cotton, linen, wool, or even silk. Always wash new fabric before dyeing; residues from the manufacturing process can interfere with dye retention. Dyeing is also a great way to salvage a favorite piece of clothing that's suffered an unfortunate stain or become faded from wear, as long as it's made with natural fibers.

A RAINBOW OF NATURAL DYES

Long before commercial dyes were an option, artists pursuing a rainbow of color developed a number of ways to naturally dye fabric and yarn. To follow the directions for dyeing with plants (on the previous pages), you'll pick leaves, shoots, or flowers, perhaps accessible right outside in the garden, harvested from the wild, or found at the grocery store. For a simpler process, you can order a multitude of powdered natural dyes and pigments from online stores. Some will even be made from insects such as cochineal, which produces a vibrant shade of scarlet. The list below is just the beginning; find out what grows naturally in your region.

Yellows:
Agrimony leaves
Barberry stem and root
Dyer's coreopsis flowers
Osage orange (dried wood shavings)
Pear leaves
St. John's wort leaves
Dyer's chamomile flowers
Weld stalk and leaves

Reds:
Bedstraw roots
Beets (whole)
Birch fresh inner bark
Common sorrel roots
Dyer's woodruff roots
Madder roots
Potentilla roots
Sandalwood (dried and powdered)

Greens:
Lily of the valley leaves
Nettle leaves

Blues:
Bilberry berries
Elder berries
Indigo (leaves put through fermentation)
Red bearberry leaves
Woad (leaves put through fermentation)

Browns:
Henna leaves (dried)
Lichens
Onionskins
Oak bark
Walnut root and green husks of nut
Coffee grounds

Purples:
Alkanet roots (processed into pigment)
Bryony berries
Cochineal (dried)
Dandelion roots
Danewort berries
Red cabbage (whole)
Hibiscus (dried petals)

Dye material from top to bottom: Osage orange, sandalwood, alkanet, cochineal, henna, indigo

SEWING

In its simplest form, sewing is the act of connecting two pieces of fabric with a needle and thread. These days, hand-sewing is usually reserved for dainty hems, quilting, and decorative work. Certainly, entire projects can be created by hand—that's how pioneers did it, after all—but a sewing machine makes faster work of it. Knowing how to tailor for fit, mend a tear, or sew a button can extend the lifetime of your favorite garment.

The Basics

The first step in sewing success is to choose the proper fabric for your project. (Sturdy canvas is great for outdoor cushion covers, but not so great as a scarf.) Fabric is sold by the yard. Standard widths are 45 inches and 60 inches, though there are variations. For beginning sewers, cotton fabric is a good choice that is easy to work with. Easy beginner projects include cloth napkins, pillowcases, tablecloths, and curtains.

In sewing, we often refer to the "right" and "wrong" sides of the fabric, in reference to the printed side of the fabric (right) and the side that has a faded, less vivid coloring (wrong). The difference is easily visible in most patterned fabrics, but can be harder to discern on solid fabrics.

In most cases, you'll sew fabric with right sides facing each other so that when the project is finished, the seams are on the inside. Just know this: If you forget, you will not be the first (or the last) person to make this mistake. (That's what stitch rippers are for!)

How to Save on Fabric

Instead of buying fabric by the yard, check out the bedding section at your favorite department store. Flat sheets come in a variety of patterns and types of fabric. They can be a less expensive source for large pieces of cloth. If you don't mind secondhand fabric, or want a more environmentally friendly option, visit your local thrift store. In addition to sheets, look for large skirts and loose dresses that can be cut apart and used for small projects.

DIY

Sewing Buttons

Knowing how to reattach a button can save your favorite shirt from being sent to the thrift store.

You'll Need:
Pencil
Needle
Thread, about 24 inches
Button (if you've lost one from a shirt, check inside the front placket, there's often an extra there)

1. Use the pencil to mark the button's location with a dot.
2. Thread the needle, pulling the ends even. Tie the ends together in a knot. This will prevent the thread from pulling all the way through the fabric.
3. Starting on the right side of the fabric, push the tip of the needle into your pencil mark, and back up on the other side. Pull the thread all the way through to the knot.
4. Push the needle through any hole in the underside of the button. Slide the button down the thread and set it in place. Push the needle down into the opposite buttonhole, all the way through the fabric, and back up again in the first buttonhole. If you're working with a four-hole button, you can work parallel or cross the threads in an X pattern, but be consistent.

5. Continue until the button is secure.
6. To tie it off, come up through a buttonhole for the last time. Push the needle through the opposite buttonhole but not through the fabric. Insert the needle into the fabric and out again directly beneath the button. Pull the threads until there's a small loop near the button. Insert the needle through the loop and pull it taut to secure the button.
7. Trim threads.

DIY

Cloth Napkins

Switching to cloth napkins is a great way to reduce waste in your home. We made the change when my kids were quite young, and we would never go back. Cloth napkins are an easy sewing project for beginners and a good lesson in hemming.

You'll Need:
Light cotton fabric cut into 12-inch squares
Matching thread
Needle and thread or a sewing machine
Sheet of card stock
Iron and ironing board
Straight pins

1. Set a square of napkin fabric wrong side up on the ironing board.
2. Place the card stock on the napkin, ¼ inch from one edge. Fold the fabric edge over the card stock, ironing it down.
3. Repeat on all sides.
4. Now make a second fold the same way, just slightly deeper to roll over the first fold. The cut edge of the fabric will now be tucked neatly underneath the clean crease. Repeat on all four sides.
5. Use straight pins to secure folds in place.
6. **To hand-hem:** Starting at the left lower corner, push the needle through the folded edge, from the underside, pulling the thread all the way through. Make a second stitch, catching just a bit of the fabric below the fold, and come up through the folded edge just above the first stitch. Aim for stitches no more than ⅛ inch. Try to stay close to the fold as you continue repeating this stitch all the way around the edge of the napkin. When the circuit is complete, make another stitch and pull the thread until a small loop remains. Push the needle through the loop and pull taut. Repeat a couple more times to secure the thread.

Overlapping corners on hemmed cloth napkins

7. **To machine-hem:** Place the edge of the napkin under the presser foot with the folded edge to the right. Position the needle so that it sits just inside the folded hem. Using a straight stitch, sew along each edge until you reach a corner. At the corner, slow your speed and stop the needle in the down position just as you cross into the next folded hem. Lift the presser foot, spin the napkin on the needle, and drop the presser foot. Repeat on the remaining sides. At the end, use the backstitch function to secure the stitches.
8. Trim the threads.

Backstitch

The backstitch function on a sewing machine switches it into reverse. Backstitching at the end of a seam locks the threads in place so they won't unravel.

Stitch Ripper

A stitch ripper is a hand tool that has a two-pronged tip with a sharp blade. It's used to cut a seam holding two pieces of fabric together, usually to undo a sewing mistake.

Seems We're Talking About Seams

Most cut fabric unravels if it's left unfinished. (The selvage, or finished edges of the fabric that form during manufacturing, does not.) This isn't a problem on hemmed edges, as the cut end of the fabric is sewn securely inside the hem. But when making seams, the raw edges are visible. You can prevent unraveling by making a second pass along the seam with a zigzag stitch between the straight stitch and the edge of the fabric. Some higher-end machines have a function that creates an overlock stitch, but basic machines do not. A simple beginner machine—Singer is a good brand—can be had for around a hundred dollars.

The seam allowance is the space between the seam and the edge of the fabric. When you turn a pair of pants inside out, you can see the seam allowance on the inside leg. Seam allowances are generally ⅝ inch or less when constructing sewing projects but are often trimmed to be narrower.

It's a good practice to press fresh seams with a hot iron to remove any puckering that may occur at the seams, and doing so helps set the stitches.

DIY

Make a Pillowcase

Pillowcases make for easy home decor—there's a whole world of fabric to conquer, from elegant patterns to cartoon characters. They make easy gifts too; it's fun to tuck kids into bed with a pillow decked out in their favorite character or latest hobby.

Pillows are a simple sewing project that adds flair to a bed.

You'll Need:
Lightweight cotton fabric, two pieces 21-by-31 inches
Matching thread
Scissors
Straight pins

1. Pin the fabric pieces together, right sides facing.
2. Using a straight stitch and a ¼-inch seam allowance, sew down the longest side. Stop with the needle in the down position ¼ inch from the end. Lift the presser foot, spin the fabric on the needle, and drop the presser foot. Continue sewing along the short side, and repeat for the second long side. Backstitch at the end to secure the thread.
3. Using the hemming technique described on page 85, make a ½-inch hem to finish the open end of the pillowcase.

DIY

Reusable Produce Bags

Homemade cloth bags can be laundered repeatedly and will serve you for years. They are much more sustainable options than disposable plastic grocery bags. This drawstring bag is made much like a pillowcase, but finished with French seams. I've made these from light cotton fabric and upcycled sheer curtains.

You'll Need:
Lightweight fabric, 2 (12-by-14-inch pieces)
Matching thread
Scissors
Straight pins
Iron
Light cord or ribbon for the drawstring
Safety pin

1. With the wrong sides facing (note that this is different than before!), sew a straight stitch along the two long sides and one short side using a ⅛-inch seam allowance. Turn out the wrong sides, and press the seams with an iron.
2. Now use a ⅜-inch seam allowance to again sew all three sides. This French seam essentially secures the loose ends inside the seam.

Overlock Stitch

An overlock stitch creates a seam as well as a second stitch that sews over the edge of the fabric, preventing unraveling. A machine that has this function may also cut away excess fabric at the same time. This is how the seams of most commercially made clothing are finished.

3. Hem the opening by folding the fabric over twice, about ½ inch each time. Stitch close to the fold.
4. Turn the bag right side out. The seams are inside, but there are no raw edges to fray.
5. Use the scissors to carefully snip a ¼-inch cut in the outside layer of the top hem. Make another snip on the opposite side of the bag. It's easier if you avoid making your snips near the seams. Make sure you don't accidentally cut through both layers.
6. Cut two 24-inch lengths of cording or ribbon. Secure a safety pin to one end of the cord. Push it into one opening, and use it to pull the cord all the way through the top hem and out the same hole. Tie the ends together. Now do the same thing with the hole in the opposite side of the bag. When you pull both cords simultaneously, the top of the bag draws closed and stays closed without the use of a twist tie.

Reusable cloth produce bags are good for the environment, reducing the need for single-use plastic bags.

PATCHWORK & QUILTING

The time-honored tradition of making patchwork quilts grew out of necessity. In a "waste not, want not" society, when fabric was in short supply—as on the great American frontier—every piece of cloth was valuable. When clothing became worn beyond mending, salvageable pieces of fabric could be patched together into a new form. Whether you begin with new fabric you pick out at the store or prefer to use salvaged material, the basic idea is the same: Cut the fabric into assorted pieces and reassemble it to create a pattern or design. Completed patchwork is most commonly used as the top for a quilt, but it works for creating other items—say curtains, aprons, or skirts—as well.

Choosing Fabric

The ideal fabric for quilting is 100 percent cotton. It's sturdy, but it softens with use. Quilters who work with new fabric may choose a special quilters' weight cotton, but home decor cotton is another good choice. If you're upcycling scraps from worn clothing, aim for material that is similar in weight. Cotton scraps make for a great quilt, but experiment! After all, the original intent with patchwork quilting was to utilize what's on hand to prevent waste.

Fabric stores typically sell by the yard, and you'll need to cut to size at home. Resembling a pizza cutter, rotary cutters easily cut through several layers of fabric in a single stroke. They're a quiltmaker's dream; they make it easy to cut accurate pieces. To use one, place the fabric on a cutting mat and roll the cutter across the fabric using even pressure.

DIY

Nine-Patch Strip Method

A nine-patch block pattern is the simplest of designs, but variations on this method make it incredibly versatile. It is an easy way to make use of fabric scraps, and if you're new to patchwork, this basic checkerboard of two tones is a great place to start. The size of your squares will determine the ultimate size of your block, and blocks can be pieced together as large as a pillowcase, a baby blanket, or a full quilt. You could cut out each square individually, but the "strip" method is a faster way to create these blocks.

Choosing fabric is the first creative step in quiltmaking.

You'll Need:
Three strips of dark fabric
Three strips of light fabric

1. Measure and cut your strips. To create a finished square measuring 8 inches by 8 inches, your strips will be 3 inches wide. Precise measurement is key to aligning the squares into a neat checkerboard.
2. Right sides together, use a ¼-inch seam allowance to sew a dark strip to a light strip. Repeat once more.

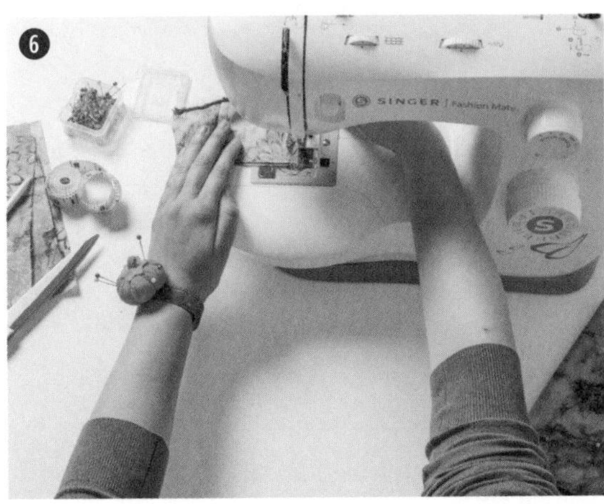

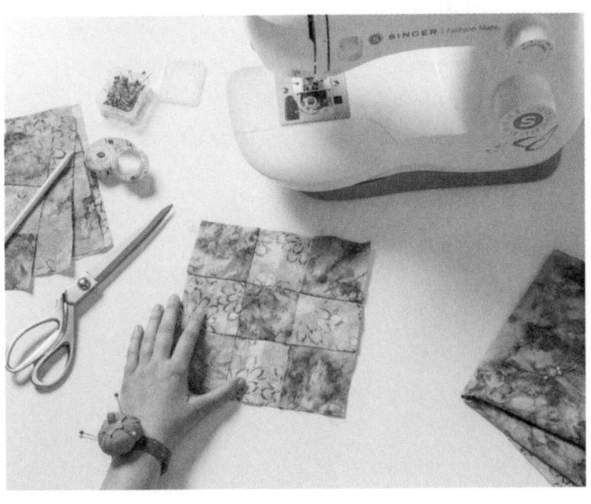

3. Sew one of the remaining strips to each of the sets of two, to create an alternating pattern.
4. Cut across each set of strips. The width of your cuts should be the same as the width of the original strips, in this case, 3 inches. You'll end up with a collection of light-dark-light strips and dark-light-dark strips.
5. Assemble by sewing alternating strips together into the nine-block pattern.
6. Sew along the seams.

A wooden embroidery ring secures layers together for easier hand-quilting.

DIY

Quilting the Patchwork

Although patchwork and quilting often go hand in hand, they are not the same. Quilting is the act of sandwiching a layer of batting between two layers of fabric and stitching through the layers to hold them all together. When crafting a patchwork quilt, the patchwork will be the top layer. The bottom or backing layer is often a single piece of fabric such as muslin.

You'll Need:
A patchwork piece
A backing piece
A sheet of batting
Large safety pins
An embroidery ring, 12 inches or larger
Needle, midsize
Thread, 28-weight cotton
Thimble
Iron (for binding step)

1. Cut batting the same size as your patchwork top piece.
2. Cut backing 1½ inches wider than the top piece on every side. This extra width will become the binding.
3. Spread out the project on a flat surface, as smoothly as possible, centering the batting and patchwork on top of the slightly larger backing, right sides facing out. Use large safety pins to secure the layers together. Place them every 12 to 15 inches or so.
4. Separate the embroidery ring. Slide the inner ring under all three layers to the center point of the project. Align the outer ring on top of the project and push it down over the inner ring and tighten, sandwiching the fabric and batting between the two rings. You'll work the section of the quilt inside the ring first.
5. Thread your needle, tying a knot in one end of the thread.

Batting

Batting is the filler that gives a quilt its thickness. Available in cotton, wool, bamboo, or synthetic fiber, batting comes in sheets and varies in thickness. Thinner batting is easier to work with and produces a coverlet-style end product. Thicker batting produces a puffier comforter.

Stitch in the Ditch

First-time quilters will find the "stitch in the ditch" pattern easiest to follow. This means that your quilting stitches will follow the pattern of the patchwork, with the stitches at the seams.

6. Position your needle at the edge of a seam (see the sidebar on "Stitch in the Ditch"). Push the needle up from the bottom of the quilt and pull the thread through. Give the knot a little tug so that it disappears through the bottom layer of fabric. The knot will catch on the batting inside but will be hidden from the outside view. Using a thimble to help push the needle through multiple layers of fabric will prevent sore fingers.
7. Now push the point of the needle down through the quilting, catching all three layers, and back up through the top layer in a shallow stitch. Pull the thread through and repeat. Aim for small, uniformly sized stitches. When you near the end of the thread, push the needle to the bottom of the quilt and tie a knot as close to the fabric as possible. Hide the knot by again giving it a little tug to pull it back inside the quilt.
8. When you've quilted all of the area within the embroidery ring, unlock the ring and shift it over about 10 inches. Working around that central point, continue stitching from the middle of the quilt outward. Working from the center of the quilt outward keeps the layers as smooth as possible.
9. Once the entire piece is quilted, you'll bind it. Fold one edge of the backing ½ inch in toward the batting. Press in place. Press over again, so the fold of the backing is at the edge of the batting and patchwork. Sew the binding down by hand or with a straight stitch on your sewing machine.

A homemade quilt is perfect for snuggling under—but one made with fabric scraps can become a memento of a lifetime.

WASTE-FREE FOOD STORAGE

Guests in my home have been known to wander from kitchen drawer to kitchen drawer, perplexed that they cannot find any plastic wrap. For us, it's been easy to give up. Instead, we keep plenty of reusable containers on hand for leftovers. But covering big bowls, sealing up half an avocado, or wrapping sandwiches to go without the use of cling wrap requires breaking long-held habits for some of us.

Beeswax wraps are a great environmentally friendly alternative to plastic wrap that is good for only one use. The pine resin can be a challenge to find locally, but it is available online. It's the ingredient that makes the beeswax wraps "clingy" so you'll want to use it. These beeswax wraps can be made with upcycled fabric (cotton sheets work well) or a fun print you find at the fabric store. This recipe comes from Chris Dalziel, author of *The Beeswax Workshop.*

DIY

Beeswax Wraps

It will take you about an hour to make several wraps. Not a bad use of your time to cut the cost and waste that comes with using cling wrap in your kitchen. Want to share the love? Double the recipe and make some for gifts, or make a set for each member of the family!

Beeswax wraps made from cotton cloth

Refresh Your Wraps

After regular use, the coating on the beeswax wraps can start to look a bit worn. To revive them, place each wrap between two pieces of parchment paper and run a warm iron over them. This will melt and redistribute the beeswax coating. Remove from the parchment paper and allow to cool.

Use your beeswax wraps in place of plastic wrap or aluminum foil. They seal nicely over a sliced avocado or an unfinished melon returned to the fridge or around a sandwich or snack in your lunch box.

You'll Need:

½ cup beeswax pellets (available at craft stores)
¼ cup pine resin
¼ cup jojoba oil
1 yard lightweight cotton fabric, 45 inches wide
Parchment paper
Paintbrush, 2 to 3 inches wide

1. Wash the fabric to remove the manufacturer's finish if you're starting with new fabric.
2. Use pinking shears—scissors with a decorative cutting pattern—to cut fabric into the desired size. A 12-inch square is a good all-purpose size for wrapping sandwiches and smaller items. Think about the bowls you might want to cover with these, and cut a variety of sizes accordingly.
3. Cover a baking sheet with parchment paper. Put one piece of fabric on the parchment and set aside.

4. Preheat oven to 225°F.
5. Cover your work area with newspaper.
6. Combine the beeswax and pine resin in a melt-and-pour can (see page 74). Set it in a saucepan with water that reaches halfway up the can. Warm over low heat, scraping the pine resin off the bottom of the can as necessary. It can be a bit sticky, but that's the reason we're using it!
7. Once the beeswax and resin are melted, stir in the jojoba oil.
8. Use the paintbrush to spread a thin layer of the melted beeswax mixture over the first piece of fabric. It will begin to harden.
9. Place the baking sheet in the oven until the beeswax just melts and begins to glisten, 30 to 45 seconds or so.
10. Remove the baking sheet from the oven and use the brush to evenly distribute the beeswax on the fabric.
11. Set a second piece of fabric atop the saturated fabric and use your hands to press the dry piece of fabric onto the waxy one to blot any excess wax.
12. Flip both pieces of fabric over (still conjoined), then put the baking sheet back in the oven to melt the wax again. This allows excess wax to transfer from the first piece of fabric to the second.
13. Remove the baking sheet from the oven, lift the top sheet of fabric off, and hang the beeswax-coated piece to dry.
14. Work on the piece of fabric on the baking sheet next, repeating the previous steps.
15. Allow all of the wraps to dry thoroughly, then wipe with a damp cloth to remove residual wax.

When using the wraps, it helps to warm them with your hands as you press them into place. Clean the beeswax wraps by washing them in warm water with a bit of dish soap. Don't allow them to soak in water. Avoid using the wraps for food products like raw meat, because you cannot sterilize them in hot enough water without melting the beeswax coating.

Replacing plastic cling wrap with beeswax wraps in lunchboxes and for short-term food storage reduces waste.

WOOL FELTING

When you picture felt, you might think of the brightly colored acrylic squares in classrooms and craft stores. But felt has a long history. Traditionally made from wool, it's been used for thousands of years and is considered to be one of the earliest forms of textile production. Felted wool is used to make hats, boots and boot liners, coats, pool table tops, and is even used to cover yurts used by nomadic people of north-central Asia.

Under certain conditions, wool binds to itself, creating a thick mat. If you've ever accidentally washed a wool sweater, you've seen felting in action. By intentionally applying the friction needed to work wool into felt, you can transform loose fiber into a flat sheet—or, for more experienced felt artists, a shaped project such as a hat, slippers, or a stuffed animal.

Repurposing Felt for Crafting

There's always something satisfying about turning something old into a new resource. You can recycle out-of-style or moth-eaten wool sweaters for craft projects. Running these castoffs through the laundry creates friction, felting the wool with little effort from you. To try it, put a sweater into a pillowcase along with a hand towel. Tie it securely near the opening of the pillowcase; this traps the woolly fibers inside as they work loose from the sweater. Toss the pillowcase into the washing machine, with soap (and other laundry if you want!) and run on hot. Remove the sweater from the pillowcase and run it through the dryer.

Felted wool should not unravel when it's cut. Test the sweater by snipping along a seam. If the weave is easy to unravel, repeat the process. Depending on the sweater, you may need to wash it a few times. Check it between each load to see if it's done. Once felted, cut off the seams and cuffs. Use the remaining flat sections of felt for craft projects. It's perfect for handmade mittens or slippers, toy making, pillows, a glasses case, or pretty bags.

> **Roving**
>
> Wool roving is a long, narrow bundle of fiber—usually prepared for spinning—that can be used in various fiber arts.

DIY

Long-Lasting Felted Soap

A bar of soap encased in a layer of felt is a bit like having a washcloth and bar of soap in one. (Less laundry!) While a plain bar of soap can get soggy and melt away in a bathtub, felting prevents this and helps soap bars last longer. Felted soap is less slippery, too, so it's great for kids.

You'll Need:

Wool roving (one ounce will cover several bars of soap)
Bar of soap (nonglycerin)
Hot water

1. Spread the wool into a somewhat flat layer.
2. Wrap the wool around a bar of soap, much like you'd wrap a gift package. Wrap in two different directions to cover all sides. Stretch and pull the wool gently to cover any gaps.
3. If you'd like to add a second color of wool for decoration, add that now. Stretch bits of wool into skinny lengths and wrap around the base color, add a second color to just one side of the soap, or roll wool into little balls to add "dots."
4. Fill a bowl with hot water. Use your hands to drizzle water onto the wool-wrapped bar. Pat the wool to the soap, adding a bit of water as you go. Using too much water at this stage can make the

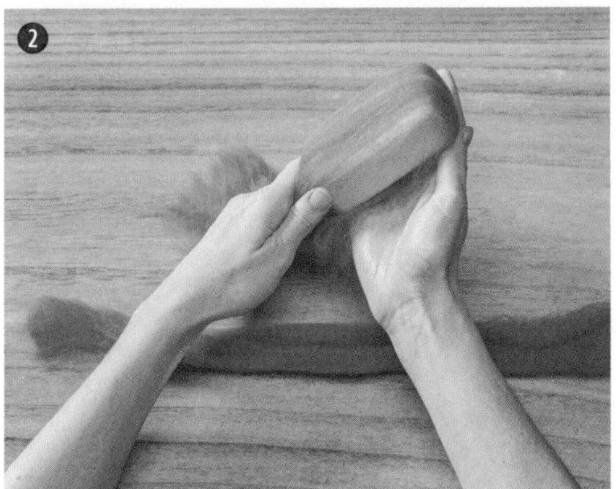

wool slip from the soap. Be patient, continuing to pat and drizzle.

5. When the wool begins to be saturated, it will start to wrinkle into a pocket around the soap. You can get a bit more aggressive with it now, pressing and rubbing the wool. Add water as necessary. The soap will begin to lather quite a bit. Keep working the wool on all sides until the wool forms a tight case around the soap.
6. Rinse off the suds under cool running water and allow to dry. Use as you would a "naked" bar of soap.

BASKETMAKING

Basketry is the art of weaving or sewing materials into a larger piece. Often, these are vessels to hold items; sometimes they're purely decorative. For centuries, natural items like twigs, grasses, and pine needles have been primary materials for making baskets. Coiled baskets made of cotton rope are made much like the longleaf pine needle baskets originally handcrafted by Native Americans, particularly nations in the Southeast.

The longleaf pine was nearly exterminated due to logging and industry in the late 20th century. Restoration initiatives are under way to save the trees, but it is best to utilize alternative materials to create these versatile baskets. Once you've mastered the coil technique, try your hand at using recycled materials, such as lengths of denim or old T-shirts.

DIY

Coiled Rope Basket

You can make a coil basket as large or as small as you like; the instructions are the same. Just choose cotton rope in a thickness that will give you the look you like. (Cotton clothesline is a good gauge to start with, and it's easy to find.) How much rope you need will depend on the size of the basket you opt to make. A 12-inch diameter would make a lovely breadbasket; a slightly bigger base with upright sides is perfect for storing potatoes, and is much more attractive on the counter than the plastic cellophane sack that store-bought potatoes come in.

You'll Need:
Cotton clothesline
Embroidery floss
Scissors
Darning needle
Thimble

1. Thread the needle with a 3-foot length of embroidery floss; tie a knot in one end. (Don't separate the multithreaded floss; use all the strands as one.) The floss secures the rope into the shape of a basket. The stitches will be visible, so choose a color that matches the rope or go with a complementary contrasting color.
2. To start, set the rope on a table or flat surface. Twist the end tightly, wrapping the rope around itself to create a spiral.

The initial stitches for a coiled rope basket

Woven Baskets

Other methods of basketmaking use a weaving technique, much as fabric is made, with a warp and weft. Wicker and plaited baskets begin with a sturdy foundation; bundles of fiber are woven in and out of this base. Plaited work is a bit like elaborate braiding, with fibers woven over and under each other.

A coiled basket can be made as large or as small as you like, and from a variety of materials.

3. With a couple of rotations complete, you'll have a small circle. Push the needle through the diameter of the circle, parallel to the table. You'll go through all of the layers of cord. Repeat this step perpendicular to the first pass. This step is easier to do with a thimble.
4. With that section secured, you can begin adding more rows to enlarge the base of the basket (you'll still be working flat). Run the loose end of cord around the circle to add the next ring. Pass the needle and thread around the two outer rings, then push it down between the coils. As you stitch, catch just a bit of the rope with the needle. This creates a sturdier basket. Precise measurement isn't important, but your stitches should be no more than ¼ inch apart.
5. Add a bit more coil as you continue stitching, crossing two coils at a time with the embroidery floss as you make the circle bigger.
6. When you reach the end of the floss, tie it off in a knot and start with a newly threaded needle from the same spot. Switch colors of floss as desired to create a colorful pattern.
7. Continue in this manner until the circle is the desired size of your basket base.
8. To begin building up the sides, gradually raise the rope above the level of the base on your next coil. The angle on this depends on what shape you're going for. Imagine the completed basket and work toward that shape as you add coils and raise the sides.
9. When you reach the desired height of the basket, finish the circle ending directly above the spot where you started building up the sides. Trim the end of the rope at an angle and secure it with stitching. Tie off the embroidery floss in a knot and trim any loose ends.

MACRAMÉ

Macramé is a method of knotting cord or string in a pattern. It can be decorative or functional, and made small or large. Heavy cotton cord or rough jute twine will result in a bulky end product such as plant hangers and wall hangings. Use embroidery floss for dainty projects like friendship bracelets and other jewelry. Special macramé cord comes in a wide range of colors. Or dye white cotton cording using the instructions on page 79.

Setting Up a Practice Project

Although crafters often use different terms for the strings, or cords, in a project, it's important to know that macramé involves *active* and *passive* cords. The active cords are what you'll make each knot with. The cords that you are knotting *onto* are the passive cords. These tend to stay put, but without them, the knotting wouldn't be possible. While there are numerous knotting methods used in macramé, start with a couple of the basics: the square knot and the half knot. A simple bracelet requires just four strands, while a wall hanging could have a multitude of strands woven together.

Before beginning the macramé plant hanger on the next page, take some time to practice knotting to get a good feel for how to do it. Prepping the cords and workspace for a macramé project are essential to avoid getting tangled and to keep the necessary tension to tie your knots.

1. Select a base to anchor your project. A dowel, pencil, or ring all work well.
2. Position the dowel (for example) between the handles of two coffee mugs, or hang your project from the back of a chair or a curtain rod.
3. Cut two 4-foot lengths of cord. Holding them together, fold them in half. You now have two loops and four dangling ends. Slide the folded end of cording around the dowel.
4. Insert the loose ends into the loop. Pull to secure the knot. This is called a reverse lark's head knot or a cow hitch.
5. Choose two cords as the passive cords; tying a weight near the ends of the passive cords holds them taut, making it easier to work, but this step is optional. The two remaining cords are your active cords.

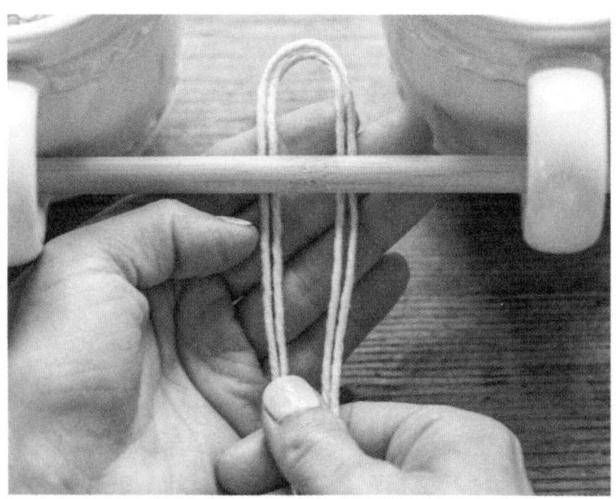

Loop cord under a length of dowel.

Insert loose ends into the loop.

Tying a Half Knot

The half knot is simple—it starts with four-ply cording—and the repetitive knotting results in a fancy-looking twisted spiral.

1. For a twisted half knot pattern, hold one active cord on each side of the passive cords.
2. Fold the left active cord over the passive cords (imagine making the number 4) and under the right active cord.
3. Push the end of the right active cord under the passive cords and over the left active cord, pulling the cord *through* the imaginary number 4. Pull both active cords taut.
4. Repeat, always starting with the left side first. As you continue knotting, the pattern will begin to twist. As it twists, the active cords will change position; just always work from the left.

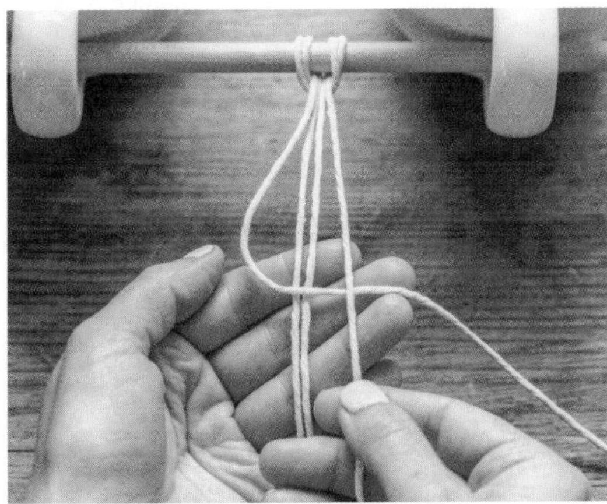

Fold left cord over two center (passive) cords.

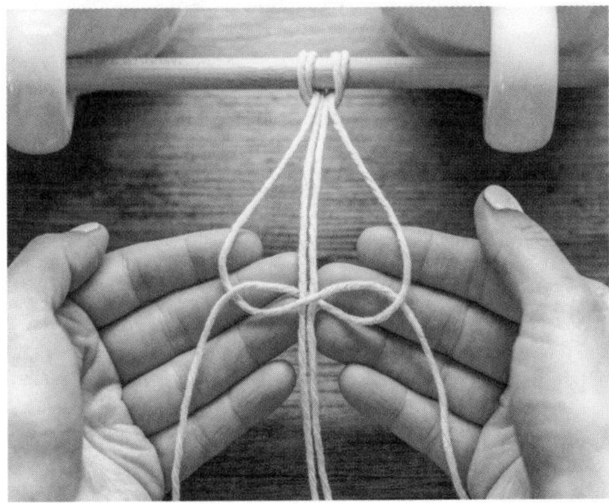

Push right cord under passive cords and through the left loop.

DIY

Making a Paracord Bracelet

A bracelet made of parachute cord (paracord) is an unobtrusive way to keep a length of rope with you. If you find yourself in need of cord, simply undo the macramé. This project could be done with thinner cord or embroidery floss for a narrower band.

You'll Need:
⅛-inch paracord, 10 feet long
Tape measure
Side-release buckle
A lighter

1. Measure and make note of the circumference of your wrist.
2. Fold paracord in half and use a lark's head knot to attach it to the female end of the buckle.
3. Take the buckle apart, and thread the loose paracord ends through the male end of the buckle, sliding it toward the secured end.
4. Slide the male buckle into position so that the distance from the outside of the female buckle to the flat part of the male buckle (don't measure the prongs) measures the circumference of your wrist plus 1 inch.
5. Beginning at the male end, tie square knots down the length of the bracelet until reaching the end. For this knot, start as you did with the half knot but alternate sides for making the "4" shape so you're pulling left-right-left. This will create a flat band rather than a twist.
6. Trim the active ends, one at a time. Use the lighter to slightly burn each end. While each end is still hot, use scissors to press the end flat against the bracelet. This will secure it in place.

Square Knot

For a flat square knot, start as you did with the half-knot—but instead of always knotting in the same direction, alternate sides, so you're pulling left-right-left.

A macramé hanger displaying plants or succulents adds beauty as well as a bit of air purification to a home.

DIY

Macramé Plant Hanger

Macramé plant hangers can be made in different designs to suit your style. This hanger will work well with an 8- to 10-inch pot. You can adjust the size to fit your planter by shortening or lengthening the distance between the knots.

You'll Need:
2-inch metal ring
(8) 10-foot lengths of cotton cord (available at craft or hardware stores)
Measuring tape

1. Set up the project: Gather cords together with ends lined up. Fold the entire bundle exactly in half and follow the directions on page 98 for Setting Up a Practice Project to knot the cords to an anchored metal ring. You will have 16 dangling cords.
2. Measure and mark 10 inches and 20 inches from the ring on all of the cords.
3. Divide the cords into four groups of four. Choose one group of cords to work first, and tie two square knots at the 10-inch mark. Repeat with the other three groups of cord.
4. Tie two square knots at the 20-inch mark. Repeat with the other three groups of cord.
5. You'll now split your loose ends into four new groups. Place two of the sets of cords side by side, so eight cords are laying flat. The four strands in the center will be a new group. The two remaining cords on each side will pair up with two adjacent cords, and the remaining four cords will make up the last new group.
6. Measure and mark 6 inches from the lowest square knot. Tie two square knots at this mark, and repeat with remaining groups.
7. To finish the hanger, create an overhand knot with all of the cords. Holding the cords neatly, form a loop and push the ends through it. Adjust the knot so that it's about 6 inches below the last set of square knots and pull to tighten.
8. Insert your potted plant and hang from a hook in the ceiling.

Endless Possibilities

One fun thing about macramé is that the projects you make can be sized up or down by using thicker or thinner cord and adjusting the length of the cording and distance between knots. Make the macramé plant hanger smaller and it becomes a carrier for your reusable water bottle. Make a larger one and hang your yoga ball out of the way.

Embellish macramé knots by adding assorted beads.

You can gussy up any macramé project by adding beads and baubles. You can string beads on individual cords, or weave them into your knots. You'll need to find beads with large enough holes to accommodate two cords at a time to do this. Large wooden beads are often a good bet.

To add a bead to a square knot, make half the knot, then slide a bead up the two passive cords. Finish the second half of the square knot, snugging the bead in place. If you want the beads to be placed evenly on the plant hanger (or other macramé project), be sure to count the knots and add a bead at the same place on each strand.

You can add beads in succession, one bead strung into each knot, or even add several beads at once. Your imagination is the only limit!

LEATHERWORK

You *could* jot down your thoughts in a boring spiral-bound notebook, but making a beautiful leather journal is an easy project that will bring you joy every time you pull it out, whether to track your garden growth, keep a diary or travel journal, or log a list of backyard birds. Have fun with it and make extras—they make great gifts!

Sourcing Leather

Many craft stores carry sheets of leather in various sizes and thicknesses. Your local thrift store can also be a gold mine for materials: Leather purses, briefcases, and jackets are often sold at a fraction of their original value and can be disassembled to create pieces of leather for small projects in fun colors. Simply cut along seams with a box knife and remove any embellishments.

DIY

Leatherbound Journal

This journal is a nice size to pack along on nature excursions. Tuck some colored pencils in your pack as well, and you can sketch the plants, animals, and birds you see along the way.

You'll Need:

- 50 sheets of letter-size paper (choose a good-quality paper, colored paper, or graph paper from a stationery or office supply store)
- Leather, 9 × 17 inches (3- to 4-ounce weight)
- 18 to 22 inches of thin leather or ribbon
- Waxed thread
- Darning needle
- Hammer and nail
- Scrap piece of wood (for hammering on)
- Sturdy scissors

1. Separate paper into stacks of five. Fold each stack in half.
2. On the spine of each bundle, make a mark ½ inch from the top and bottom of the fold. Add two more marks between the first two, an equal distance apart.
3. Punch a small hole in each booklet at the pencil marks. I do this by laying the booklet open flat on a piece of scrap wood, using a hammer and nail to pierce the paper. Repeat with remaining paper booklets. The holes in all the booklets should align.
4. Set the leather, right side down, on a flat surface. Position one of the folded bundles of paper on the leather, with edges ½ inch from the top, bottom, and left side of the leather (the right side will be longer). Use the pencil or chalk to mark the position of the four holes.
5. Stack the paper booklets and measure the thickness of the spine. Using this measurement, cut short slits of matching width in the leather at the measurements you've marked. You'll sew through these slits to attach the paper to the leather.
6. Thread the needle with waxed thread. Tie a knot in the end and leave a 3-inch tail.
7. Place the first bundle onto the leather, open, aligning the holes with the slits. Insert the needle in the bottom hole and through the slit. Pull the thread through to the knot. Insert the needle through the second slit and hole, pulling it back inside the bundle, then back down into the next hole and slit. Continue in this manner until you reach the top hole. Stitch back to the bottom in

Make It Vegan

Prefer not to use leather? You can use heavy canvas fabric or upcycled denim for the cover instead.

the same alternating pattern, filling in the blank spaces. When you reach your starting point, tie the thread to the tail in a tight square knot as close to the paper as you can.

8. Repeat with remaining bundles of paper until all are sewn in place, and tie off the thread.

9. The longer right side will become the overlapping cover. Cut a ½-inch slit about an inch from the right edge. Tie a knot on one end of a length of thin leather and thread the opposite end through the slit. Fold around the journal and wrap the loose end of the knot to secure cover.

MOSAICS

Ancient civilizations of the Near East used mosaics to decorate floors and walls. During the era of the Greek and Roman Empires, artists began crafting representational imagery. Materials like pebbles and, later, cut tile and glass were mortared in place to depict people, animals, and detailed quiltlike designs. Adventurous travelers marvel at mosaic World Heritage sites such as the great European basilicas, floors of Roman villas restored by archaeologists, and the completely tiled exterior of the Jameh Mosque in Iran.

Creating mosaics is easy to do in *this* century, and it's a great way to use materials that might otherwise go to waste. Use upcycled bits of tile and pottery to craft a pretty trivet, tile backsplash, patio tabletop, garden planter, or candleholder.

Designing a Mosaic

A mosaic project is unique to its creator; no two are alike. Mark out a design on your base—perhaps a square of plywood for a trivet or a clay pot for a garden planter. (Don't worry; the sketch won't be visible on the final product.)

If you're working with a flat project, it's a good idea to lay all of the tesserae out on the pattern *before* setting them in place to make sure you like how it looks before committing yourself with glue. You cannot really do this with a three-dimensional design, but you can lay out the materials in a rough pattern on a table before securing them.

You can also set your tesserae randomly without following any sort of pattern. Just choose materials and colors that look good together and glue them in place free-form as you go, varying the sizes of tesserae for visual interest.

Tesserae

The materials with which mosaic are created—small tiles or bits of pottery—are called *tesserae*.

DIY

Mosaic Trivet

Trivets sit under a hot dish to protect the table surface beneath. In just a few hours, you can transform a board—or even one of those ugly wooden thrift store plaques—into a fun and colorful mosaic trivet to brighten up any dinner table. Add a hook to the trivet and you can even display it on the wall.

You'll Need:

- Board for a base, round or square, roughly 8 to 12 inches across and at least ¼ inch thick
- Weldbond (or other very strong glue)
- Tile grout
- Tesserae of your choice
- Colored markers, optional
- Rags
- Disposable gloves

1. If you're planning a pattern rather than a random display, use markers to draw it on the board.
2. Lay out your design, rearranging tesserae until you're happy with how it looks. Allow about a ⅛-inch gap between pieces and at the edges.
3. Lift one piece at a time, squeeze a dab of Weldbond to the back, and set it in place. Once all pieces are glued down, allow to dry overnight.
4. Mix tile grout according to package directions.
5. Wearing disposable gloves, scoop some grout onto the trivet. Grout is a soft material that you can easily spread and push into cracks between the tesserae and around outer pieces to finish the edges.

Sketching out a design and placing tesserae on the pattern before gluing in place allows you to make necessary adjustments.

6. Scrape as much excess grout off of the tesserae as you can, then use a damp rag to clean the surface and smooth the cracks. As you do this, you might notice some low spots. Fill these in with more grout as needed.
7. Once the grout is smooth, allow to dry overnight.

Resizing Your Bits and Bobs

Some of your materials might need to be broken into smaller pieces—a chipped teacup, say. To break porcelain or ceramic pieces into random bits, place inside an old pillowcase and tap with a hammer until you have the size pieces you desire. The same method works for glass, but use a heavy brown shopping bag so that you can throw it away when you're done. Use extreme caution to avoid being cut by tiny shards and sharp pieces of glass.

For more precise shapes, you'll need a special hand tool. A mosaic tile nipper, available at craft or building supply stores, will cut tile into smaller pieces. For glass, a wheeled, plier-like tool cuts glass with minimal splintering. When cutting glass, do so with your hands inside a lidded box. It's a bit awkward, but using this method will help contain the inevitable shards. When your project is done, be sure to clean the area thoroughly.

Ten Mosaic Materials to Upcycle

Looking for materials? Try garage sales, thrift stores, and the waste bin at construction sites or tile shops:

- Broken or chipped cups and saucers
- Seashells
- Beads
- Broken tiles
- Scrap glass or glass tiles
- Broken mirror pieces
- Marbles (flat or round)
- Pebbles and stones
- Jewelry
- Bottle caps

BLOCK PRINTING

Long before the printing press was invented and modern laser printers were a household fixture, images were duplicated in a more rustic manner. Woodblock prints were a way to replicate an image, used to embellish fabric or create playing cards. From simple to elaborate, block printing allows makers to create a custom, personalized pattern that can be used again and again.

Cut a raised pattern into a potato for a quick and easy stamp.

Block Materials

Before you start carving out your pattern, you'll need to decide what material you'd like to use as your base.

- **Wood** is environmentally friendly, but its density makes it one of the more difficult materials to carve. Basswood is commonly available in premade blocks.
- **Bamboo** is used in Hawaii to create long, narrow designs for printing on kapa, a traditional cloth made of fibers from the paper mulberry tree.
- **Synthetic blocks** come in a variety of densities and materials. Linoleum blocks are common, but for easier carving seek out a softer product, such as those sold under the names of Soft-Kut or E-Z Cut. (Visit *dick blick.com* for a wide variety.)
- **Styrofoam trays** can be upcycled for printing, though you'll be limited by the size of the tray.
- **Potatoes** are an easy-to-carve option and great for small, simple patterns. Unlike the other options they cannot be reused for long.

Carving Tools

The type of tool you'll use to carve depends on the material you're carving. Special wood gouges or linoleum carving tools come in sets with several blades and are used, respectively, for cutting wood or linoleum blocks. An X-acto blade works well for bamboo. Soft foam can be "carved" with a chopstick or the end of a paintbrush. And a kitchen knife works on potatoes.

DIY

Block Printing

Prints can be made on paper, fabric, or a variety of smooth surfaces. It's the perfect way to upcycle plain boxes or brown bags into pretty packaging, or to make a gift card. Block printing is also a fun way to decorate clothing and tote bags, or to create a design on a wall.

You'll Need:
A block to carve
Carving tools
Paper
Pencil
Marker
Paint
Paintbrush or brayer

1. Sketch a design on a sheet of paper the same size as your block. Remember that your design will print in reverse.
2. To make your own transfer paper, use the pencil to completely cover another sheet of paper with graphite. Place the paper onto the block, graphite side down. Set the sheet with your design

Stencil Printing

Stencils are other common printing tools. Cut your design from card stock or paper, then use a paintbrush to lightly fill in the stencil, or place the stencil beneath a screen-printing frame and apply ink or paint with a squeegee. This makes for an even application and allows you to layer colors or produce many copies.

faceup on top of the transfer paper and use a pencil to firmly trace the pattern, transferring it to the block.

3. Use a marker to make the pencil lines on the block darker. (Once you start carving, pencil lines alone become harder to track.)
4. Decide if you want the lines to be white or colored. If you carve out the lines themselves, they will appear white on your print. If you want the lines to be colored, you'll remove the negative space *between* the lines.
5. Choose a carving tool and begin carving your pattern. Take your time, so you don't accidentally carve out an area that you had intended to keep.
6. When your block is finished, cover it with paint. Avoid getting paint in the carved-out sections. A brayer—a smooth roller—makes this easier, but with a little care, a paintbrush works fine.
7. Press a piece of paper onto the painted block, using your hands to smooth the paper so that it makes contact with the entire surface.
8. Alternatively, pick up the block and press it onto another surface. To make this easier, glue the carved design to a larger block of wood. This allows you to pick up the carved print and press it to another surface more easily.

Making blocks for printing allows you to go into great detail once, and then easily replicate the design on fabric, walls, or paper.

• *chapter three* •

CLEAN

CLEAN

Often, when we think about a healthy lifestyle, the first thing that comes to mind is what we eat. We avoid unhealthy foods or produce that's been sprayed with pesticides, or attempt to add more fiber and vegetables to our diet. But what about the products we use to clean our bodies and our homes?

From lotions and shampoo to laundry detergent and deodorizers, our bodies are constantly being exposed to unfamiliar—and often dangerous—ingredients. Even something that sounds as innocuous as "fragrance" can contribute to our chemical body burden—in other words, the toxins that build up over a lifetime and impact our health. Persistent organic pollutants found in some pesticides and industrial chemicals, for example, can accumulate in fatty tissue; repeated exposure has been implicated in cancer, nervous system damage, reproductive disorders, and disruption of the immune system.

Wondering how you can eliminate harsh chemicals from your life while still maintaining a clean environment? The answer is simple: Do it yourself! The recipes in this chapter call for everyday items like shea butter in soap, avocado as a hair mask, and vinegar as a cleaning agent.

In this chapter, you'll learn about alternative options for personal care products, household cleaners, and nontoxic household pest control. Embracing a clean and simple lifestyle is easily extended to your medicine cabinet, too, especially for common ailments like colds, congestion, and abrasions. Herbal medicine has been practiced for centuries and is still widely used in much of the world. It is important to educate yourself on proper usage and risk, but you can reap real benefits by exploring the fascinating world of plant-based natural remedies.

Start with just one of these recipes and slowly begin to replace commercial products with homemade alternatives.

• CONTENTS •

Previous pages: *Handmade soap with natural ingredients (see page 112)*
Opposite: *Fire cider ingredients (see page 132)*

SOAPMAKING

Synthetic fragrances and dyes can be irritants for many people; if you're trying to eliminate them from your household, you may have already switched to gentler soap made with natural ingredients and scented with essential oils. But handmade soaps can get expensive. By learning to make your own, you can save money and create whatever scent combinations you like. Customized soap bars also make excellent gifts.

Soapmaking was on my list of skills to conquer for years before I finally made my first batch. Not surprisingly, the idea of using a caustic ingredient like sodium hydroxide—commonly known as lye—has prevented even the most intrepid do-it-yourselfers from learning how to make soap. Turns out, it's one of those projects that is amazingly easy once you've gotten over your initial trepidation.

Like baking, soapmaking requires careful measurement and mixing of ingredients. Soap is a little less forgiving than cookies or cake, though. It's important that you don't deviate from the recipe. Weigh ingredients using a kitchen scale; accurate measurements are required for saponification to happen.

Saponification is the process that transforms ingredients into a cleaning tool. It's a chemical reaction that occurs when oils and fats are exposed to a strong alkali like lye. Every oil needs a different amount of lye to be transformed into soap. If you must make changes to a recipe, or want to develop one of your own, it's essential to use a lye calculator to make sure that the ratios will produce a successful batch of soap.

Important Safety Notes:

Making soap is simple, but you do need to follow some safety precautions:

- When lye is added to water, an exothermic reaction occurs. It's not visible—there's no foaming or color changing—but the water becomes very hot.
- Always add the sodium hydroxide—or lye—to the liquid. Adding the liquid to the lye can cause a reaction resulting in an eruption of materials.
- When working with lye, always wear protective gear and work in a well-ventilated area—outside, if possible. If you must work inside, be sure to open a window and avoid breathing in the fumes.
- If your skin comes into contact with lye, run it under cold water for 15 minutes. If you get lye in your eyes or on a large area of skin, seek medical attention immediately.
- Never leave heating fats unattended, as they are flammable. The purpose of heating oils in soapmaking is strictly to liquefy solid oils and butters. Once that occurs, remove from heat.

What You'll Need for Making Soap

Most of the ingredients required for making soap are readily available, but sodium hydroxide can be a bit elusive. Hardware and farm supply stores are good bets, or you can order it online. Just be sure that sodium hydroxide is the only ingredient listed. Some drain cleaners tout their product as lye, but have added ingredients that you don't want in your soap. In addition to the ingredients for your soap, you'll need a handful of tools:

- **Heatproof pitcher:** The spout will make it easier to safely pour the lye mixture. Use stainless steel or plastic.

Dry handmade soap on a wire rack for four to six weeks before using.

■ **Immersion blender:** You can stir the soap batter by hand, but an immersion blender makes the process much faster. Be careful that you keep the head of the blender submerged and upright to avoid splattering liquid. An inexpensive immersion blender runs less than $20 and is a worthwhile investment if you intend to take up regular soapmaking.

■ **Digital kitchen scale:** Soap ingredients—even liquids—should be measured by weight, and not volume, for accurate results.

■ **Thermometer:** A digital instant-read thermometer allows you to check temperatures quickly; a candy thermometer works in a pinch.

■ **Long-handled stainless steel or silicone spoon:** Use for stirring the ingredients.

■ **Rubber spatula:** This helps you scrape the soap batter into the molds.

■ **Molds:** You can purchase silicone molds in a variety of shapes and patterns, or upcycle containers for forming soap. Cardboard milk cartons, small cardboard boxes, and yogurt containers are recycled options that work well.

Is Lye Safe?

Lye is a corrosive ingredient and must be used with respect (much in the way you use caution with bleach). It's also crucial to the soapmaking process. Each molecule of lye reacts with molecules of oil, both becoming an entirely new material: soap plus glycerin. When fats and oils are combined with lye in the right proportions and cured properly, the chemical process of saponification results in soap with no trace of lye remaining. While you're using it, it's important to take precautions by wearing a long-sleeved shirt, safety goggles, and gloves, and precise measurements are a must. Mixing the lye into water creates fumes, so work in a well-ventilated space.

Choosing Your Oils

Many oils and fats can be used in soapmaking, and the cost of the different options varies widely. Common cooking oils like olive, coconut, and avocado work well; you can combine these with products like shea butter or cocoa butter to make soaps that serve different purposes and offer a wide range of benefits.

Beautiful Soap

Once you've mastered a basic bar, start experimenting! Customize soap with the addition of natural coloring (find a great guide at *lovelygreens.com/how-to-naturally-color-handmade-soap*) or exfoliants like oatmeal or coffee grounds. Add swirls of color, texture the surface, use molds in unique shapes, or press flower petals into the bars for fancy soaps.

Coconut and castor oils are good for sudsy soaps; shea butter is moisturizing. Olive oil provides a creamy lather and makes a long-lasting bar. Sunflower oil, which is high in essential fatty acids and vitamin E, is nourishing for the skin. Some oils should only be used in small percentages. If you want to develop your own custom soap recipes, you'll need to get familiar with the benefits and limitations of these ingredients.

Although palm oil is a common ingredient in soaps and shampoos, I don't recommend using it in your own products, as massive deforestation (and thus, loss of habitat for both humans and animals) is occurring in regions with palm plantations. Tallow is an excellent substitute for palm oil in soap recipes, and is much gentler on the environment.

Cold Process or Hot Process?

The basic ingredients for soapmaking are the same regardless of the process you use. Cold process soaps are made by blending ingredients together and

Essential oils add fragrance to soap.

Silicone molds made especially for soap are useful for forming loaves.

allowing them to harden and cure for an extended period of time.

Hot process soaps require the additional step of cooking the ingredients in a slow cooker or double boiler. Heat speeds up the saponification process, so hot process soap can be used in just a few days. In this chapter, we focus on cold process soaps, as they are a good option for beginning soapmakers.

Preparing Soap Molds

Some soap molds—wooden molds and upcycled cardboard boxes—need to be lined. This makes it easy to remove the soap loaf. Freezer paper or parchment paper work well for lining molds. To keep the liner as smooth and wrinkle-free as possible, cut two separate strips. One strip should be as wide as the long length of the mold, the other as wide as the narrow length. Both should be long enough to extend beyond the top of the mold. Place the paper in the molds so they overlap (with the shiny side facing up if you're using freezer paper).

Silicone molds don't require that you take this step. One thing to note, though: Silicone molds can retain moisture, adding another day or so before soap can be removed from the mold.

Finishing Your Soap

Once you've poured the soap batter into molds, cover the loaves with parchment paper and a towel for insulation. Set aside to harden for 24 to 48 hours, checking them occasionally. If the soap begins to form cracks, it's getting too hot. Uncover and move it to a cooler location. When the soap feels cool and solid to the touch, it's ready to be unmolded.

When the soap is completely set, turn it out of the mold. Remove loaves from wooden molds by lifting the parchment paper's overhanging edges. For silicone molds, press the soap up from the bottom until it releases. Individual soaps are ready to dry; use a sharp knife (not a serrated one) to cut loaves into any size bar you like.

Set the bars on stainless steel or coated wire racks to cure and dry. (Other metals can discolor the finished soap.) This allows the bars to firm and finish saponification. Bars are safe to touch with bare skin after 48 hours but won't be ready to use for four to six weeks.

DIY

Pure Tallow Soap

For soapmaking on a budget, tallow soap can't be beat. You can find tallow at some supermarkets or learn to render your own. Tallow is a by-product of butchering, made from beef fat, and is a more sustainable option than many other fats or oils—especially because it can often be sourced locally. And don't worry: This soap doesn't smell like meat! This recipe can also be made with lard (from pork fat). I prefer to use tallow from grass-fed cows; I get it at my local butcher shop.

You'll Need:

32 ounces tallow or lard
4.33 ounces sodium hydroxide (lye)
11.2 ounces distilled water
1 to 2 teaspoons essential oils (optional)

1. Prepare your molds (see previous page).
2. Melt the tallow in a saucepan until it's liquefied, then remove from heat.
3. Wearing a long-sleeved shirt, safety goggles, and gloves, carefully pour lye into the water. Stir well, being careful not to splash.

Experiment with colorants to create vivid swirls and dark-colored bars.

4. When the tallow cools to between 100°F and 125°F, pour the lye solution into the tallow. Ideally, the lye solution will be within 10 degrees of the temperature of the melted tallow. Be careful not to splash while combining the mixtures.
5. Use an immersion blender to mix the soap batter until the mixture reaches trace and the soap begins to hold its shape.
6. Stir in essential oils, if desired.
7. Pour the raw soap into molds and follow directions for finishing the soap.

DIY

Moisturizing Soap Bar

Regular soap bars can be drying on the skin, especially on the face and sensitive décolletage. Using shea butter results in a gentle cleansing bar with moisturizing properties.

You'll Need:
12.5 ounces water
5.5 ounces sodium hydroxide (lye)
8 ounces coconut oil
8 ounces cocoa butter
4 ounces shea butter
4 ounces avocado oil
1 ounces jojoba oil
16 ounces olive oil
1 to 2 teaspoons essential oils (optional)

1. Prepare your molds (see page 115).
2. Measure water into a heatproof pitcher.
3. Wearing a long-sleeved shirt, safety goggles, and gloves, carefully pour lye into the water. Stir well, being careful not to splash. The lye will react with the water and get hot.
4. Set the lye mixture aside.
5. Combine the coconut oil, cocoa butter, and shea butter in a saucepan and heat gently. Once liquefied, remove from heat and stir in the liquid oils. This helps to bring down the temperature of the melted oils.
6. When the temperature of the oils reaches between 100°F and 125°F, pour the lye solution into the oils. Ideally, the lye solution will be within 10 degrees of the temperature of the oils. Be careful not to splash.
7. Use an immersion blender to mix the soap batter until the mixture reaches trace.
8. Stir in essential oils, if desired.
9. Pour raw soap into molds and follow directions for finishing the soap.

Superfatting

Lye molecules convert fat molecules into soap. If there are more oil molecules than fat molecules, some of these will remain in the soap. Superfatting is the process of intentionally calculating for extra oil in a recipe. This is done when creating a moisturizing bar.

What Is Trace?

Soapmakers use the term "trace" to describe the consistency of the soap batter when it's ready to be poured into molds. When the soap begins to look like cooked custard and holds its shape across the top, you've achieved trace. Note that there isn't an exact science to this, and the level of trace can range from light (thinner) to heavy (thicker). Mixing the batter until it reaches heavy trace allows for layering soap of different colors, as it holds its shape to support additional layers.

Imperfections

It's not uncommon for soap to crack or "volcano" as it hardens, pushing a hole in its exterior. Different combinations of ingredients can be more prone to this, and the temperature of the soap as it cures can also impact the curing soap. The good news is that your soap is perfectly fine to use with these blemishes.

Cleanup

When you're done making a batch of soap, you'll be left with equipment that's covered with raw batter. Use recycled newspapers to wipe as much of it from the utensils as possible. Toss the newspaper in the trash. Soak the equipment in a sink filled with very hot, soapy water. Use a dishrag or sponge dedicated to cleaning up soaping messes and your gear. To clean the immersion blender, run it in a container of hot soapy water, then thoroughly wipe it down.

SKIN CARE

A good skin care routine doesn't require a lot of bells and whistles, but a little extra pampering never hurts. The following homemade products allow you to indulge in some of your favorite skin care routines with all-natural ingredients. Globally, we spend an estimated $130 billion on skin care. Other factors to consider beyond the monetary cost of caring for our skin are the additives that cause concern for both human health and the environment. We chase younger, more supple skin with parabens, microbeads, and phthalates. Phthalates, for instance, have been linked to potential reproductive issues. Microbeads are teeny, tiny bits of synthetic plastic used in skin care products that wash down the drain and end up in our oceans—and in the fish that live there.

We have natural alternatives to these environmentally unsound products. Ingredients like oils, beeswax, shea butter, and essential oils can form the base of beautiful, healthy skin care products without synthetic chemicals.

Skin Care Basics

Everyone's skin responds differently to treatments. Even if you are a no-frills, zero-cosmetics person, you can take several tactics to keep your skin—your body's largest organ—healthy.

■ **Diet** Eat right and your skin will shine. A healthy diet complete with plenty of fruits and vegetables (and a sufficient amount of water) is good for you and your complexion.

■ **Sun Protection** Choose a sunscreen you're comfortable with and use it every day, even if it's cloudy! Chemical sunscreens offer high SPF protection, but skin can absorb the chemicals in these products; moreover, several of the most common chemical sunscreen ingredients have been found to be hormone disrupters. These sunscreens have also been implicated in causing damage to coral reefs. Physical sunscreens use mineral barriers like zinc oxide and titanium dioxide to deflect the sun's rays. But even products that proclaim to use natural ingredients can contain harmful ones. Always read labels on sunscreen to make sure you're comfortable with all the ingredients. Alternatively? Wear a big floppy hat and long sleeves and avoid being out in the sun during the hottest part of the day.

DIY

No-Mess Lotion Bars

Lotion bars are solid at room temperature. But when held in your hands for a few minutes, your body heat warms them, converting them into lotion. Handy for traveling, these lotion bars are especially ideal if you're flying and limited in the amount of liquids you can carry on. When made with various essential oil blends, they can do double duty by offering headache relief, stress relief, or antimicrobial properties.

You'll Need:
Coconut oil
Shea butter or cocoa butter
Beeswax
Essential oils (optional)
Melt-and-pour container (see page 74)
Molds or upcycled candy tins

1. Combine equal parts coconut oil, shea butter, and beeswax in the melt-and-pour can.
2. Set the can in a small saucepan, then add water outside the can so that it reaches about halfway up the can. Warm over medium heat.
3. When the ingredients are melted, remove from heat and stir in 10 to 20 drops of essential oils, if desired.

Solid lotion bars moisturize skin. Stored in a recycled tin, they are perfect for tucking into a carry-on travel bag.

4. Pour liquid into molds or candy tins and allow to harden.
5. To use, hold a lotion bar in your hands until it begins to melt, then rub it in. For lotion bars poured directly into tins, wash and dry your hands, then rub the pad of your thumb across the top, warming the bar until it's softened.

DIY

Deodorant Cream

Usnea is a lichen that has been used medicinally for centuries. Intrepid foragers can harvest usnea from the wild (it's common throughout the United States), but it's also available from online herb purveyors or health food stores. Its antimicrobial properties can help keep your pits odor free and help reduce exposure to aluminum, a common ingredient in commercial antiperspirants that's been linked to a possible increase in risk for breast cancer.

You'll Need:

¼ cup arrowroot powder
⅛ cup baking soda
⅛ cup dried usnea, packed
1 tablespoon shea butter
2½ tablespoons coconut oil
Contents of one vitamin E capsule (or ⅛ teaspoon)
10 to 20 drops essential oil (optional)
Food processor
Small jars

1. Combine all ingredients except the essential oil in a food processor. Pulse until the shea butter is well crumbled.
2. Continue blending, scraping down the sides, until the ingredients become creamy.
3. Stir in the essential oil.
4. Transfer to a jar with a lid.
5. To use, rub a small amount of deodorant in your armpit until absorbed.

DIY

Coconut Oil Salt Scrub

A salt scrub works wonders for exfoliating dead, dry skin. Even rough, calloused feet will feel soft and new when treated to a little extra care.

You'll Need:
1 cup sea salt or pink Himalayan salt
½ cup coconut oil
10 drops essential oil
2 teaspoons dried herbs or flowers (optional)
Small airtight container

1. Measure the salt and coconut oil into a mixing bowl. Use a fork or pastry blender to mix until well combined.
2. Stir in your favorite essential oil. Lavender is soothing, peppermint offers an astringent pick-me-up, and grapefruit can aid with detoxification.
3. If desired, add dried herbs or flower petals to the scrub. This makes the scrub prettier for gift giving but is not necessary.
4. Store in an airtight container.
5. To use, scoop a couple teaspoons of the scrub into the palm of your hands and use it to scrub wet skin. Use extreme care if you choose to do so in the bathtub, as the oil will cause the tub to become slippery.

Scent Blends to Try

Fragrance is a highly individual preference. You might opt for no fragrance at all in your personal care products, and that's just fine. If you decide to add essential oils, you can customize the scent strength by limiting the amount you add or combine different oils to create a signature scent.

- Patchouli + vetiver + cedarwood = earthy
- Jasmine + rose + bergamot = floral
- Ginger + orange + cinnamon = spicy
- Cypress + white fir + sandalwood = woodsy
- Lemon + orange + rosemary = citrusy
- Peppermint + eucalyptus = decongestant
- Tea tree + orange = antimicrobial
- Clary sage + lavender + lemon = stress relief
- Peppermint + lavender + marjoram = headache relief

Indulge in a little soothing self-care with a salt scrub.

DIY

Tallow Moisturizer

Tell people that you're moisturizing your face with beef fat and their first reaction is likely to be less than favorable. That was my reaction when I first heard of tallow moisturizer, but now I use it daily. Although this isn't a good option for vegetarians, tallow is easily absorbed; this moisturizer leaves skin soft and supple without being greasy. Opt for tallow from pastured, grass-fed beef (available at natural food stores).

You'll Need:
½ cup tallow
1 tablespoon olive oil
1 tablespoon cocoa butter
1 tablespoon beeswax pellets (available at craft stores)
20 to 30 drops essential oil for fragrance
Melt-and-pour container (see page 74)
Small jars

1. Combine tallow, olive oil, cocoa butter, and beeswax in a melt-and-pour can.
2. Set the can in a small saucepan, then add water outside the can so that it reaches about halfway up the can. Warm over medium heat, stirring occasionally until melted.
3. Remove from heat and stir in the essential oil.
4. Pour into small jars and allow to cool.

DIY

Soothing Body Butter

Dry skin—especially dry hands—can be downright uncomfortable. This body butter soothes and softens chapped skin from fingers to toes. This recipe can be made with various oils: Grape seed, sweet almond, and sunflower all work well. You can use infused oils, too. Oils infused with rose, calendula, lavender, or chamomile make great additions to this body butter. (See page 130 for how to infuse oils.)

You'll Need:
¼ cup cocoa butter
¼ cup shea butter
¼ cup oil
2 teaspoons tapioca starch (optional)
15 drops essential oil (optional)
Melt-and-pour container (see page 74)

1. Combine cocoa butter, shea butter, and oil in a melt-and-pour container.
2. Set the container in a small saucepan, then add water outside the can so that it reaches about halfway up the can. Warm over medium heat.
3. Remove from heat and stir in the tapioca starch, if desired. This prevents the body butter from feeling greasy as it goes on, but it is optional.
4. Pour into a small mixing bowl and refrigerate until it begins to firm, about 45 minutes.
5. Beat with a fork until it's light and fluffy, or use an immersion blender for an extra-fluffy product.
6. Add the essential oil, and stir until combined.
7. Transfer to an airtight container and store in a cool, dark place for up to 6 months.

Butter Me Up

Shea butter and cocoa butter are derived from the nuts and fruits of tropical trees.

1

2

3

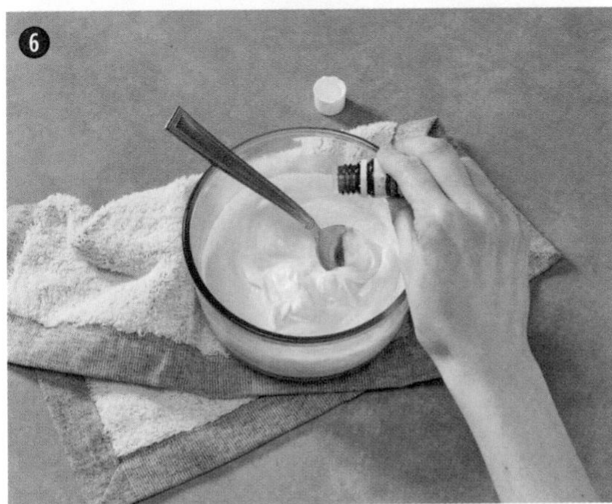
6

NATURAL HAIR CARE

When you use shampoo, you're removing sebum—a natural oil—from hair. Sebum protects the hair and hair follicles, but it can also make hair feel greasy when too much builds up. Shampooing makes our hair feel clean by stripping off that greasiness, but it also signals our body to produce more sebum to protect the hair follicles, thus creating the desire to shampoo again. It's a vicious, daily cycle that can expose us to ingredients like parabens or preservatives that release formaldehyde. Shampooing less frequently is one easy way to interrupt that cycle.

Although the idea of caring for your hair without lots of "product" might concern your hairdresser, you might consider a number of gentler methods for maintaining gorgeous locks.

Cleaner Shampoo

With the exception of colorants, cosmetic ingredients don't require Food and Drug Administration (FDA) approval before they hit the market. Ingredients like parabens, butane, fragrance, methylisothiazolinone, and other unpronounceable additives make their way into hair care products with nary a glance from the FDA. The Environmental Working Group *(ewg.org)* rates cosmetics (including shampoo) for their safety. EWG gives brands like Avalon Organics, Beautycounter, and Attitude high marks for safety. Check how your go-to shampoo scores—and if it doesn't make the grade, look for an alternative.

But even natural shampoo can leave you with a disposable plastic bottle. Check your local health food store; many offer natural shampoos in a bulk section, where you can bring your own bottle and refill it. Or consider switching to a shampoo bar—a bar of soap formulated specifically for use on hair. These usually come packaged in a compostable paper wrapper.

DIY

Time-Saving Dry Shampoo

If you're too busy to wash your hair or are trying to extend the length of time between shampooing, a dry shampoo can help. It essentially absorbs some of the oiliness. Using dry shampoo can be a good environmental move, too. By stretching the length of time between sudsing up, you'll save water and use less shampoo, creating less packaging waste.

You'll Need:

For light hair:
¼ cup organic cornstarch
1 teaspoon cinnamon
5 drops essential oil (optional)

For medium-to-dark hair:
¼ cup organic cornstarch
1 to 2 tablespoons cocoa
5 drops essential oil (optional)

1. Mix ingredients. The cocoa and cinnamon are colorants. They'll help prevent the cornstarch from being visible in your hair. Use less colorant for lighter hair, more for darker hair. Experiment with the amount until you're happy with it.
2. Store in an airtight container.
3. To use, create a part in your hair to expose the scalp. Sprinkle a small amount of the powder along the part, or use a makeup brush to apply. Repeat several times in different locations on your scalp. Use your fingers to gently work in the powder, and then brush your hair out.

The "No-Poo" Method?

The "no-poo" method is a two-pronged approach that calls for using baking soda and a vinegar rinse instead of shampoo, along with cleaning your hair less frequently. Some people rave about this method,

Keeping a jar of this dry shampoo on hand can shorten your beauty routine when you're pinched for time.

Ingredients like eggs, oil, and avocado are standard in many kitchens, but—surprise!—they're good for hair health, too.

claiming that their hair has never felt better. Others have found that the alkalinity of the baking soda is damaging in the long run. Another option? Skip the shampoo and the baking soda and vinegar. Simply scrubbing the scalp and hair with hot water works well for some people.

DIY

Hydrating Avocado Hair Mask

Avocados are good for more than just guacamole! The natural oils in these green fruits help to moisturize dry hair. All natural hair care made from fresh ingredients means less packaging, too!

You'll Need:
½ ripe avocado
1 egg
2 tablespoons jojoba oil
15 drops lavender essential oil
1 tablespoon apple cider vinegar

1. Combine all ingredients in a blender or food processor. Pulse until well combined.
2. Beginning at the roots, work the mixture into dry hair all the way down to the tips. Allow to sit for 15 minutes.
3. Rinse and shampoo to remove mask. Use this hydrating mask monthly, especially during the dry winter months.

Essentials Oils for Healthy Hair

Essential oils add fragrance, and they can also improve the health of your hair. Adding oils to your DIY hair products is optional, but if you want a little extra boost, give these a try:

- **Healthy hair:** Sage, lavender, sandalwood, rosemary, peppermint
- **Treating dandruff:** Rose geranium, lemon, Atlas cedar, juniper berry, tea tree
- **Improved hair growth:** Sage, basil, lavender, peppermint, vetiver
- **Treating oily hair:** Lemongrass, sage, rose geranium
- **Treating lice*:** Spearmint, clove, citronella, tea tree, eucalyptus

** Used in conjunction with other natural treatments for lice infestation*

DIY

Leave-In Hair Moisturizer

This oil-based hair moisturizer works particularly well on dry, curly hair like mine. It also works to tame the frizzies for those times you need to freshen up your 'do quickly sticking with natural—pronounceable!—ingredients.

You'll Need:
1 tablespoon avocado oil
1 tablespoon argan oil
10 to 15 drops essential oil
Small bottle with an eyedropper

1. Combine the oils in a bottle. Try lavender or rosemary essential oil, or choose your favorite.
2. Shake the bottle to combine the ingredients.
3. Use on either damp or dry hair. Put several drops of oil on your fingertips and work into hair. Avoid putting moisturizer directly onto the scalp, where your body is already producing its own oils.

Dandruff Control

A number of factors can cause dandruff—those embarrassing white, flaky bits that drift from scalp to shoulder. Ironically, both dry and oily scalps can lead to dandruff. Flaky, dry skin is an obvious source of dandruff, but oily scalps can harbor a yeastlike fungus called malassezia that causes excessive skin cell production. Another possible cause? Sensitivity to hair care products.

If you find yourself opting for white shirts to avoid the telltale signs of dandruff, see if these natural tactics solve the problem before going the medicated shampoo route.

The antibacterial and antifungal properties of honey can help ease the itching and dry skin that results in dandruff. Mix raw honey with a small amount of warm water—roughly 90 percent honey, 10 percent water—and massage into the scalp. Leave the honey in place for three hours; rinse with warm running water until the honey is completely washed away. Apply several times a week for a month.

Adding several drops of certain essential oils to your shampoo may help, too (see sidebar).

Another avenue to explore? Probiotics. It may come as a surprise, but adding fermented foods that are rich in probiotics to your diet may ease symptoms when dandruff is related to a yeastlike fungus (malassezia) on the scalp. See page 36 to start making some of your own healthy ferments.

4
Nettle
Sage
2
Lavender
6
5
Echinacea
3
Calendula
8
Rose
Rosemary
7
Fennel
9
10
Peppermint

❶
Chamomile

MEDICINAL HERBS

With their different medicinal properties, herbs can be used in a variety of ways. You'll use whole or crushed dried herbs for making infused oils or tinctures. Herbs such as calendula and comfrey can be blended with a bit of hot water to make a poultice for wrapping sprains. Some may be consumed in tea or other foods or simply bottled for their scent.

❶ **Chamomile** *(Matricaria recutita)* This lightly sedative herb is wonderful to aid digestion and abdominal cramping. The essential oil is antiseptic and anti-inflammatory.

❷ **Sage** *(Salvia officinalis)* Sage is an excellent herb for painful, swollen throats, hot flashes, and night sweats.

❸ **Calendula** *(Calendula officinalis)* Chiefly known as the wound-healing herb, calendula treats cuts or bruises. It's an excellent addition to soothing salves and creams.

❹ **Nettle** (*Urtica* sp.) This highly nutritive herb is worth the trouble it takes to harvest it. It is a stellar herb for urinary tract complaints.

❺ **Echinacea** (*Echinacea* sp.) Tremendous for the immune system, echinacea also assists with oral health.

❻ **Lavender** *(Lavandula angustifolia)* With a scent known to calm anxiety, lavender also soothes achy muscles.

❼ **Rosemary** *(Rosmarinus officinalis)* The piney resinous scent of this herb opens airways and encourages memory recall and cognition. Rosemary also soothes aches and pains and makes a nice hair treatment.

❽ **Rose** (*Rosa* sp.) Rose soothes worries and stress tension, while also promoting a radiant, firm complexion.

❾ **Fennel** *(Foeniculum vulgare)* Fennel provides near-instantaneous relief for indigestion.

❿ **Peppermint** *(Mentha × piperita)* Peppermint quells nausea, reduces aches and sore muscles, and, of course, gives us fresh breath. The flavor of peppermint makes even the most bitter herbal formulas more palatable.

HERBALISM

When you embrace herbalism for dealing with minor ailments, you'll start to see little treasures everywhere. As you'll discover, each different herb offers a separate set of nutrients and benefits; what works for one body might not be ideal for another. Start with some of the basic recipes here, but don't hesitate to fiddle with the herbal blends once you have an idea of what works well for you.

Learn about the different properties of herbs and double-check to make sure they are right for you. (Some herbs can interfere with pharmaceutical drugs; for instance, St. John's wort can interact with oral contraceptives.)

DIY

Making Herbal Tinctures

Crafting your own tinctures at home will save you a bundle of money, especially if you're growing or foraging your own herbs. Dosages for adults are generally 30 to 60 drops (usually 1 to 2 droppers full) in a small amount of water; take up to three times daily.

You'll Need:
Fresh or dried herbs
Glass jar
Vodka or brandy, 80 proof
Cheesecloth and funnel
Dark-tinted bottles with droppers

1. Chop fresh herbs or crush dried herbs. If you're using the roots of herbs (such as dandelion), clean them thoroughly and chop into small pieces.
2. Put herbs in a glass jar.
3. Pour alcohol over the herbs to cover. Dry herbs will absorb liquid and expand, so monitor the liquid level to make certain that the herbs remain covered, adding more as necessary.
4. Screw on a lid and set in a cool, dark cupboard for 4 to 6 weeks. Shake the jar every few days.
5. Strain the mixture through cheesecloth into a bowl or second jar. Gather the cheesecloth around herbs and squeeze as much liquid as possible from them.
6. Allow the liquid to settle overnight and strain a second time to remove tiny particles.
7. Transfer the tincture to dark-tinted bottles, and store away from the light. Finished tinctures will last for years.

Storing Dry Herbs

Although it's not always practical to store herbs and spices in their whole form, they'll last longer if you can. For example, mustard seeds have a much longer shelf life than ground mustard.

If you're growing and drying your own herbs or foraging for wild medicinals, make sure the herbs are completely dry before storing them. Any moisture remaining in the leaves can lead to mold on an entire batch. Check for moisture by rubbing a few leaves between your fingers. They should feel crispy and crumble into bits when totally dry.

Tinctures and Extracts

Concentrating herbs in a liquid form makes them easy to take; the two main options are tinctures and extracts. Tinctures are made using alcohol, while extracts are made with water, vinegar, or glycerin as their base. You can use dried or fresh herbs to create a tincture or extract. Fresh herbs yield a stronger flavor, but dried herbs may be more readily available.

Tincturing herbs in alcohol preserves their properties.

Once the herbs are ready for storage, choose airtight containers. I prefer glass over plastic, as it tends to be more airtight. Canning jars work well, as do jars with a locking bail and wire lid.

Label each jar with the name of the herb (I include a botanical name to avoid confusion) and the harvest date. Although they won't go bad in the sense that some foods do, they will lose potency. This varies, but the shelf life of herbs is generally one to three years.

Find a cool, dark place to store your bottles of dried herbs; light can degrade their potency. Opaque containers can help here, too.

DIY

Make Infused Oil in a Slow Cooker

Infused oils are useful for everything from healing salves to flavored salad dressing with a medicinal benefit. Making these useful blends is easy to do with a slow cooker.

You'll Need:
2 to 3 ounces dried herbs
½ cup oil (olive, almond, or jojoba are good options)
Funnel and cheesecloth

1. Place a folded towel in the bottom of a slow cooker. Add 3 inches of water.
2. Combine herbs and oil in a glass canning jar and screw on a lid.
3. Place the jar on top of the towel in the slow cooker and cook on low for 10 to 12 hours or overnight. You can prepare several different herbal blends in individual jars and warm them all at the same time.
4. Line the funnel with several layers of cheesecloth. Pour the oil through the lined funnel into a clean jar. Lift the cheesecloth and squeeze the remaining herbs to extract as much oil as possible before composting them.
5. Store in an airtight container in a cool, dark place.

Hydrosols

The concentrated oils in the leaves and flowers of plants are the basis of their fragrances. That sweet summer rose, the brightly scented peppermint, and the soothing smell of lavender all come from plant oils. These oils dissipate quickly in the air; distilled essential oils capture that fragrance and the plant's properties.

Commercial producers rely on elaborate steam distillers—or in some cases, harsh solvents—to produce essential oils and hydrosols. Hydrosols are clear, lightly fragrant liquids derived from plant material during that distillation process. Capturing the fragrance of your favorite plant materials at home is a bit less precise. Although you may not obtain all of the aromatic compounds, this method results in a lightly fragrant liquid that you can use in various ways.

Give your face a light spritz with chamomile, lavender, or vetiver hydrosol for a calming effect. Plant materials with antibacterial properties, like peppermint, eucalyptus, and rosemary, net a hydrosol that combats odor. Use your favorite scent as a linen or garment spray to impart a gentle fragrance.

Uses for hydrosols abound. Try soaking a washcloth in the fragrant liquid to make a soothing cold compress for headaches. You can also use hydrosols as a natural hair rinse (rosemary is especially good for this). Hydrosols are great additions to homemade personal care or cleaning products; simply use one in place of the water called for in a recipe to impart a light fragrance.

DIY

Making a Hydrosol

Some plant materials are easier to distill fragrance from than others because of their high oil content. Highly fragrant plants like lavender, peppermint, and rosemary are good options to start. If you're growing a lush herb garden (or can find herbs at the farmers market), here's your chance to capture your favorite herbal fragrance in a bottle.

You'll Need:
2 to 3 cups fresh plant material
Ice
Stockpot or slow cooker with a domed lid and a wire rack that fits inside
A small heatproof bowl or measuring cup
Dark glass spray bottle

1. Set the wire rack on the bottom of the stockpot or slow cooker.
2. Set a bowl or measuring cup on top of the rack in the center of the pot.

3. Pour water into the pot—outside the bowl—to within 2 inches of the bowl rim.
4. Sprinkle the plant material on top of the water around the bowl.
5. Place the lid on the pot, upside down. Cover the lid with ice. This is the trick to collecting the hydrosol. When the heated water creates steam, it will condense on the cold lid and drip down into the bowl.
6. In a stockpot, bring to a boil over medium-high heat, then reduce heat to maintain a simmer. In a slow cooker, cook on high for 3 to 4 hours. Keep a close eye on the process.
7. When the bowl is full, carefully remove it. Transfer the liquid to a larger bowl and return the bowl to the stockpot or slow cooker to continue the process.
8. As the steam condenses, the water level in the pot will become lower. Do not allow all the water to evaporate, but when it's substantially reduced, turn off the heat and allow the pot to cool.
9. If you'd like, you can add more plant materials as the first batch cooks down, but this is not necessary.
10. Discard the water in the lid. The liquid in the bowl is your homemade hydrosol. Transfer it to a dark-colored glass bottle (to protect it from the light), and store in a cool, dry place.

When steam rises to meet cold ice, condensation forms inside the inverted lid, making it easy to collect the hydrosol.

NATURAL REMEDIES

A wholesome diet and lifestyle goes a long way toward helping your body remain healthy—but even the healthiest people get sick every once in a while. Germs become airborne when a sick person coughs, sneezes, or even talks. The germs last longest on hard surfaces like plastic and metal. That shopping cart you just pushed up and down the supermarket aisles? The gas pump? To reduce exposure, use the wipes offered at the entrance of the store to clean the cart handle before you use it.

Giving the immune system a natural boost during cold and flu season can help prevent or lessen the severity of an illness. Some holistic tricks can make a minor illness more bearable, too.

RECIPE

Knock-Your-Socks-Off Fire Cider

Makes 3 to 4 cups

An herbal folk remedy, fire cider is crafted by steeping potent ingredients in vinegar to create a warming tonic that is said to boost natural health and stimulate digestion. At the very least, it will clear your sinuses! Try taking a tablespoon straight up every morning. Stir it into your favorite salad dressing, or add it to vegetable juice or a smoothie. This base recipe will get you started, but don't hesitate to improvise with your favorite herbs and spices. Fire cider can be stored in a cool, dark place for up to a year.

You'll Need:
½ cup ginger root, grated
½ cup horseradish, grated
1 cup yellow onion, chopped
10 garlic cloves, crushed
1 whole lemon, cut into 1-inch pieces
1 tablespoon turmeric powder
¼ teaspoon cayenne pepper
3 to 4 cups raw apple cider vinegar
¼ cup honey, plus more if you prefer sweeter results

1. In a quart-size jar with a lid, combine the ginger root, horseradish, onion, garlic, lemon, turmeric powder, and cayenne pepper.
2. Pour the apple cider vinegar over the seasonings until everything is submerged and the vinegar reaches the top of the jar. Screw on the lid and shake well.
3. Place the jar in a cool, dark place for 4 weeks, remembering to shake daily.
4. Strain through a cheesecloth, squeezing as much liquid as possible from the solids.
5. Stir in the honey to taste.
6. Decant into jars with lids.

RECIPE

Elderberry Syrup

During cold and flu season, adding elderberries to your routine can boost your immunity and potentially shorten the duration of an illness. This elderberry syrup can be made with berries you've foraged, grown at home, or purchased from an herb store. Take it daily during cold and flu season; dosage is a half to one teaspoon for children under 12, and two to three tablespoons for adults. Store elderberry syrup in the refrigerator for three months or freeze for six months.

You'll Need:
1 cup dried or 2 cups fresh elderberries
1 cinnamon stick
¼ cup fresh orange peel
2 tablespoons ginger, grated
1 cup raw honey
Special equipment: cheesecloth

1. In a large saucepan, combine 5 cups water with the elderberries, cinnamon stick, orange peel,

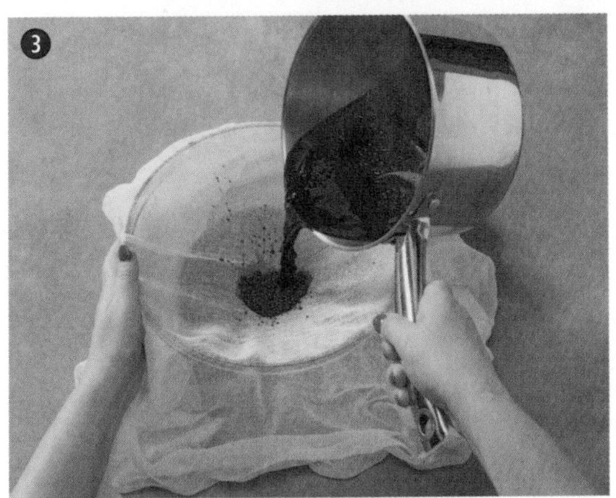

and grated ginger. Bring the mixture to a boil over medium-high heat.

2. Immediately turn down the heat and let simmer for 30 minutes.
3. Strain the mixture through several layers of cheesecloth into a bowl.
4. Let cool slightly, then squeeze as much of the juice as possible out of the cheesecloth and into the bowl. Be careful not to release the solids.
5. Stir in the honey to taste. This is easier to do while the juice is still warm.
6. Decant into jars with lids.

Sinus Decongestant

One of the easiest ways to clear your sinuses is to eat something spicy. Horseradish and cayenne pepper can do a number on a stuffy nose. So can a cup of hot chili-spiced broth.

If you haven't tried a neti pot yet, it's a good way to clear out the gunk. It can take some getting used to—water up the nose and all—but it's effective.

Inhaling strong essential oils like eucalyptus or mint can help clear the sinuses, too. One of the easiest ways to do this is to simply put a few drops of essential oil on a cotton ball and hold it near your nose. (Be careful not to get the strong oils on your skin.)

DIY

Decongestant Chest Rub

Heaviness in the chest, difficulty breathing, and a deep racking cough? If it goes on for long, you might want to see a doctor. If you're sure that it's just a cold running its course, a steamy shower and a steaming hot mug of lemon and honey can help. For persistent chest congestion, though, you'll find some relief with a bold chest rub. Eucalyptus and peppermint oils can be quite strong, and are not recommended for young children. To make a lighter, child-friendly version, choose essential oils like Fragonia, pine, or cedar, and use half as many drops.

You'll Need:

3 tablespoons avocado or olive oil
1 tablespoon beeswax pellets
20 to 30 drops peppermint essential oil
20 to 30 drops eucalyptus essential oil
Melt-and-pour container (see page 74)

1. Combine oil and beeswax in a melt-and-pour container.
2. Set the can in a small saucepan. Add water outside the can so that it reaches about halfway up the can. Warm over medium heat, stirring occasionally.
3. When the beeswax is melted, stir in the essential oils. Transfer the warm oil to a small jar with a lid and allow to cool.
4. To use, rub a small amount onto your chest.

Fill a neti pot with a saline solution made from distilled water for nasal irrigation.

DIY

Soothing Healing Salve

Scrapes and superficial wounds are inevitable if you're a gardener, hiker, or do-it-yourselfer. Natural salves can be customized to suit your needs, but whether you choose ingredients for their antiseptic, antibacterial, or soothing properties, the basic method remains the same.

You'll Need:
1 cup infused oil
2 tablespoons beeswax pastilles or grated beeswax
5 drops essential oil (optional)
Melt-and-pour container (see page 74)
Wooden chopstick
Small containers

1. Combine the oil and beeswax together in the melt-and-pour container. Place the tin can in a saucepan filled with 2 to 3 inches of water. Be sure that you don't get any water in the oil.

Headache Remedies and Prevention

Although severe headaches that interrupt your day require medical attention, less severe variations can often be treated at home. How successful these methods are may depend on the severity of the pain and your own personal constitution. If your head pain is coupled with double vision, vomiting, weakness, paralysis, vertigo, or hearing loss, seek immediate medical attention.

- Chew on a small piece of fresh ginger root, or steep the root in hot water to make ginger tea.
- Daily doses of feverfew (usually in the form of an extract) lessen the number and severity of migraines for some patients.
- Brew a cup of chamomile, peppermint, spearmint, rose hip, meadowsweet, or lemon balm tea. Adding a tiny bit of cayenne pepper to tea can also help.
- Gently massage lavender oil into your temples.
- Drink more water. Mild dehydration can trigger headaches.
- Be sure to eat! Skipping meals can trigger hunger headaches.
- Avoid excessive caffeine and alcohol consumption.

Simple steam therapy can ease congestion.

2. Set the saucepan over medium heat until the beeswax is melted, stirring with the chopstick to combine.
3. Use the stirring stick to test the consistency of the salve. Let the salve dry on the chopstick; if it feels too soft, sprinkle in a bit more beeswax. If it's firmer than you like, add a little oil.
4. Pour the salve into small containers. Recycled mint tins or small glass jars work well.
5. Store in a cool, dry place for 6 to 12 months.

DIY

Aromatic Steam Therapy

Steam inhalation coupled with essential oils can help with both sinus and chest congestion. This homemade remedy is as easy as making a cup of tea, and eases discomfort quickly.

You'll Need:
5 to 7 drops of essential oils
A heatproof bowl (a glass mixing bowl works well)
Bath towel

1. Boil approximately 4 to 5 cups water.
2. Pour the boiling water into a heatproof bowl on a table.
3. Add the essential oils. Eucalyptus, thyme, or tea tree oils are good choices for congestion.
4. Sit with your face close to the bowl and cover your head with a towel to capture the steam.
5. Breathe slowly and deeply to inhale the steam.

CLEANING & LAUNDRY

From disinfectants and detergents to deodorizers and bleach, the array of household cleaners available on the market is mind-boggling. But perhaps more surprising is the fact that most of these products are not tested for safety. (When the Environmental Protection Agency tests products, it focuses on individual chemicals, rather than the combination of chemicals touted as the only way to get our homes truly clean.)

These ready-to-use products frequently include known carcinogens, endocrine disrupters, and lung irritants damaging to you and to the environment as well, but only a small percentage of cleaning products actually list ingredients on the bottle.

Using harsh disinfectants and sanitizers (regulated as pesticides by the EPA, by the way) might make sense in the case of an infectious outbreak. And certainly, they're necessary in hospital settings. But for everyday cleaning, less toxic options can be safer, more sustainable choices. You probably have the ingredients for some of these recipes on hand already.

Vinegar, the Greener Cleaner

To make a simple and effective spray for cleaning, mix equal parts vinegar and water in a spray bottle. Spray it on surfaces, allow to sit for a minute or so, and wipe with a damp rag. If you don't like the smell of vinegar, add about 10 drops of essential oil for a more fragrant variation. Don't use this on marble though.

White distilled vinegar (5 percent) can stand in when you need to disinfect, too. The easiest method is to use undiluted vinegar in a spray bottle. To be effective as a disinfectant, clean the area first, then thoroughly spray with vinegar and allow to stand for a full 10 minutes before wiping away. White distilled vinegar won't remove all hard-to-kill bacteria but will take out many common germs. It becomes a more effective disinfecting agent if first heated in a saucepan to 150°F. Use a funnel to carefully pour the hot liquid into your spray bottle and use immediately.

Cleaning Versus Disinfecting and Sanitizing

Scrubbing with water, a cleaner, and good old elbow grease will wash offending grime down the drain. Sanitizing and disinfecting *kill* germs with antimicrobial pesticides.

DIY

Citrus Scrubbing Cleaner

This gentle scrubbing cleaner is good for sinks and tubs but can also be used to remove tough dirt on dry surfaces. It's easy to make with just a couple household ingredients and gets its gentle aroma from natural citrus peel rather than synthetic fragrances.

You'll Need:
1 cup baking soda
⅓ cup liquid castile soap
2 tablespoons citrus peel, dried and ground
Airtight container

1. Peel oranges or grapefruit and allow the peels to dry at room temperature or by using a dehydrator (see page 18).
2. Once fully dried, use a food processor equipped with a metal S-blade to reduce them to a fine powder.
3. Combine 2 tablespoons ground citrus peel with remaining ingredients in a bowl, stirring well.
4. Transfer to an airtight container and tighten on a lid. As the mixture sits, it may expand, so allow an inch or so of headspace.
5. To use, scoop a small amount onto a cleaning rag or scrub brush and work into the dirty surface, then rinse or wipe away with a clean cloth.

Natural ingredients combine to make a scrubbing cleaner without toxic chemicals.

Keeping ready-made wipes on hand makes quick work of accidental spills.

DIY

Ready-Made Cleaning Wipes

If you like the idea of ready-to-use wipes for fast cleanups but cringe at the waste they create, try making your own! Add tea tree oil for its antimicrobial properties; lemongrass and orange are antifungal and antibacterial. These will cost you far less than the overpriced options at the supermarket, too.

You'll Need:
1 cup water
1 cup vinegar
20 drops essential oil
Cloth rags
Large airtight jar or container

1. You can use washcloths for these wipes (just choose a dedicated color to keep them separate from your bathroom linens) or rags torn from old flannel sheets or towels. Fabric with a bit of heft works best.
2. Put four or five cloths into the jar.
3. Combine the water, vinegar, and essential oil in a bowl. Pour over the cloths in the jar. If necessary, add a bit more water to ensure that the cloths are moistened all the way through. Seal the jar.
4. Remove wipes as needed to clean up spills.
5. Toss used wipes in the laundry.
6. Create a fresh batch of wipes as necessary. Note that you could make a bigger batch, but it's a good idea to make only as many as you'll use in a week or so. If left longer, you risk introducing bacteria to the container of wipes.

On the Go

These wipes are handy to keep around the house, but consider keeping some in your car. Use them—especially during cold and flu season—to wipe your hands to prevent the spread of germs.

DIY

Dishwasher Soap

I've fiddled with various recipes for making my own dishwasher soap, and in the end, the simplest recipe seems to work the best. This homemade alternative allows you to skip some of the harsh ingredients in commercial products, plus it will save you some cash. You can find washing soda at most hardware stores or online.

You'll Need:
1 cup washing soda
½ cup citric acid

1. Measure the ingredients into a bowl. Use a fork to thoroughly mix the washing soda and citric acid. (If your powders are at all chunky, either sift them or blend the ingredients in a food processor.)
2. Store in an airtight container. Use 1 to 2 tablespoons powder for each dishwasher load.

Laundry

There's no question that commercial laundry detergent gets clothes clean. But it often comes with harsh chemical ingredients like sulfates, fragrances, and even petroleum products.

Making laundry soap at home to replace the commercial version is easy, but does it work? In my experience, it does the job for most everyday laundry, but I sometimes fall back on commercial detergents for greasy items (the kind that result from engine work). Another option is to give homemade laundry soap a "boost" with a product that contains plant-based surfactants. Dr. Bronner's Sal Suds is one such option.

Detergent Versus Soap

Soap is made from natural ingredients. Detergents are made from manufactured ingredients and often include synthetic surfactants, which make oils and dirt easier to remove. Many synthetic surfactants get a big fat F from the Environmental Working Group and are known to be carcinogenic.

Do You Need a Rinse Aid?

Dishwasher manufacturers like to suggest synthetic rinse aids to prevent water spots on your clean dishes. Instead of opting for the commercially available options, give vinegar a try to prevent buildup on your dishes.

DIY

Powdered Laundry Soap

Commercial laundry soap gets your clothes clean, but it also emits volatile organic compounds (VOCs) every time you use it. According to the EPA, there's no safe level for these air pollutants. That spring fresh scent? Skip it and try this homemade alternative instead. It does the job without compromising your health.

You'll Need:
5 (3-ounce) bars of castile soap (or homemade tallow soap, page 116)
2½ cups washing soda (usually sold in the supermarket's laundry section)
5 cups borax
1¼ cup citric acid (optional, as a laundry booster)
Food processor

1. Chop the soap into small chunks. Put half the soap in a food processor along with half the washing soda. Process with a metal S-blade until the soap is very fine. Repeat with the remaining soap and washing soda.
2. Combine all ingredients in a large bowl. Store in an airtight container.
3. Use 2 to 3 tablespoons of laundry soap per load.

DIY

Stain Remover

It's inevitable that you'll end up with spills and stains on your clothing. If you notice right away, it's always a good idea to rinse with water to remove as much of the stain as possible, then squeeze on a bit of this handy liquid.

You'll Need:
½ cup hydrogen peroxide
¼ cup liquid castile soap
1 tablespoon baking soda
Squeeze bottle

1. Combine all the ingredients in a bowl. Stir gently to combine and dissolve the baking soda.
2. Transfer the mixture to an upcycled plastic squeeze bottle.
3. To use, gently shake the bottle, then squeeze a bit on stains. Rub the fabric together to work the stain remover into the fibers, then launder as usual.

AIR FRESHENERS

Air fresheners commonly available at the supermarket might disguise unsavory scents with synthetic fragrances like "ocean breeze" or "strawberry fields." But when you spritz a room, you may be inhaling ingredients like benzisothiazolinone and parabens, in addition to synthetic fragrances. Ditto for the plug-in or countertop solid versions. More natural approaches will eliminate stuffy, stinky air without the harsh chemicals.

Offensive odors can be alkaline or acid in nature. Acidic odors (like cigarette smoke) can be neutralized with a small container of baking soda, while alkaline odors like fish are improved with vinegar.

DIY

Fresh Air Spray

Brand-name odor eliminators and their synthetic fragrances can cause respiratory problems; this DIY fresh air spray is made of all natural ingredients.

You'll Need:
½ cup water
½ cup vinegar
20 drops essential oil
Small spray bottle

1. Combine all ingredients in the spray bottle. Shake gently.
2. To use, set the bottle to mist (not stream) and spritz the air.

DIY

Linen Spray

This light spray freshens fabric, combating musty odors that can come from lack of airflow. And the light touch of scent might just lighten your mood! A lavender-scented spray is great for bedding, as the fragrance is calming. I'm also partial to vetiver; sometimes called the "oil of tranquility," it has a rich earthy scent.

You'll Need:
2 tablespoons rubbing alcohol (or vodka)
20 drops essential oil
¾ cup water
8-ounce spray bottle

1. Combine the rubbing alcohol and essential oils in bottle. Swirl to mix.
2. Add water.
3. Use it to freshen clothing, bedding, curtains, quilts, or upholstered furniture.

Houseplants

One easy way to foster cleaner air inside your home? Add some houseplants. Thriving greenery can help remove toxins like formaldehyde, benzene, and ammonia from the air.

Store homemade sprays in opaque bottles.

Commercial air fresheners can emit harmful air pollutants; a homemade diffuser is a nontoxic way to clear the air.

DIY

Scent Diffuser

Try an oil-based diffuser to bring some pleasant scents into your home. This is an easy way to change up the aroma to suit your mood. Peppermint and citrus essential oils are energizing; frankincense and chamomile are calming.

You'll Need:
¼ cup sweet almond oil
30 drops essential oil
1 tablespoon vodka
6 to 8 bamboo skewers
Small vase or upcycled glass jar

Use Caution With Pets

Essential oils are natural but can be dangerous for some pets. This varies widely based on the concentration and type of oil. If you have indoor animals and are concerned about their safety, check with your veterinarian.

1. Combine all liquids in the vase.
2. Put skewers in the vase until one end is saturated, then flip the skewers over.
3. Set the diffuser on a bathroom countertop or tucked away in a room that tends to get stuffy.

Carpet Freshener

To help remove carpet odors, sprinkle some odor-absorbing baking soda on your carpet and let it sit for a half hour or so before you vacuum. The offending odors will be vacuumed up along with the loose powder.

HOUSEHOLD PEST CONTROL

Pests inside the home: Nobody wants them. Getting rid of interlopers like mice, ants, or cockroaches isn't always easy. And when you're trying to avoid harsh chemicals in your household, it's even more of a challenge. A number of different approaches help control unwanted household pests. One of the best ways to eliminate them is to prevent them in the first place. Closing obvious entryways into your home is a good first step. Window screens will prevent mosquitoes, and sealing gaps can deter mice from squeezing in.

Storing food in airtight containers will also help keep pests at bay, while keeping counters and floors devoid of food crumbs prevents pests from turning your kitchen into a buffet. But let's be honest here: Pests inside the home aren't necessarily a judgment of cleanliness. Cockroaches, for instance, will dine on wallpaper glue, hair, and paper items. No matter how clean your home, pests can still find something to nosh on. (That's not to say you should leave last night's pizza on the counter!)

Natural Pest Repellents

Making your home and yard undesirable to pests is one way to deter them. Repellents come in many forms, with varying success rates. What works in one region might not work in another, which makes experimenting necessary. When it comes to four-legged pests like mice and rats, I consider my cats to be some of the best repellents I have. They don't do much for creepy crawlies, though.

Diatomaceous Earth

Diatomaceous earth (DE) is made of the silica-rich, fossilized skeletons of minute aquatic organisms called diatoms. The remains of these diatoms settled in sediment, creating silica deposits that are the source of natural diatomaceous earth. The Food and Drug Administration classifies DE as "generally recognized as safe" for use as a pesticide.

This finely powdered dust doesn't poison insects; it dries them out by absorbing oils from their exoskeletons. The sharp edges of diatomaceous earth particles are abrasive and will roughen the exoskeleton, speeding up the drying process. Opt for food-grade diatomaceous earth and take care not to breathe the dust as you apply it. DE is effective as long as it remains dry.

To prevent ants, cockroaches, and other crawling insects from entering your home, regularly sprinkle diatomaceous earth around your home's foundation or around each pier block supporting your home. Inside the home, sprinkle DE along baseboards and in cupboards or drawers where you see signs of infestation. Out-of-the-way areas like behind the refrigerator or water heater are also good places to sprinkle it; the fine white powder will sift down into cracks and crevices. Sprinkle a little DE in your pet's bedding to keep fleas at bay. It won't harm your animal.

Encourage the Good Guys

Whether you're dealing with household pests or garden pests, encouraging the predators that eat them can help keep things under control. Lizards, frogs, and toads will eat ants and cockroaches. Bats consume massive numbers of mosquitoes every night and are completely harmless, despite their depiction in spooky movies. And cats, of course, hunt small rodents.

Burning citronella oil in outdoor torches can repel mosquitoes and other insects.

Cockroaches

Ants are frustrating, mice are icky, but cockroaches take the cake when it comes to household pests. They carry bacteria that can cause salmonella, staphylococcus, and streptococcus when transferred to food. For some, cockroach droppings may trigger asthma attacks.

These bugs are insidious and hard to get rid of; before you know it, one random roach will morph into an infestation. Roaches come in a variety of sizes, but all are difficult to evict once they've decided that your place suits them just fine, thanks. The following tactics will discourage a welcoming environment.

First, watch what you bring in. Packaging—especially corrugated cardboard—can harbor cockroach egg cases. These brown, rectangular eggs cases are called oothecae and can contain from a dozen to 50 eggs, depending upon the species of cockroach. Learn to recognize the oothecae, and give boxes a once-over before you bring them inside. Empty shipping boxes immediately, and remove the cardboard from your home. If you do find oothecae, don't just throw them away; squash them immediately to prevent them from hatching.

Second, remember that cockroaches are drawn to water. Although it's difficult to eliminate moisture entirely—hello, kitchen sink—you can avoid drawing them to otherwise dry parts of the house. Make sure that dishes are thoroughly dry before putting them away, avoid leaving glasses of water in bedrooms, and pick up wet laundry.

Although you won't always see cockroaches, they tend to leave behind a couple of signs. Small, dark brown, round droppings or brown streaks on surfaces (spittle) can indicate the presence of cockroaches. You might notice a musty smell along with their droppings. Roach poop has special pheromones to attract more roaches, so you'll want to remove the droppings as soon as you notice them. Vacuum them up, dispose of them, and thoroughly wash the area with soap and water.

Five Pest-Repellent Plants

Planting pest-repellent specimens near your house or in patio containers can help reduce the population of unwanted visitors:

- Artemisia repels insects and even small animals.
- Basil repels flies and mosquitoes.
- Catnip leaves (dried) make an ant-repelling sachet.
- Citronella grass is the source of mosquito-repelling citronella. (This is different than the citronella-scented geranium that's less effective as a repellent.)
- Lavender repels fleas and moths.

Add insect repellent plants like lavender to your landscape.

If you discover that you have roaches, it's crucial that you tackle the problem immediately or they will quickly multiply. Sticky traps are a good, natural way to take roaches out of service, though their efficacy can vary by brand. If you live in a region that is prone to cockroaches, it's not a bad idea to keep several sticky traps in play at all times. Boric acid lures are a less toxic commercial solution. But for persistent infestations, you may have to resort to roach poison. If you do, be sure to place it completely out of reach of children and pets.

Scent as a Deterrent

A variety of DIY pesticides are worth employing. The strong scent of peppermint, eucalyptus, and citrus essential oils can deter a variety of pests. Both ants and mice are said to avoid peppermint. Put a few drops of peppermint essential oil on cotton balls and tuck them into drawers or in the corners of your cupboards.

DIY

Fruit Fly Traps

Fruit flies tend to be most problematic in the late summer, when warm weather and abundant produce makes it easy for them to reproduce rapidly. Fruit fly eggs or larvae hitchhike in on the fruit you bring home, then hatch right in your kitchen. This easy trap will help disrupt their life cycle and reduce their numbers. If vinegar doesn't seem to be the right attractant, you can try fruit juice, wine, or soy sauce.

You'll Need:
Vinegar
Liquid dish soap
Glass jar
Saucer
Sheet of paper

1. Put about an inch of vinegar in a glass jar, and add a few drops of liquid dish soap.
2. Set the saucer on the sheet of paper and trace around it with a pencil. Cut out the circle. Fold the circle into quarters. Unfold and mark the center of the circle.
3. Cut along one fold line to the center of the circle.
4. Overlap the cut edges to form a paper cone, leaving a small opening at the tip.
5. Set the cone in the jar, pointed end down. Place near the fruit fly infestation. Be sure to remove any other attractants that might divert them from this DIY fruit fly trap, such as rotting fruit or compost.

Trapping fruit flies in a homemade trap will prevent them from breeding and continuing the cycle.

PART II

OUTDOORS

GROW | FARM | TREK

chapter four

GROW

GROW

Growing at least some of your own food is a sure route to a simpler life. On a summer evening, nothing is better than plucking and eating a warm tomato straight from the vine of the plant that produced it. A thriving vegetable garden—bees humming, flowers blooming, and colorful produce bursting from rich, loamy soil—is the perfect refuge from the stresses of everyday life. Harvesting fresh, vibrant produce for your table is almost just a bonus.

Backyard gardening is a great way to put organically grown food on the table for a fraction of the cost. It's also an excellent activity for families focused on a healthier lifestyle, for a number of reasons. Working to plant and harvest a garden gets the entire family outside breathing fresh air, being active, and spending time on a shared project. Growing food gives kids a greater understanding of where their meals come from. And the resulting produce is packed with nutrition and—if you use natural gardening methods—free of concerning chemical pesticide residues.

If you've been considering exactly how to get your food closer to home, a backyard garden might be the answer. You don't have to start big; a couple containers planted with vegetables can be just the encouragement you need to embrace the concept. In this chapter, urbanites will find inspiration for projects like growing microgreens in a jar, building a salad tower for fresh greens, or creating space-saving trellises for a small backyard. Those with a bit more room can begin to experiment with different crops and build their botanical knowledge as they expand the garden to include unusual heirloom varieties that aren't found in any supermarket. But I have to warn you: Gardening can be addictive! You'll be a convert once you've experienced plucking a ripe, zebra-striped tomato off the vine or sampling a deep purple carrot fresh from the soil.

• CONTENTS •

Previous pages: *Harvesting Swiss chard, carrots, and beets*
Opposite: *Heirloom tomatoes come in a variety of colors.*

PLANNING A GARDEN

Many things should be considered when planning a garden; deciding what, where, and how much to plant requires some forethought. Whether you're a beginner or an experienced grower, planning ahead will assure a greater level of success. That said, it's important to give yourself permission to make mistakes. Poor seed germination, strange weather, or pesky plant diseases can seem like failures, but try to see them as lessons in the long view. In the end, the experience you gain is more important than achieving perfection. Year after year, your knowledge (and harvests!) will grow.

Size Up the Possibilities

Get started by thinking about how big you want your garden to be. If you're new to growing your own food, heed some advice: Be realistic. Although you might dream of a garden that provides all the produce your family needs, can you plausibly manage a garden of that size? It might not be feasible to harvest hundreds of pounds of produce in one season, particularly if you've never gardened before. Start small, or at least smallish; modestly sized plots are easier to maintain, but still offer large rewards. The bigger your garden, the more effort it will take to prep the area and stay on top of your harvest.

Location, Location, Location

The following are important things to consider when deciding where to plant your vegetable garden. An afternoon spent observing your yard will help you determine where the garden will be most likely to thrive.

- **Sunshine and shade:** As a general rule, vegetables need a nice, sunny spot to thrive. Plants grown for their fruit (tomatoes, peppers) crave sunshine. Aim for a location that provides six to eight hours of sunshine during the summer months. Pay attention to trees and structures that cast shade in your yard, too; a little bit of filtered shade can ease summertime heat, but too much will impair plant growth. Some vegetables do well in shady conditions—plants grown for their roots (radish, turnip) or leaves (lettuce, chard)—but the list is pretty short.

- **Drainage:** Although you'll want to maintain steady moisture in your garden beds, soggy soil can cause problems. Make sure your garden area has good drainage. If the sunniest spot in your yard is also a low spot that retains water, create a swale—a very shallow trench—to divert water from the area, or consider raised beds to get plants up above the wet ground.

Rainbow chard is tasty and pretty in the garden.

Good drainage is crucial for a healthy garden; remedy soggy soil issues before planting.

Growing herbs in containers is a fun way to keep flavor on hand and is perfect for balcony gardens.

■ **Accessibility** You don't want to have to hike to the back forty to harvest green beans for dinner, so make sure you situate your garden reasonably close to your kitchen. If the area must be some distance from the house, consider keeping a planter full of things you use the most—your favorite herbs and lettuce, maybe—right outside the door for easy access.

■ **The root of the problem:** Grab a shovel and dig some test holes in the area you wish to transform into a productive vegetable garden. If you hit a lot of rocks or roots from nearby trees, this will be a hard place to dig beds. However, raised beds, built on top of the root-choked area and filled with good soil, will help sidestep this problem.

Seasonal Crops

No matter what time of year you plant your garden, you'll be harvesting fresh produce in 30 to 90 days from the time it's planted.

Plant these cool-weather crops in early spring and fall:

- Broccoli
- Cabbage
- Carrots
- Cauliflower
- Kohlrabi
- Leafy greens
- Lettuce
- Peas
- Radish

Warm-weather crops to plant in late spring:

- Beans
- Corn
- Cucumbers
- Eggplant
- Okra
- Peppers
- Summer squash
- Tomatoes
- Winter squash

Choose Your Crops

It's easy to get caught up in garden fever, but focus on creating a lineup that will work for you and your family. Have a plan before heading to the nursery for seeds and seedlings. Probably the most important thing to consider when choosing crops is what your family likes to eat. Of course, part of the fun in gardening is trying new things—but all the same, packing a garden with experimental vegetables might not be the best idea. A huge okra harvest isn't going to serve you well if nobody in your family will eat it. What fresh produce do you find yourself using on a regular basis? Start with those!

Be sure to talk to local gardeners to find out what grows well in your region. Plants that thrive in your neighbor's yard are a good bet for success in yours. Most home gardeners put lettuce, tomatoes, radishes, cucumbers, and zucchini on their list of "bulletproof" vegetables; they'll grow easily in most climates.

Planting Seasons

Young plants thrive in the warming spring sunshine, so it's common for garden centers to feature row upon row of vegetable seedlings this time of year. But that's not the only time you can plant. Cool-season crops are good to go in both the spring and fall. A spring planting allows them to run their course early in the year, avoiding the high summer heat that tends to make them wilt. As fall approaches, gardeners can sprout a second crop that will enjoy end-of-the-season cool weather, ripening just as frost threatens. Warm-season crops don't like cold soil, so it doesn't do any good to set them in the ground early; they'll just sit there and sulk until the weather turns warm.

Harvesting cabbage from the garden

Plant Enough

Whether you're planting beans or zucchini, you'll want to know how much you can expect from a single plant to decide how many to grow. A single bush bean plant simply won't provide enough food for a family of four; a single zucchini plant might. The following are rough yields per five-foot row (though this will vary based on your local conditions and plant varieties):

- Beets—5 pounds (roots)
- Bush beans—4 pounds
- Broccoli—3 pounds
- Carrots—5 pounds
- Cucumbers—6 pounds
- Eggplant—3 pounds
- Green onions—5 pounds
- Kale—3 pounds
- Lettuce (leaf)—2 pounds
- Melon—5 melons
- Onions—5 pounds
- Peas (snap)—1 pound
- Squash (summer)—10 pounds
- Tomatoes—7 pounds
- Peppers—2 pounds
- Turnips—2 pounds (roots)

Extending Your Harvest

If you're going to the trouble of planting a garden, you'll want to get the most out of all your work. That means being able to harvest and eat fresh produce for as long as possible. The easiest way to make this happen is to diversify. Instead of planting only one variety of beans, choose several varieties with different ripening times. Seeds labeled "early" will be ready to harvest sooner than those labeled "late." Plant some of each, and you'll pace your harvest over a longer period of time.

Another way to make sure to have fresh produce throughout the season is to utilize succession planting. This practice is especially effective with crops that ripen quickly, like radishes and lettuce. If you plant all your radish seeds at once, they'll be ready at roughly the same time; if you stagger planting time by putting seeds in the ground every two weeks during growing season, the radish harvest will stretch longer.

To really extend your growing season, consider a cold frame or row covers. These methods are a bit more labor intensive but allow growers in cold climates to plant earlier and extend the harvest past the first frost by creating a covered area that retains heat. A row cover—sometimes called a low tunnel or hoop—is made of fabric and allows sunlight to penetrate while protecting crops from the cold. A cold frame is essentially a covered bottomless box that allows sunlight in to warm a confined area.

The temperature inside a cold frame is generally about 5 to 10 degrees warmer than outside the frame. The timing for moving seedlings into a cold frame depends on the type of vegetable. Tomatoes need a minimum soil temperature of 55°F, whereas cool-season crops like cabbage and lettuce can handle temperatures in the 40s. Use a thermometer to check nighttime air temperatures; move seedlings into the cold frame when the temperature is ideal for your crop. In the fall, set a cold frame up around frost-tender vegetables when frost threatens.

DIY

The Simplest Cold Frame

Sometimes, you just need an easy project that will get you growing quickly. Instead of fussing with building a wooden cold frame, this easy alternative comes together with straw bales (that will eventually end up in your compost) and a recycled window:

1. Place four straw bales in a square.
2. Set a recycled glass window or sturdy clear plastic over the top.

As you'll see, the clear top allows sunshine to reach your plants and warm the area inside. The straw insulates the area inside the "box," trapping that warmth.

A simple cold frame helps extend the growing season.

Five Must-Have Garden Tools

- **Trowel:** You'll use a trowel—like a little hand-size shovel—to dig holes for transplanting seedlings into the garden.
- **Shovel:** Good for scooping and lifting, a shovel works for digging holes and moving soil. A spade has a narrower head than a shovel and is made for cutting and scraping.
- **Hoe:** Available in many sizes and shapes, hoes are good for loosening soil and weeding. Try a stirrup hoe for eradicating small weeds without disturbing the soil in a newly planted bed.
- **Hand pruners:** Use these for trimming off dead leaves and branches in the garden or for harvesting vegetables with sturdy stems, like eggplant or squash.
- **Garden rake:** Valuable for leveling and smoothing garden beds, a garden rake's metal tines will help collect small rocks for removal from the garden area.

You can make a bigger cold frame by simply adding more straw bales to make it long and narrow. Set one up around an existing planting to protect it from fall frost, or use it for setting seedlings into the garden earlier.

If you expect temperatures to dip into the 30s, use a blanket to insulate the glass. You will need to tilt the window up to allow air to escape on warmer days; it can get very hot inside. The straw bales will deteriorate over time. Add them to your compost pile or use them as mulch in your garden beds.

Timing Is Everything

After long months of perusing seed catalogs to pass the cold winter days, some gardeners tend to become a bit antsy about getting outside and digging into the soil. But try to restrain yourself. Planting your entire spring crop on the first sunny day of the year could be one of the biggest gardening mistakes you make. Here's why: Even though it's starting to warm up and feels like gardening weather, a frost may still be in the forecast. Frost kills new sprouts and seedlings. The key here is to know your region's first and last frost date; these dates help determine when it's safe to plant outside. Most seed packets offer advice like "start two weeks before last frost." Every region has a different frost date. Check with your local cooperative extension office to determine yours. No extension office in your region? Check them out online at *articles.extension.org*.

If you're anxious to start planting, look for cool-season crops that suggest planting "as soon as soil can be worked." These crops won't mind the frost, and in fact, some crops prefer the cooler weather (see list on page 154).

Climate Zones

The U.S. Department of Agriculture has mapped the United States into climate zones so every gardener from Vermont to Texas can determine when to start seeds for transplanting (see Appendix A on page 306). The Urban Farmer website *(www.ufseeds.com)* offers a concise planting schedule for each zone. You can also narrow it down by city and state.

Growing fresh produce in the backyard means vegetables can go from harvest to table in mere hours.

1
Roots
2
Heads
4
Leaves

❸ Fruits

ROOTS, FRUITS & LEAVES

Which part of a plant is edible? Creative cooks know that some crops—like beets and radishes—can be eaten in their entirety, while others have specific edible parts.

❶ **Roots:** Just as you'd imagine, root crops grow underground; the roots sustain the plant as it grows to become your next meal. Harvesting root crops entails pulling the entire plant, so it will not keep producing. Common root crops include radishes, onions, beets, turnips, and potatoes. Less commonly planted are sweet potatoes, rutabaga, kohlrabies, and yacon.

❷ **Flower buds and heads:** Although you might not think of broccoli and cauliflower as flowers, left on the plant, those heads would form flowers and then seeds. Brussels sprouts are a biennial plant, but left unharvested for a couple of years, they too would flower. The small flowers of cruciferous vegetables like kale, cabbage, collard greens, and radishes offer a flavor resembling that of the plant itself, though often milder. Squash blossoms are another bonus crop; fill them with ricotta cheese and fry them up for an unexpected garden meal.

❸ **Fruits:** Plants that produce fruit (even though we may call them a vegetable) include tomatoes, zucchini, beans, peas, eggplant, peppers, and okra. These plants produce for weeks or months, allowing you to harvest again and again during their growing season.

❹ **Leaves:** Grown for their edible leaves, plants like lettuce, cabbage, kale, and arugula will keep your salad bowl full. Swiss chard, bok choy, and collards are excellent as cooked greens. A few, like head lettuce and cabbage, are harvested in their entirety. Others can be grown as "cut and come again" crops by harvesting just what you need so the plant can continue growing and producing more leaves. Use scissors to snip mature leaves from the outer (or lower) part of the plant. The crown will grow and produce new leaves for weeks until finally going to seed.

WATERWISE GROWING

Water usage in a garden will vary by region. In some areas, the last spring rain means a months-long dry spell that requires supplemental watering in the garden; in other areas, rain falls even during the hot summer months. No matter where you live, using water responsibly is simply good stewardship and may become even more important as our climate and weather patterns continue to change. You can reduce the amount of water your garden needs by using efficient watering methods and improving your soil's structure so that it retains moisture and reduces evaporation.

Free Water

Installing a rain barrel—or a few—keeps some of your precious rainfall on site for use in your garden. Using rainwater allows you to avoid some of the chemicals that may be present in municipal water. Meant to kill bacteria in our drinking water, these additives can also kill beneficial bacteria in garden soil. Your local water municipality should provide a list of additives in the public water.

Wastewater from household routines like showers, baths, and dishwashing—essentially, everything except toilet water—is considered "gray water." Although no longer pure enough for drinking, it can be diverted to the garden if you use environmentally safe soaps. Of course, capturing and diverting this gray water requires some alternative plumbing. But if you live in a drought-prone area, it might be worthwhile.

Stop Sprinkling

Although sprinkling the soil surface is necessary for germination when starting seeds, once plants are established it's most waterwise to direct water right to the roots. Soaker hoses are porous tubes that mount to a standard spigot, allowing water to seep out slowly along the length of the hose. Place it along rows so it delivers water right to the root zone.

A drip irrigation system requires specialized equipment, including various sizes of tubing and drip emitters. A system like this works well for distributing exactly the right amount of water to a plant. Each emitter is installed alongside individual plants, so it's best used in a more permanent situation, like a berry patch or perennial vegetable garden. Rearranging emitters every few months for seasonal crops isn't feasible.

DIY

Terra-Cotta Olla

An olla irrigation system is a traditional method of deep watering. Submerge an olla—a porous vessel—into the ground near the base of your plants. Fill the olla with water and it will slowly seep into the ground, becoming available as plants need it. Although ollas are available premade, you can also make your own.

An olla buried in the ground directs water to plant roots.

Capturing roof runoff in a rain barrel provides a source of chlorine-free water for your garden.

This DIY version is made from terra-cotta pots and costs substantially less to make.

You'll Need:
8-inch terra-cotta pot
8-inch terra-cotta saucer
Sandpaper
Waterproof silicone sealant

1. Sand the lip of the pot and saucer to roughen the surface. This will help the silicone to adhere better.
2. Use a rag to wipe away any residue, then generously cover the lip of the pot with silicone.
3. Place saucer upside down onto the silicone, pressing it in place so there are no visible gaps. Allow to dry overnight.
4. Double-check for gaps; if any, fill these with more silicone, to prevent water from leaking out.
5. Bury the olla in the garden, saucer side down, about a foot from the base of a vegetable plant, allowing the drainage hole in the pot to remain visible.
6. Pour water into the drainage hole until the pot is full. Cover the drainage hole with a small rock to prevent mosquitoes from turning the olla into a breeding ground.
7. Add water as necessary to keep the olla full.

Set a Timer

Install a battery-operated timer on the garden spout. The automatic shutoff prevents accidental overwatering. You can also set it to go off in the early morning hours—when you're still tucked in bed—to reduce the evaporation that happens when you water in the heat of the day.

ANNUAL CROPS

Summer annuals like petunias and snapdragons are familiar flowers, perfect for perking up a patio with their colorful blooms. Many productive vegetable crops are annuals, too. An annual plant—flower or vegetable—is one that completes its entire life cycle in a single season. From germination to production of the next generation of seeds, these plants are Mother Nature's one-hit wonders.

Annuals generally germinate during spring and reach maturity by autumn. A plant that "goes to seed" is signaling the end of its life cycle by producing the means to regenerate itself for the next growing season. We eat some of those seeds—think about corn, tomatoes, and peas—while others, like radish or lettuce seeds, are only valuable for replanting.

Annual vegetable crops are most often grown during summer months, but gardeners can stretch the season by knowing which crops will thrive in cooler spring or fall conditions.

Annual Vegetables for Your Garden

Although we may use generic terms like "tomato" or "corn" when we talk about our vegetables, each garden crop is available in a multitude of varieties featuring different growing habits, fruit shapes, and climate needs. Once you've determined that you want to grow tomatoes, for example, you'll need to decide if you want to grow cherry tomatoes or large slicing tomatoes; red tomatoes or yellow; solid or striped; sweet or acidic. Pondering the pages of a colorful seed catalog to compare vegetable varieties is a great way to get a head start on your garden during the cold winter months.

■ **Beans *(Phaseolus vulgaris)*** Easy to grow from seed, these legumes come in bush or pole varieties. Bush beans grow low and do not need to be staked. Pole beans can reach eight feet in height and need a trellis on which to climb. Both are wonderfully productive; choose the type that works best for your space. Once soil has warmed to at least 60°F, sow bean seeds directly in the garden. As the weather warms, the plants will take off quickly. Commonly grown and harvested as tender young green beans, the pods can be allowed to mature for their edible dry seeds. This is the plant that gives us the common kidney, pinto, and black beans, though you can choose from a multitude of varieties. Good for direct sowing (see page 180).

■ **Bok Choy *(Brassica chinensis)*** Also known as pak choi or pok choi, this Chinese cabbage has dark green leaves and large white ribs that stand fairly upright in the garden. Sow seeds in spring and again in late summer for a fall harvest. Soil temperature should be a minimum of 50°F for best germination. Slugs can be a persistent problem on bok choy (and other brassicas); dust the plants with diatomaceous earth to deter them.

■ **Cucumber *(Cucumis sativus)*** Easy to grow and prolific, cucumbers are a great addition to a summer garden. For best results, plant seeds directly in your garden when the soil temperature is a consistent 70°F. Choose between vining or bush cucumbers. Vining cucumbers can be left to spread on the ground, but you'll save space and avoid slug damage if you give the plants a trellis to climb on. Bush cucumbers are a good option for small gardens or container gardening. No matter what variety you choose, give

Eggplant is an eye-catching crop in the garden, available in purple, orange, yellow, and white.

cucumber plants plenty of sun and maintain consistent soil moisture. Cucumbers come in lots of shapes and sizes, from roundish to long and slender. Be sure to harvest cukes regularly so vines will continue to produce.

■ **Eggplant *(Solanum melongena)*** The stunning eggplant fruit comes in a variety of shapes, sizes, and colors. From the familiar oblong purple eggplant to orange orbs or long white fruit, the beauty of an eggplant cannot be dismissed. Ranging from two to four feet in height, they are great plants for front-yard gardens! Eggplants need a long growing season, so it's best to start seeds indoors in advance of warm weather or opt for nursery-grown seedlings. Provide well-drained soil, and consider mulching to maintain steady soil moisture. If you live in a cool climate, growing eggplants in dark containers can provide the warm soil they crave.

■ **Green onions *(Allium)*** Mildly flavored green onions are not necessarily a particular variety of onion, but rather the result of how they're harvested. Any type of onion can be harvested when young and used as green onions. Sow onions in the fall or early spring in rich, loamy soil. If you intend to allow some of the onions to grow into full-size bulbs, pull and eat young green onions, allowing four inches between each remaining bulb. You can also just snip off the green as you need it, allowing the onion roots to remain. This method allows for a continuous harvest.

■ **Kale *(Brassica oleracea)*** A member of the cabbage family, kale is a cool-season crop. Planted early in springtime, kale will produce leaves until the weather gets too hot. Get a second crop by planting more as autumn approaches and the weather cools. In mild regions, kale can produce its curly or elongated leaves throughout the winter. Harvest leaves from the bottom up, discarding any that are yellowed.

■ **Lettuce *(Lactuca sativa)*** Standard fare for salads, lettuce prefers mild weather and will even tolerate some shade. Seeds germinate in 40°F soil, making them ideal for early spring or late season planting. (Lettuce won't germinate at all in soil that's 80°F or warmer.) Give it nitrogen-rich soil for tender leaves. Iceberg lettuce forms a head, while other varieties form loose heads or are considered leaf lettuce. The latter can be harvested by cutting the outer leaves, leaving the rosette in place. This method allows for a continuous lettuce harvest over the course of several months.

The flavor of garden-grown melons is exceptional.

■ **Melon (*Cucumis melo* or *Citrullus vulgaris*)** If you can provide three months of heat, plenty of moisture, and lots of sunshine, melons can be a very rewarding crop. Cantaloupe, honeydew, and watermelon are standard fare, but there are so many melon varieties to choose from! How about a watermelon with white, orange, or yellow flesh? Or maybe striped or serpent-shaped melons? Be sure to give melons plenty of room by spacing plants three to four feet apart because they tend to really spread out. Another alternative is to trellis the plants, but you'll need to manually tie the vines, as they don't have tendrils. Protect fruit from rot and pest damage by eliminating soil contact. To do this, slide a piece of cardboard under each melon or use a layer of hay.

■ **Okra *(Abelmoschus esculentus)*** Another warm-season vegetable, okra likes lots of sunshine and soil rich in organic matter. Gardeners can get a jump on growing okra by planting seedlings out, but treat them gently. Okra has fragile taproots that you'll need to keep intact. Okra plants can reach six to eight feet tall. Be sure that you give them enough room, and don't plant them where they'll shade other sun-loving crops. Harvest pods when they're two to four inches long; any bigger and they'll get tough and stringy.

■ **Peas *(Pisum sativum)*** Like beans, peas come in bush or climbing varieties; choose what works best in the space you have. Peas like cool weather. Plant them as soon as your soil can be worked in the springtime to harvest a good crop before summer heat sets in. Soak pea seeds in water for 12 to 24 hours before planting to encourage better germination. Shelling peas are grown for the peas inside a pod. Harvest pods when they're full and plump, and remove the shells to reveal rows of peas. Snow and snap peas have sweet, edible pods. Harvest edible pea pods when they are young and tender.

■ **Peppers *(Capsicum)*** Sweet peppers come in a rainbow of colors; hot peppers can be mildly spicy or mouth-numbingly hot. Both sweet and hot peppers like a long growing season. Don't set them out in your garden until warm weather has arrived for good. Peppers need regular watering, well-drained soil, and six to eight hours of sunlight daily to thrive. They are relatively compact plants and do well in containers, making them a great item to add to a balcony garden. It's not unusual for peppers to produce right up until frost. If frost threatens while there are still peppers on your plants, harvest them all to prevent loss.

■ **Spinach *(Spinacia oleracea)*** A cool-season annual harvested for its leaves, spinach tends to bolt (send up flower heads) quickly in warm weather, which makes the leaves less tasty. To avoid this, sow spinach in the spring and fall in fertile, well-drained soil. Spinach can tolerate some shade and likes a sufficient amount of moisture in the soil. Harvest leaves as needed by cutting them from the outer portion on the plant.

Handling Hot Peppers

Capsaicin is the compound in hot peppers that gives them their heat. The heat is concentrated in the seeds and inner membranes and can burn skin and eyes. Everyone reacts differently, but use extreme caution when working with hot peppers. Using gloves will protect your hands, but be careful! The heat of capsaicin is easy to pass from your hands to your eyes, nose, and mouth. Clean your tools and wash your hands thoroughly after cutting hot peppers to avoid a painful lesson. Rarely will a hot pepper burn cause damage that requires medical intervention, but the searing pain can last for hours.

A vivid yellow variety of summer squash

■ **Summer squash *(Cucurbita)*** As the name implies, this is a crop that does well in summertime heat. Zucchini is known for being prolific, and that fame is well deserved. A few plants will keep a household in squash all summer long, no matter the variety. Squash plants can take up a good amount of space in the garden; allow three to six feet between plants, depending on variety. If your space is tight, encourage squash plants to grow more upright by placing a tomato cage over young plants. The large broad leaves of squash do a great job of shading the area below the plant to retain moisture and hold down weeds. Zucchini is best harvested at six to eight inches long, but don't be surprised when you find one the size of a baseball bat hiding among the plant's leaves.

■ **Tomato *(Solanum lycopersicum)*** Tomatoes come in a variety of sizes, shapes, and colors, ranging from red to yellow, orange, green, and even purple. Late spring or early summer are good times to plant tomatoes in most regions. (Hurrying them into the ground before it's warm enough is an exercise in futility and will not result in an earlier crop.) Work compost and calcium-rich crushed eggshells into each planting hole, setting plants deeply. Tomatoes can grow two to eight feet tall; some will need support in the form of a trellis or tomato cage. When buying tomato seeds or plants, you'll need to know if you want determinate or indeterminate plants. Shorter determinate varieties reach their full height and stop growing, making them a good choice for container gardens. Tomatoes ripen within a short one- to two-month window, meaning lots of ripe tomatoes at once. Indeterminate varieties continue to grow and put out new growth and tomatoes until frost hits. These can get quite large in the garden.

■ **Tomatillo *(Physalis philadelphica)***
Popular in Mexican cuisine, tomatillos may be a bit unusual, but they are worth adding to your garden, especially if you live in a region with extremely hot summers. Often called a husk tomato, the fruit can be green or purple and is encased in a papery husk. Remove the husk and use the fruit in fresh salsa or cook it into chili verde. When planting a tomatillo, set plants deeply, burying a good portion of the stalk. Roots will emerge from the stalk, giving the plant a sturdier footing. Choose a sunny, well-drained spot. Tomatillo plants grow much like a tomato, and benefit from staking. Harvest tomatillos when they have completely filled out their husk.

DIY

Salad Tower

This simple vertical planter allows you to grow more than a dozen plants in one square foot of space. It's easy to make using materials from a building supply store, but if you know someone in the construction industry, you might be able to salvage what you need, as I did. The diameter of pipe for this project is a bit flexible, which allows you to choose what works best for you.

You'll Need:

PVC pipe, 8-inch diameter by 4 feet long
PVC pipe, 2-inch diameter by 4 feet long
Cordless or electric drill
1½-inch hole saw for drill
¼-inch drill bit
Tape measure
Potting soil
16 pieces of recycled cardboard, roughly 2 inches square
17 seedlings of lettuce and mixed greens

1. Mark four evenly spaced lines vertically down the large pipe. These will serve as guides for the holes you'll drill.
2. Measure 12 inches from one end and mark a line around the circumference of the pipe. For reference, mark this end of the pipe "DOWN" so you'll remember that this end should go down into the soil when assembling your salad tower.
3. Using the hole saw, drill one hole where a vertical line intersects with the horizontal line. Now drill a second hole directly opposite, again at the intersection of a vertical and horizontal line. (Mind you, these holes do not have to be perfectly aligned; just get them in the ballpark.)
4. Drill three more holes along the same vertical lines, leaving about 10 inches between holes. You now have two lines of four drilled holes.
5. Drill three holes on each of the remaining vertical lines, offsetting each new hole so that it's placed diagonally from those adjacent to it, making an alternating pattern.
6. To use in the garden: Use shovel to dig a 10-inch-deep hole in the ground and bury the bottom end of the pipe almost to the first hole.

A tower garden lets you grow many plants in a small space.

Tomatillos are less common in a backyard garden than tomatoes, but are another great ingredient for making salsa.

7. To use on a patio or balcony: Drill several holes in the bottom of a 5-gallon bucket or large planter and fill halfway with gravel. Place the pipe on top of the gravel and add soil around the pipe, to the top of the container.
8. Now take the thinner PVC pipe and drill about 30 randomly placed ¼-inch holes. Insert it inside the erected, wider pipe so that the top of the inner pipe is slightly higher than the outer pipe. (Add a bit of soil inside the wide PVC to elevate the thin pipe if necessary.) Eventually, filling this inner pipe with water aids in getting moisture to the roots of the seedlings you're about to plant.
9. Fill the large pipe with potting soil up to the bottom of the lowest holes, keeping the inner pipe centered.
10. Fold a piece of cardboard into a V and use it as a funnel to slide a seedling into one of the lowest holes. Gently push the piece of cardboard into the hole. This helps to prevent potting soil from escaping. Do the other hole on the first tier then add more soil to reach the next set of holes. Lightly water seedlings in, to settle the soil. Continue in this manner until each hole is planted.
11. Add a few more plants in the top of the tower.
12. Water the tower slowly from the top as well as into the interior pipe.
13. Harvest leafy greens as they mature.

RECIPE

Tomatillo Salsa

Makes about 2 cups

I started making this tomatillo salsa as a stand-in for my usual garden salsa when my tomato crop wasn't producing well. My family likes the tangy, zippy flavor so much that we continue to make it even when tomatoes are plentiful. Serve it straight from your garden, with chips or alongside chicken or fish. Store salsa in a sealed container for up to a week in the refrigerator.

You'll Need:

2 cups fresh tomatillos, rinsed and husked
¼ cup onion
½ jalapeño pepper
Juice of ½ lemon or lime
½ teaspoon salt
½ teaspoon black pepper

1. Chop all vegetables into ¼-inch dice by hand or with a small food processor.
2. In a bowl, stir together all the ingredients.

PERENNIAL CROPS

A perennial plant is one that lives for at least two seasons—and sometimes much, much longer. Perennials tend to be sturdier plants than annuals. Flower beds are often filled with perennials like daylilies, chrysanthemum, and hosta that will bloom year after year. But some fruits and vegetables are perennial, too. Think about that: These are plants that will produce food year after year without replanting or tilling or starting over each spring.

Plant them once, then harvest the crops every year. In colder regions, some perennials may die down during the winter and send out new growth in the springtime. This varies widely based on climate.

Start Right

Because you won't be amending the soil annually as you might with your vegetable garden, it's important to do a thorough job of preparing the soil for perennial planting. Incorporate some rich compost into each planting hole to boost the soil (for more on soil improvement, see page 198). If your soil seems short on nutrients—maybe you see plants failing to thrive—consider picking up a soil test kit at your local nursery to find out what you can add to improve it. You can get a more detailed soil test through your local cooperative extension office, a college agriculture department, or by mail.

To set perennials in the garden, remove your plant from its container, carefully loosen the root ball, and set it into a planting hole, backfilling so that the top of the root ball is level with the soil. Add a thick layer of mulch around the base of each plant. Wood chips, straw, or dry leaves work well to help keep the weeds down, retain moisture, and add nutrients to the soil.

What grows well for you will depend entirely on your climate zone (see page 306), so be sure to do a little research on which of these will thrive in your garden. Some perennials thrive in temperate climates but can only be grown as an annual in cooler regions. For instance, most gardeners grow peppers as an annual vegetable, but in the right climate they can live for more than one season.

Cultivate asparagus for a spring garden delight.

One of the drawbacks to perennial vegetable and fruit crops is that they can take a year or two to become established. Be patient! Once they start producing, they'll do so for years, saving you plenty of time.

Where to Plant Your Perennial Crops

You can plant perennials in a garden bed, just as you plant annual crops like tomatoes, beans, and corn. But it's not necessary. Because perennials are a more permanent garden addition, consider planting these vegetables or fruits at the perimeter of your garden beds. Some will even help keep the weeds at bay.

Industrially cultivated strawberries are notorious for pesticide residue; grow organic berries for a delicious treat.

When planting berries in your perennial fruit garden, thornless varieties will yield an easier harvest.

Perennial Fruits

No space for an orchard? Add some of these fruiting perennials to your yard to sweeten up your harvest. In some cases, you'll have to wait a year or two for a good crop, but your first homegrown strawberry shortcake or blueberry pancakes? Totally worth the wait.

■ **Strawberries *(Fragaria)*** You can choose from a number of varieties of strawberries, but your biggest decision is between ever-bearing (they'll produce for several months during the spring/summer) or June-bearing (a large crop comes in one big batch around June). Most people who grow strawberries do so in a large patch and use lots of straw mulch to help keep the berries themselves from rotting against wet soil. Of course, the berries are fabulous, but strawberry plants make a beautiful ground cover, too. Your strawberry bed is the perfect place to give companion planting a try. Make the most of your space by growing strawberries and asparagus together. This increases your harvest from one garden bed. Also, the requirements for each are similar, and you'll be able to side-dress and mulch both at the same time, saving you some work. The asparagus spears will poke up through the strawberry plants in the springtime.

■ **Blueberries *(Vaccinium)*** Blueberry plants are attractive, making them an option for front-yard gardeners. They'll provide fresh berries for you during the early summer months and continue bearing for years. If you live in a cold region with short summers, consider haskaps, a highly nutritious berry in the honeysuckle family.

■ **Raspberries and Blackberries *(Rosaceae)*** The most important thing to know when planting raspberries or blackberries is that they can become invasive. Their roots spread underground, sending up shoots as they travel. Plant them in large containers or in an area where you can easily watch for suckers and remove them as they appear. Opt for thornless varieties to make harvesting easier. Gardeners with small spaces can grow this summertime fruit by choosing dwarf varieties that are less invasive.

■ **Grapes *(Vitis vinifera)*** Bring a little taste of Tuscany to your backyard landscape by planting grapes. Choose from red, purple, or white grapes, seeded or seedless. Grapes will provide fruit year after year and are a good option for growing on an arbor because they need support. The deciduous vines will create summertime shade and lose their leaves in the winter, allowing warm rays of winter sunshine through.

Perennial Vegetables

Sometimes a summertime garden just isn't in the cards. Plant some perennial vegetable crops, and you'll have a backup plan for when life gets in the way of a backyard harvest.

■ **Asparagus *(Asparagus officinalis)*** A productive asparagus bed is a beautiful thing, but you'll need patience. Grown from seed, asparagus will take three years to start producing. Shorten that time by opting for one-year-old crowns (often sold during bare-root season). Martha Washington is a well-recognized variety, but all-male hybrid asparagus varieties like Jersey Giant and Jersey Knight are a relatively new option for gardeners, and they're getting high marks for productivity.

■ **Artichokes *(Cynara scolymus)*** An artichoke is, simply, a thistle. The vegetable that we love to eat leaf by leaf is actually a big flower bud. Left unharvested, it blooms into a large, purple thistle flower. Artichoke plants grow to about three feet high and wide, so give them a fair amount of space when setting them in the ground. The Green Globe artichoke variety is commonly planted, but you can choose from other varieties as well. Purple Italian Globe is more tolerant of heat and cold than Green Globe and it adds a punch of color. Emerald artichokes also tolerate a range of temperatures and grow to five feet tall.

■ **Rhubarb *(Rheum)*** Plant it once and you'll have rhubarb forever. The platter-size leaves of rhubarb are very decorative in the landscape, but also poisonous. The red stems are tangy and fresh, great for pie and jam.

■ **Malabar spinach *(Basella alba)*** This fast-growing, soft-stemmed vine has leaves that are slightly mucilaginous. Malabar spinach is quite different from the leafy green most people call spinach. It's a heat-loving plant that can be grown as an annual in cooler climates.

■ **Okinawan spinach *(Gynura crepioides)*** This is another plant that's not actually spinach but is called such. This vining green is good for adding to stir-fry dishes and has a slightly fishy taste. Grow it as a perennial in temperate climates or an annual in cooler regions.

Artichokes—as we eat them—are immature flower heads.

REAPING THE HARVEST

An established garden can provide an abundance of fresh vegetables. Although most gardeners want to try a little bit of everything, some crops are more giving than others. They all have merit, but knowing how different crops produce can help you plan to get the most out of each. This is especially important to keep in mind if you're trying to grow most (or all) of the fruits and vegetables for your household.

Once and Done Vegetables

Some plants you sow, grow, and harvest in their entirety. In other words, to harvest the crop, you pull the entire plant. Radishes, carrots, beets, turnips, head lettuce, and cabbage are examples of this. Other "once and done" vegetables include onions, garlic, potatoes, and sweet potatoes.

Cut and Come Again Vegetables

With some crops, you can cut—or harvest—a portion without harvesting the entire plant. Leaf lettuce, kale, spinach, and bok choy are all greens that can keep producing in the garden for months. Instead of pulling the plants, snip off the outer leaves as you need them, leaving the center in place. The plant will continue to produce new leaves until it starts to go to seed.

Continual Harvest

Once some plants start bearing fruit, you'll be able to harvest from the same plant for an extended time. Tomato plants take 50 to 60 days to start providing fruit, but once they do, they tend to be prolific and can produce for months. Whether you like your peppers hot or sweet, they'll put out fruit all season long, as will eggplant, summer squash, and cucumbers. Green beans and peas will produce for six to eight weeks if conditions are good. Harvest peas and beans regularly to encourage the plants to keep producing. Although most radishes are a "once and done" vegetable, rat-tail radishes keep on giving. Instead of pulling up a plant and getting one radish, this plant produces green pods that taste—not surprisingly—like a radish.

Green onions can be a source of flavor almost all season long; just snip off the larger stalks and leave the more immature ones in place. Both celery and Swiss chard are easier to store in the garden than in the fridge. Simply use a knife to cut the outer stalks as you need them.

RECIPE

Dried Red Pepper Flakes

Makes ½ cup dried flakes

Sprinkle these fiery flakes on pizza or into your favorite spicy recipe. Store pepper flakes in an airtight container indefinitely.

You'll Need:
1 cup hot peppers, washed and dried
Special equipment: dehydrator

1. Remove and discard the stem of each pepper, then slice the peppers into ⅛-inch rounds or in half, if the peppers are small.
2. Spread the peppers out on a dehydrator tray, with space between them.
3. Dry at 165°F until the peppers are dry and brittle, 6 to 8 hours.
4. Transfer the dried peppers to a food processor and pulse into flakes.

RECIPE

Radish Leaf Pesto

Makes about 2 cups

The green tops from radishes, beets, sweet potatoes, and turnips are often tossed to the compost pile,

Transform radish greens into a bright and tasty pesto for topping pasta or spreading in sandwiches.

but—surprise!—they're edible. This radish leaf pesto has a slightly spicy flavor and retains its color beautifully. Serve it over pasta or spread it on your favorite cracker. It keeps in the fridge for up to a week.

You'll Need:
3 cups radish greens (about 2 bunches)
2 large garlic cloves
¼ cup olive oil
⅓ cup shredded Pecorino Romano cheese
Pinch of sea salt
Special equipment: blender or food processor

1. Thoroughly wash and dry radish leaves.
2. Remove and discard any woody stems from the leaves, then place the leaves in a blender or food processor with remaining ingredients.
3. Blend until smooth.

Succession Planting

Planting an entire bed full of radishes in one go will net you a huge harvest all at once. But unless you *really* like radishes, a better bet is to utilize succession planting. This process is a great way to maintain ongoing production from many of your garden crops.

As mentioned previously, radishes mature very quickly; rather than emptying a full seed packet, plant a new row once a week and you'll have a continuous supply of ripe radishes at the ready. Other crops work well for succession planting, too.

Plant spinach and leaf lettuce weekly. Plant corn, beans, peas, and turnips every 10 to 14 days up until 8 weeks before your first expected frost. Carrots, cucumbers, and melons take longer to mature, but a second planting about a month after the first will assure a more sustained harvest season for these as well.

EDIBLE LANDSCAPING

If you love garden design or just want to get the most out of every inch of your yard, you will enjoy strategically mixing productive plants among ornamentals to create an aesthetically pleasing, edible landscape. By incorporating good-looking vegetable plants, edible flowers, and culinary herbs, you can harvest fresh produce from your decorative landscape. Some suburban homeowners' associations require that a landscape conforms to specific guidelines. Sneak some of these pretty edible plants into your front-yard borders; they'll never know that you're harvesting food.

■ **Daylily *(Hemerocallis)*** The new shoots, tubers, buds, and blossoms of this stunning, yet hardy flower are all edible. If you want to eat the roots, you can pull up the plant and harvest the potatolike tubers; be sure to set some aside for replanting. Cook the tubers like potatoes or eat them raw. The young leaves, buds, and blossoms can also be eaten raw: a perfect addition to salad. Some people batter and fry the flowers, too.

■ **Nasturtium *(Tropaeolum)*** These flowers are a bright addition to your yard and garden, and they're edible. There are both annual and perennial varieties of nasturtium. The perennial is somewhat uncommon, but the annuals reseed themselves so freely that they're almost guaranteed to come back year after year. The flower petals add a bit of color to green salads. Use the leaves as a spicy addition to salad, or stuff them much as you would grape leaves. The seeds can be pickled or fermented to make a crunchy condiment reminiscent of capers (see recipe, page 297).

■ **Artichokes *(Cynara cardunculus)*** The perennial gray-green foliage of this plant grows two to three feet high and produces many artichokes in a season.

■ **Asparagus *(Asparagus officinalis)*** You'll need to prepare a really rich bed for this one, but once it's established, plants will produce asparagus spears for several weeks each spring. After harvest season, spears are left in place and develop a wispy, fernlike foliage.

■ **Basil *(Ocimum basilicum)*** A summer staple for a lot of gardeners, basil is prolific and pretty. The bright green leaves can be harvested all summer long for pesto or as an addition to salads, pizza, or pasta.

■ **Beets *(Beta vulgaris)*** You'll probably grow beets for the bulbous root, but while it's busy growing underground it will make pretty (and edible) leaves in your flower bed.

■ **Eggplant *(Solanum melongena)*** If you've never grown eggplant, you're in for some fun. The fruit is beautiful and can come in dark purple—almost black—or light purple, striped or solid. The handsome plant itself has gray-green leaves and stands one to three feet high.

■ **Lemongrass *(Cymbopogon citratus)*** This sturdy perennial will fool most everyone into thinking it's a landscape plant. It's great for tea and may keep mosquitoes at bay.

■ **Lettuce *(Lactuca sativa)*** If you have bare spots in your border, fill them with lettuce! Butter lettuce comes in several varieties and stays nice and compact. Or try dark red Merlot lettuce for a surprising splash of color. Sprinkle a mix of lettuce seeds, keep them moist, and in no time those bare spots will be filled with pretty, edible greens. Lettuce also makes a great addition to patio containers.

Daylilies are prized flowers—and they're also entirely edible, making them a great choice for many landscapes.

■ **Peppers *(Capsicum)*** Whether you like 'em hot or sweet, peppers grow on a sturdy plant that stays lush and green all summer long. The peppers themselves can range from green to yellow to red, and from small to large. Most pepper plants grow about 12 to 15 inches high. They're beautiful ornamental plants, especially in the fall.

■ **Rhubarb *(Rheum)*** The oversize leaves of a rhubarb plant add almost a tropical feel to the landscape. They'll likely die down during cold winter months, but come springtime an established plant will provide lots of rhubarb stems. (The leaves are high in oxalic acid and can cause unpleasant side effects and, in some cases, poisoning—so don't eat those! You can, however, use them for mulch.)

■ **Summer Squash *(Cucurbita)*** Although prolific zucchini plants can tend to overwhelm a small space, a summer squash variety like pattypan grows on a more compact plant. Squash makes a great background for blossoms like marigolds and petunias.

■ **Swiss Chard *(Beta vulgaris)*** A single Swiss chard seed will grow into a plant that produces for months. It grows about 12 inches high and relatively upright, with lush green leaves. Tuck it into small bare spots in your border.

CONSIDERING CALORIES

Most experienced gardeners pack their growing space to full capacity: tomatoes, lettuce, peas, beets, carrots, green beans . . . But no matter how many of those favored veggies a garden holds, it might still be missing something crucial: calories. You can gorge yourself on fresh veggies all summer long, but that produce alone isn't enough to sustain a person. Growing some calorie-dense crops in your garden is a must if you want to stop depending on the supermarket produce aisle and transition to a homegrown diet.

Beans

Most people who have been gardening for any length of time are familiar with growing green beans. The dried beans you get at the store? They come from a plant just like this, but the pods are allowed to mature completely. The seeds—or beans—removed from the shell are dried for storage. Cowpeas, kidney beans, black beans, runner beans, even lentils—you can grow all of these right in your garden. Calorie counts vary based on variety, but a cup of cooked beans will net about 200 calories.

Corn

Growing corn requires a bit more space than most other garden crops, and corn plants are thirsty. If you've got the space and plentiful water, though, a summer corn harvest is hard to beat. Corn is a starchy grain that grows two or three corncobs per stalk. Harvest sweet corn when the silk at the top of the corn cob turns dry and brown. Don't be afraid to pull the husk aside carefully to check, though. A medium ear of corn has about 77 calories.

Dent corn grows in the same manner as sweet corn, but it's grown specifically for use as a dried grain.

Dent corn can be dried and ground into cornmeal.

Choose from a number of dent corn varieties, some that originated with Native American tribes. Dent corn is ground into fine or coarse cornmeal and used as an ingredient for making polenta, corn bread, or tortillas.

> **Edible Sweet Potato Vines**
>
> The vines of a sweet potato plant are edible, providing a bonus crop of greens for stir-fries or for adding to soups.

Potatoes

These tubers come in a wide variety, including red, purple, and white options. Although the various colors are fun and do have a subtle flavor difference, if you hope to make your potato harvest last all winter, it's better to focus more on varieties that store well, like deep purple Magic Molly or Yukon Gold. Once potato plants are well established, you can carefully dig below the plant to harvest tiny "new potatoes" for summertime meals. When the leaves begin to die off later in the season, dig up the entire plant to harvest the full-size potatoes. A medium-size potato has about 160 calories.

Squash

Winter squash and pumpkins aren't quite as calorie-dense as the aforementioned crops, but they are easy to grow and store. The vining plants take up a fair amount of space, but they produce generously. Whole pumpkins and squash will last throughout the winter season. A cup of cooked pumpkin or squash has about 50 calories.

Sweet Potatoes

In the right conditions, sweet potatoes are incredibly easy to grow. Sweet potatoes need a lengthy growing season, but if you can get them in the ground early enough, even many cold region gardeners have success with them. These plants need a minimum of 90 days from first frost to last; start sweet potato slips inside to get a jump on the season. Submerge a sweet potato halfway in water; in several weeks, it will begin to sprout. Those sprouts—or slips—can be planted in the garden when they're about a foot long. Bury the stem, leaving the top three or four leaves visible. Harvest in midsummer to late summer, depending upon your weather. Just like potatoes, sweet potatoes store well for winter use. They provide about 115 calories for a one-cup serving.

Potatoes are a calorie-dense crop that stores easily through the winter months.

GROWING FROM SEED

When starting your garden, you'll have two options: seeds or seedlings. Both have pros and cons, and most gardeners do a little bit of each. You can start planting seeds directly in the garden after the soil warms, or in containers to grow seedlings for transplanting after the last frost. Whether you plant in the ground or in pots, there's really nothing like seeing that first sprout of green emerge from the soil, full of potential. You can also purchase nursery seedlings that are ready to transplant straight into your soil.

Choosing Seeds for Your Garden

Growing plants from seed is very inexpensive. For about three bucks, you can take home enough zucchini seeds to keep you and your entire neighborhood in squash for the summer.

Every garden supply store offers a selection of seed packets from which to choose. Mail-order seed companies offer a bigger selection for gardeners who want more variety or the chance to experiment with more exotic produce. Before you buy, though, make sure you understand the different types of seeds, and choose what will work best for you.

Heirloom or **open-pollinated** varieties of seed can be saved and replanted from year to year, and the resulting fruit remains true to type, meaning that seeds planted from these crops will result in the same plant in the next generation. In other words, that funny little tomato you remember from grandma's garden? If you planted seeds saved from that tomato, you'd get the same fruit today.

Hybrid seeds are the product of crossbreeding two varieties of one type of fruit or vegetable to increase yield, pest resistance, disease resistance, flavor, or shelf life. Hybrid seeds do not grow true to type for a second season, so they're not the best choices if you hope to save seed from year to year.

Genetically engineered seeds (also called "GMO"—genetically modified organisms—and "transgenic") are often confused with hybrid seeds. Genetically engineered seeds are altered by inserting DNA from outside the species into a plant seed. Mother Nature doesn't allow such a thing to happen, but the miracle of modern technology lets scientists cross that barrier. GMO seeds are patented, and it's actually

Comparing Seeds and Seedlings

There's no right or wrong way to start growing; determine what works best for you!

The Benefits of Planting Seeds:

- Choose from many more varieties than the standard nursery fare.
- You can get started while it's still too cold outside to do other gardening projects.
- It's less expensive.
- You can use seeds saved from last year's garden, as long as they are an open-pollinated variety.
- Directly sown seeds do not have to endure the shock of transplant.

The Benefits of Starting with Seedlings:

- Starting with small plants can help avoid trouble with pests that attack tender sprouts.
- Seedlings may produce sooner than seeds planted at the same time.
- They're visible—you'll know right where they are in the garden.
- If you opt to buy seedlings at the nursery, someone else has done some of the work for you.

Direct sowing seeds works well for sturdy crops like beans and corn, as well as root vegetables like radishes and beets.

illegal to save and replant some varieties. These seeds are primarily sold to large-scale farms and are not available at the retail level.

Planting a Seed

A good general rule is to plant a seed twice the depth of its size, but seed packets should have specific instructions for seed depth. Some seeds—tomato, pepper, eggplant—should be surface sown or just barely covered with soil. Set one or two seeds into each planting hole, cover it with soil, and water.

Direct Sowing Seeds

Generally speaking, the seeds that do well sown directly in the garden are large varieties, like those of squash, peas, and beans. Root crops like radishes, beets, turnips, and carrots are also good for direct sowing. Some seeds simply dislike being transplanted, so you'll want to direct sow those. Corn, beans, carrots, peas, and radishes fall into this category.

Gardeners can plant seeds in rows, which has been the garden standard for years; scatter seeds evenly across the ground (called broadcasting); or use the square foot planting method.

To plant in rows, make a furrow for the seeds at the appropriate depth. Sow seeds spaced evenly at the distance suggested on the seed packet. Place large seeds manually; smaller seeds are a little harder to get exact, and that's okay. If you notice that the sprouts are too close together, thin them once the seedlings

Frost Dates

The last spring freeze rings in the beginning of garden season. The arrival of the first frost of the year generally spells the end. Northern regions will see frost earlier in the year, while warmer climates tend to see frost weeks later. The National Centers for Environmental Information (*www.ncei.noaa.gov*) averages 30 years of climate norms to estimate first and last frost dates across the United States.

As seedlings emerge, control weeds to prevent root competition.

have two true sets of leaves. To thin seedlings without damaging the tender roots of the ones you intend to keep, use small scissors to snip them off at the ground.

Small seeds that are planted shallowly like lettuce, carrots, and kohlrabi do well with the broadcasting method. Determine the area that you'll be planting. Rake to loosen the soil surface, then scatter seeds as evenly as possible. Lightly rake again, then spread a thin layer of sifted compost over the area. Use a fine mist to moisten the newly planted area. You'll need to maintain that moisture until seedlings sprout; on hot days, you may need to water more than once.

Starting Your Own Seedlings

Starting seedlings ahead of planting season allows gardeners to get a jump on getting vegetable plants in the ground. By replicating the spring weather that seeds need to germinate, garden plants can get a head start on the season, even when the temperature outside is too cold. The key elements for growing seeds indoors are warmth, light, and moisture. The easiest way to provide this environment is with a heated seed mat and a grow light.

DIY

Pre-Sprouting Seeds With an Old T-Shirt

Storing seeds in a cool, dry place can extend viability, but as time passes, most seeds tend to lose their oomph. If you've ever planted an envelope full of seeds only to have just a few sprouts emerge, you'll appreciate this. By pre-sprouting, you can see in advance which seeds are viable rather than planting row upon row of duds that will disappoint.

You'll Need:
An old T-shirt or scrap of cotton fabric
Tape or twine
Seeds
Plastic container or bag

1. Cut an old T-shirt into 6-inch-square sections.
2. Soak squares of fabric in water.
3. Sprinkle seeds onto the fabric's surface and fold the fabric in half. Roll it up burrito style and secure it with masking tape or twine.
4. Place the rolls in a recycled plastic container or plastic bag to help retain moisture. Place in a warm location, though sunlight is not necessary.
5. Check daily to make sure the cloth is still moist. (Be sure it's not oversaturated; this will cause the seeds to rot.)

Utilize recycled containers for starting seeds.

6. After two days, start checking for sprouting. As soon as the seeds begin to send out white tendril rootlets, carefully lift each one and plant in a soil-filled pot. The tip of a pencil or a knife can work well for moving sprouted seeds. Don't allow the sprouted seeds to linger at this stage, or they'll send little roots into the fabric, making it difficult to move them.
7. Set sprouted seeds at the depth suggested for seed planting listed on the packet. This will vary by variety.

Growing Seedlings in Pots

You don't have to have specialty containers for planting seeds. Save the cans and yogurt containers that pass through your kitchen; simply poke a few drainage holes in the bottom and you're set. Fill containers with good-quality seed starting mix to within an inch of the top.

Place your containers in a warm place (or on a heat

mat) that gets plenty of light, and wait for the seeds to sprout. Once sprouted, keep the soil moist. A spray bottle is a good way to mist fragile new seedlings. You'll need to keep seedlings inside under lights until the last frost date. Once safe to do, transplant seedlings into your garden.

DIY

Planting in Soil Blocks

As you might imagine, a soil blocker is a tool for creating a compressed block of soil. A soil blocker replaces planting pots because plants started in a soil block are planted directly in the ground. Cutting out

the transplant step means less chance of disturbing the roots of tender seedlings.

You'll Need:

Aluminum can with a lip on the bottom (rather than a rounded edge)
Can opener
Dowel, roughly 1 inch in diameter and 6 inches long (or cut a straight branch from a tree)
Jar lid, slightly smaller than the diameter of the can
Hammer
Small nail
Screw
Screwdriver
Bucket for mixing soil
Tray

1. Cut both ends from an aluminum can with a can opener. Bend down sharp edges if needed. (You could also use a recycled plastic container with straight sides.)
2. Set the jar lid on a flat surface, with the top up. Use a hammer and nail to tap a small pilot hole in the center of the lid.
3. Push a screw partway into that pilot hole so that the pointed end of the screw is visible on the inside of the lid. Use a screwdriver if needed.
4. Center one end of the dowel or twig on the screw, and use a screwdriver to attach the jar lid to the dowel. Stop tightening the screw when just ¼ inch remains above the lid. This tool becomes a tamper to press down the soil; the screw projection will leave a little indent in the soil for the seed.
5. Prepare the planting soil by adding enough water to make an oatmeal-like consistency. It should hold together when you squeeze it in your hands.
6. Set the can in a tray or cardboard box lined with plastic. Add about 3 inches of soil to the can, and use the tamper to compress it. Hold pressure on the tamper while gently lifting the can away from the soil. Repeat process to make as many soil blocks as you need.
7. Set a seed in the indentation left by the screw head. Water seed blocks with a spray bottle set to "mist" until roots begin to hold the block together. To plant in the garden, dig a hole, set the entire soil block in place, and backfill so that the top of the soil block is level with the garden soil.

From Seed to Sprout

When a seed first emerges from the soil, it has a set of embryonic leaves called cotyledons. The cotyledons nourish the seedling. These look nothing like the second set of leaves, "true leaves," that emerge as the seedling grows. The cotyledons will eventually die off, leaving only true leaves. These young seedlings are fragile; water with a mister or spray bottle to prevent knocking them over with a stream of water. If you find that you have several seedlings that sprout close together, thin them. The best way to do this is not by pulling the seedlings, which can disturb fragile roots, but rather by using a small set of scissors to snip off all but one of the seedlings.

Transplanting Your Seedlings

When seedlings have two to four (or more) sets of true leaves, they're ready to be planted out in the garden. If they've been growing under lights or in a greenhouse, you'll need to acclimate them to their new environment. This is called hardening off. Sunlight—stronger than the grow lights the seedlings have been under—can burn the plants. A light wind can stress plants or cause stems to break.

About two weeks prior to your last frost, begin transitioning seedlings to the outdoors. Start by moving them outside to a protected area for a few hours. A location that shades them from direct sun and protects them from wind or rain is ideal. If you experience a cold snap, be sure to bring them back inside. Gradually increase the time the seedlings spend outside, allowing them to receive a little sunshine during morning or evening hours when it's not as intense. After about a week or 10 days, allow the seedlings to remain outside overnight as long as you don't expect a frost.

Once they are hardened off, you can transplant the seedlings into your garden. Most seedlings should be planted so that the level of the soil in their pot or soil block is level with the soil in the ground. The exception is tomatoes and tomatillos. It's okay—and even a good idea—to plant these deeply. Their fleshy stems will send out more roots where they are buried, giving the plants more stability.

If possible, choose a calm, overcast day for transplanting so the seedlings have a chance to adjust without battling harsh sun as they transition. Alternatively, plant your seedlings in the cooler temperatures of the late afternoon or evening. Water seedlings thoroughly after transplanting.

VERTICAL GARDENING

Small urban and suburban yards can be a challenge for people who want to grow their own food. If you don't have enough space to let your garden spread out, consider growing up! Adopting some vertical gardening techniques is a great way to make the most of the space you have. It allows you to transform areas like skinny driveway planters or side yards into productive growing space. The primary purpose of vertical gardening is to increase yield, but there are several good reasons to consider implementing some of these techniques.

Gardening at ground level or in raised beds uses up the horizontal surface of your garden. Some plants in particular take up more than their fair share of space. Pumpkin plants, for instance, can spread to cover a 10-foot-square area or more. The only part of the plant that actually needs to be on the ground is the base, where it's rooted to the soil. By training pumpkin vines on a trellis, you can free up a substantial amount of growing ground.

Raising plants up off the ground also serves to increase air circulation. This aids in preventing pests and disease. And of course, fruit that sits on the ground is at risk of rotting or being chewed by bugs and is in easy range for pesky rabbits. Keeping fruit off the ground can prevent some loss.

Harvesting is also simpler when plants are grown vertically. It's hard to see vegetables among leaves when the plants are sprawling across the ground. Train them to grow in a more upright position and you'll have an easier time finding ripe fruit. Plus, less bending is easier on a gardener's back.

Cage Your Plants

Grow your summer squash in a tomato cage. Train the leaves into the cage as it grows to hold the plant more erect; this will save precious garden space. Plus, when it comes time to harvest, it will be easier to see the zucchini that are often easy to miss when they're hidden among the plant's big leaves sprawled on the ground.

Using a Trellis

You can create a trellis in a garden in any number of ways, but you might already have one in place. A garden fence is an easy way to start growing vertically. Plant seeds or seedlings along the fence line and, as they grow, train them on the fence for support.

If you want to try your hand at making your own garden trellises, seek out recycled materials for a budget-friendly plan. Tree branches and bamboo are obvious choices, but items like mattress springs, metal headboards, or bike tires mounted to a post can also be transformed into creative support for your crops. Consider the vigor of the plant you plan to trellis. A small trellis made of branches and twine can work for peas, but probably won't hold up melons.

A classic garden tepee starts with six to eight straight poles, about six feet long. Bound together at the top, the wide base and circular shape of the tepee offer a solid foundation for plants that grow exuberantly or have heavy fruit. It can also become a great outdoor play space for children.

Most trellises are seasonal, but a permanent structure can become a garden focal point offering support for a variety of crops from year to year.

DIY

Build a Sturdy Tomato Trellis

There are many methods of supporting tomatoes, and most gardeners will passionately debate their favorite one. This trellis is easy to build and offers plenty of support. It makes a great replacement for tomato cages that tend to fall over with the weight of a thriving tomato plant. It works for other vining crops, too.

Train vining plants like beans and peas on a trellis to provide support and reduce the amount of room they take up.

You'll Need:

A 16-foot rigid-wire livestock panel, 4 feet high (available at farm supply stores)
5-foot steel fence posts (also known as T posts, available at most building supply stores)
Plastic zip ties
Bolt cutters

1. Use bolt cutters to cut the panel to the length of your garden row. (This makes it easier for transporting, too.) Stand the panel up.
2. Pound posts into the ground in line with the panel for structural support. Space them 4 to 6 feet apart.
3. Use plastic zip ties to attach the panel to the posts.
4. Plant tomatoes in alternating positions on both sides of the trellis.
5. As plants grow, weave stems in and out to secure your plants to the frame.

Veggies to Trellis

Some vegetables—like peas—have tendrils and will climb a trellis naturally. Others must be manually trained to do so, but it's not hard. You can achieve it by winding vines between the trellis or by tying them in place. Strips cut from an old T-shirt are great for this, because they stretch and won't cut into the plant like twine does.

All of these vegetables are good candidates for trellising:

- Beans (pole varieties)
- Cucumbers
- Gourds
- Melons
- Peas
- Pumpkin
- Squash (winter)

Hanging Plants

The vertical space—the airspace, if you will—in your yard can be put to good use for growing veggies. As long as the area has a sufficient amount of sunshine, planting vegetables in hanging pots or in planters mounted to a wall or fence is a great way to utilize space that would otherwise be unproductive, and to add lush greenery to your yard. Small crops like lettuce, chard, and many herbs do well in hanging pots. The soil in planters like this tends to dry out quickly, especially on hot summer days; be sure to water regularly to maintain consistent soil moisture.

Consider an Arbor

More permanent garden structures, arbors add a bit of romance to a yard or garden. People tend to gravitate toward their vertical lines and dappled shade, large or small. But arbors are not just a pretty landscape element; they can also double as a base for vertical gardening. Small arbors—the kind you might see over a gate or garden entrance—can support many vining vegetables. A larger arbor—the kind built to provide shade over a patio—is a perfect place to grow some edibles that appreciate more support.

One crop to try? Grapes. A more permanent option than summer annuals, grapes need a solid support structure, but once established, they will provide fruit year after year. Place grapes about 10 to 12 feet apart, planting them at the base of an upright post so they will have support as they grow upward. If you have space, choose several different varieties that will ripen at different times of the year to extend the harvest. For example, Flame Seedless generally ripens in July, while Thompson Seedless is ready to harvest in August.

Another bonus? Growing grape vines on an arbor will provide shade during summer months but allow the warmth of the sun to penetrate once their leaves have dropped.

DIY

Upside-Down Tomato Planter

Planting tomatoes upside down puts gravity in control and utilizes empty airspace.

You'll Need:

5-gallon bucket

Electric drill with a hole saw bit (1- to 1½-inch diameter)

Scrap fabric or old T-shirt

Tomato seedling

Props for use in assembly, slightly taller than seedlings (concrete blocks or extra buckets work)

Heavy-duty hook for hanging

Planting mix: Hanging 5 gallons of heavy potting mix will put stress on the handle of the bucket. To create a lighter mix, combine roughly two parts potting soil, two parts peat moss, and one part perlite.

1. Drill a hole in the center of the bottom of a bucket. If you do not have a hole saw, you can use a large drill bit and drill several holes that merge to make an opening about the size of a quarter or a little larger.
2. Cut a piece of fabric roughly the size and shape of the base of the bucket. Cut a slit from the edge of the fabric to the center. Place the fabric

Make a Lettuce Ball

For a fun twist on those coir-lined half-baskets, fill two with good potting soil. Place a piece of cardboard over the top of one, and hold it tightly in place as you flip the basket onto the other one to make a sphere. Slide the cardboard out and wire the halves together. Use a small knife to cut slits in the coir every four inches or so, and slip a lettuce seedling into each hole. As the lettuce grows, it will obscure the baskets, becoming a beautiful, edible orb.

inside the bucket, covering the bottom. This will help hold the soil and tomato seedling in place until it is rooted in.

3. Set the bucket up on blocks to allow you to work without crushing the tomato seedling.
4. Flip the fabric back so that you can slide the upside-down tomato seedling in the hole, with the leaves hanging below the bucket.
5. Pull the edges of the fabric slit together, snug around the stem.
6. Gently add planting mix around the tomato roots, and continue adding soil until the bucket is nearly full.
7. To hang your planter, screw a heavy-duty hook into an arbor or overhang at least 6 feet from the ground. Place the handle of the bucket over the hook. If necessary, adjust the height by looping a piece of chain through the bucket handle and then onto the hook.

Growing tomatoes upside down saves space.

NATURAL WEED CONTROL

Weeds are often a gardener's enemy number one. They compete with vegetable plants, depleting moisture and nutrients in the soil, and they can quickly overtake smaller or slower growing plants. Although a few weeds here and there aren't a problem, it's best to try to keep them under control. Weeding by hand is the old standby, but you can take offensive measures in the war on weeds to make it less tedious and time consuming.

Mow the Weeds

Obviously, this only works if your garden beds are bordered by wide areas that allow access with a lawn mower. Keeping weeds cut low will prevent them from setting seed and will prevent creeping weeds from sending out their long runners that root down into moist soil to spread. Mowing will not work on weeds that have underground runners. If your lawn mower is equipped with a bag to collect the cuttings, use them to mulch around the base of trees. Seed-free clippings can also be added to your compost pile.

Mulch

Mulching in the garden offers a lot of benefits, and suppressing weeds is one of them. Once your vegetables have sprouted, spread a thick layer of mulch around them. Use lawn clippings or leaves to a depth of about six inches to really hold down weed growth. The mulch will slowly break down, improving your garden soil. When weeds begin to persist and push through the composting mulch, simply cover the weeds with more mulch. Be sure to leave some breathing room between the base of the plants and the mulch; mounding the pile directly against the stem or trunk of a plant or tree can damage it.

Many materials can be used as mulch. Grass clippings, as long as they haven't been treated with pesticides, are great mulch for a vegetable garden and are often readily available. Shredded leaves, green plant trimmings, straw, and compost are beneficial to soil and are good at holding down weeds. Wood chips can draw nitrogen from the soil as they break down. This makes using them in the vegetable garden a bit controversial; some growers swear by it, others avoid it. I use them around trees and shrubs instead (for more on making mulch see page 199).

Smother the Weeds

Suppress weeds around trees, shrubs, perennials, and other semipermanent plantings—essentially, areas where you won't be trying to dig—by smothering them with plain, untreated cardboard or newspaper. These recyclables are great to use in the garden. Flatten boxes, remove any plastic tape or packaging, and spread them around the base of trees and plants to smother weeds. Although this method is highly effective, it is ugly. To remedy this, once an area is covered with cardboard or newspaper, add a layer of

Use Caution When Importing Materials

Many municipalities grind up green waste and offer the resulting mulch for use in the community, often for free. It may sound like a great opportunity, but that mulch can become contaminated when the mix includes chemically treated pallets or plant material that's been sprayed with harsh weed killers. Persistent pesticides in straw and manure are another concern. Straw or hay that is sprayed with pesticides in the field can retain some of those chemicals; it's even been reported to survive in manure. Adding straw mulch or amending with manure contaminated by persistent pesticides can kill any plants in its path. Know your source when adding any of these items to your garden.

When pulling weeds, make every attempt to remove the entire plant—roots and all—so they don't return.

Goats are an aggressive (and cute!) way to rid overgrown areas of brushy undergrowth.

wood chips. (These are typically available bagged at garden centers, but here's a frugal tip: Contact tree trimmers and volunteer as a drop-off for their wood chip waste when they're in your neighborhood.) As the cardboard and newspaper break down, the weeds will eventually start to come back. Simply repeat the process.

Burn the Weeds

Fence lines and edges are the areas where a lot of people fall back on using poisonous weed killers. A weed burner is a tool that attaches to a propane tank. You can pick one up for less than the cost of a gallon of herbicide, and it can be just as effective, so long as it's not at risk of causing a wildfire. Focus the flame on weeds at the base of a fence or nonflammable edge until they begin to wither. Over the course of several days, the weeds will turn brown and die. For the most effective weed-killing action, repeat the process soon after you see new weeds beginning to sprout again.

Chicken Scratch

Chickens are natural weed killers. If you keep chickens, their natural tendency to scratch and peck for bugs can be the death knell for weeds. Set up a portable chicken cage or chicken tractor to contain them to the area in need of weeding and toss out a handful of scratch. They'll spend the day happily decimating weeds. Another trick? To encourage hens to work on specific weedy spots—the fence line, say—scatter scratch in those areas.

Goats

Goats can completely clear an area in no time flat. They're probably not a good bet for the suburbs or an apartment balcony—but if you have a sizable piece of land that is overrun with brushy growth, goats can save a lot of backbreaking work. If you don't want to own goats or go to the trouble of installing fencing, find out if there's a "rent a goat" operation near you—they will bring the goats and portable fencing.

Solarize

You can use the power of the sun to kill your weeds. It's not a quick fix, though. Spread a dark tarp over the area where you want to kill weeds—note that this method will kill everything under the tarp. Set a few rocks on the tarp to hold it in place, then walk away. Depending on the sun, it can take two weeks to a month to kill the weeds under the tarp, but it's definitely a low-effort solution.

Shade the Weeds

Many common weeds don't like shade. You can take advantage of this and plant accordingly. Tighten up the spacing between your vegetable plants to shade and crowd out weeds below. Set vegetable plants close enough that at full size, their leaves will just touch and shade the ground. Edge garden beds with plants that grow wide and low to the ground. Comfrey works well, as does plantain. (Plantain can be considered a weed, but it's one that can be useful—and it's removed easily if you decide you no longer want it.)

Boiling Water

This isn't practical for a big project, but when there's boiling water in the kitchen—from cooking pasta or canning, say—take it outside and pour it on weeds. Because this method can damage the roots of nearby plants, reserve it for weeds in the driveway or those growing in cracks in the concrete.

Rototillers can be useful in weed removal.

Eat the Weeds

Another way to deal with weeds is to embrace them. Many common weeds are actually edible and can be good sources of early spring greens. Consider these:

- Dandelion
- Miner's lettuce
- Nettles
- Plantain
- Purslane
- Ramps

Rototilling

Tilling is a mechanical method of turning soil. A rototiller knocks down weeds and loosens the soil, making it easy to manually remove weeds. A small tiller can be very handy for weed control, even if you prefer to use no-till gardening methods.

Salt

Salt kills plants. All plants. Don't use this method anywhere that you might want to grow in the future. But for dealing with weeds poking through pavers, patio cracks, and driveways, it's a keeper. Scatter salt on offending plants. Some plants will respond to the salt treatment alone, whereas others won't wilt until the salt has been wet down a bit.

What About Chemical Weed Killers?

Herbicides are convenient, sure. And easy. But here's the trouble: Although we simply don't know the health implications of these poisons, there are concerns. High doses of the widely used herbicide glyphosate have been linked to developmental and reproductive issues in lab rats; it has also shown potential to be carcinogenic. And juries in recent court cases have awarded millions to plaintiffs suffering from cancer related to use of glyphosate weed killer. The verdict is in on another issue, though: In their quest to survive, weeds are becoming more and more resistant to glyphosate-based herbicides. As that happens, growers continue to increase the amount of herbicides sprayed to combat these superweeds. Since the late 1970s, the use of glyphosate-based herbicides has increased approximately a hundredfold, and some growers are now mixing stronger chemical cocktails to try to combat the problem.

CONTAINER GARDENING

Growing veggies in containers can be a great way to get started with a garden. Suburbanites with limited growing space can make the most of their area by adopting this tactic, growing productive crops in pretty—and functional—raised beds, patio planters, or pots. Even apartment dwellers can grow some food in containers on a sunny balcony. Raised beds are a method of container gardening that provides numerous benefits. These can be built to perfectly fit your space using a variety of materials, including lumberyard boards if your budget allows or salvaged materials for a more cost-effective option.

Reasons to Consider Raised Beds

Building a box-style raised bed—essentially, an open-bottomed box you can fill with soil—allows you to exclude some frustrating garden pests. Install sturdy wire at the bottom to prevent gophers and moles from burrowing in and decimating your beds. Use what's called hardware cloth; chicken wire is not strong enough to keep them out, and it will rot quickly. You can also line the bed with weed cloth to keep creeping grasses from invading.

Improving a plot that has poor or rocky soil requires a lot of backbreaking work. By installing raised beds and importing a truckload of good-quality soil, you can grow crops above the ground, rather than trying to fix what's there. Likewise, if you have an oversize driveway or parking area, set up a couple of raised beds right on top of the concrete to transform it into productive space. This is a great way for renters to set up a temporary garden, as the beds can be easily removed and relocated.

Probably one of the most convincing arguments for raised beds is that your back will thank you. Raising the level of your garden means you won't have to bend down so far to work.

Container gardening is easier for people with mobility issues.

DIY

Simple Raised Garden Box

Cedarwood is more rot-resistant than other varieties, but any type of lumber will work. To avoid unwanted chemicals in your food garden, opt for unfinished, untreated wood.

You'll Need:

(1) 4 × 4-inch post, 4 feet long
(4) 2 × 12-inch boards, 6 feet long
(2) 2 × 12-inch boards, 4 feet long
(2) 2 × 2 grade stakes, 24 inches long
(24) 3½-inch deck screws (6 screws per post)
(6) 2-inch deck screws (optional)
Screwdriver or cordless drill with screw head
Wooden stakes (often called survey stakes)
Circular saw
Weed cloth (optional)
U nails or staple gun (optional)

1. Cut the 4-foot post into four 12-inch sections to make corner posts. (You'll have a little piece left over.)
2. Assemble the short sides for the raised bed first.

Building a simple, raised garden is easy—and can prevent tunneling pests from ruining your crops.

Use three 3½-inch deck screws to attach a 4-foot board to a corner post, aligning the post with the bottom and end of the board. Repeat this step until you've mounted a corner post at each end of both short boards in the same manner.

3. Stand the assembled short sides upright, facing each other with the corner post to the inside. Screw the long boards to the corner posts, aligning the ends of the boards to make a corner.
4. If you wish to add wire or hardware cloth (to keep gophers out of the bed) or weed cloth (to prevent unwanted growth), now is the time to add it. Cut the wire or weed cloth slightly bigger than your box. Flip the box over and use U nails (for wire) or a staple gun (for weed cloth) and attach securely to the bottom the bed.
5. Set your garden box upright and position it where you want it.
6. Measure and mark the middle of each long side. Pound a grade stake into the ground, alongside the garden bed. Use 2-inch deck screws to secure the stake to the garden bed for added stability.
7. Fill the box with a good-quality planter mix.

Woodworking Tip

Cut the boards to the appropriate length using a circular saw. If you don't have a circular saw, your lumberyard might cut the materials to size for you if you note the specific measurements.

Designing Your Raised Garden Area

No matter what material you use to create your raised beds, you'll need to think about how to lay out your garden area.

If you have easy access to power tools, raised beds made from lumber can be adapted to fit any space.

Think about how much space you need between garden beds and what those paths will look like. Do you use a garden cart for hauling materials around? Make sure the space between beds allows for that. If you'll let grass grow on the paths, you'll need enough space for your lawn mower. (Remember to leave room for turning corners, too!)

Raised beds can be made to fit any space, but you'll want to make sure that they're not too wide. A good rule of thumb is that the middle of the bed should be no more than an arm's length from the outer edge. This allows you to be able to reach the entire bed for planting, harvesting, and weeding.

Feed Your Veggies

Fertilize your container gardens two to three times each month to keep them healthy. Use one tablespoon fish emulsion per gallon of water, or make up a batch of compost tea. To do that, tie about two cups of compost into an old sock and soak in a gallon of water overnight.

Free Raised Beds

Using lumber to build a raised bed creates a more refined end product. But keep in mind that utilizing materials you might already have on hand makes for a more cost-effective project. Plus, you'll reduce the carbon footprint of your raised beds.

One of the simplest ways to create a raised bed is to use good-size logs from downed trees. Simply lay them out where you want your garden bed and fill with good-quality soil. The bigger the diameter of the log, the taller the raised bed will be. Alternatively, you can use shorter lengths of logs or branches sunk into the ground vertically in a tight line. Dig a trench and bury logs in the ground at least 12 inches deep to ensure that the end result is sturdy enough.

Rocks are another easy way to create a raised garden bed. The limitation here is that they are heavy and you might need to stack the rocks to achieve the height you desire. A dry stack wall allows for more height and is a beautiful thing, but be sure it's stable before adding soil. Rocks are a good option for building raised beds on uneven ground, too. By stacking one side of the bed higher than another, a raised bed can effectively "level" your planting area by creating a sort of terrace.

You can use two pallets to create a square raised bed. Cut the pallets in half, across the inner braces, and assemble them into a bottomless box. The construction method will vary depending upon your pallets, but take a cue from the raised garden box instructions in this chapter, and screw the pallets to wood braces in each of the four corners. Line the box with weed cloth to retain soil and exclude weeds, and fill with good-quality soil.

Pallets can be used individually as planters, too. Place a pallet face down and use landscape fabric to cover the back and four sides. Turn it over and fill with potting soil. Shake the pallet as you add soil so that it settles into all of the gaps. Plant seedlings in each row; a planter like this is great for growing greens. You can use this planter flat, or carefully lift it into an upright position so it's more of a vertical garden. If you have trouble with soil falling out of some of the gaps, temporarily slide some pieces of cardboard over each row, tucking it under the pallet boards. As the plants root in, they'll hold the soil in place.

Stacked stone makes a pretty raised bed.

Fun growing containers can be pulled from the recycle bin.

Growing Food in Pots

If you don't have room for a large in-ground garden, you can grow aboveground in containers. The beauty of containers is that you can plant in just about anything, so long as it has a drainage hole. Baskets, tin cans, five-gallon buckets, wooden boxes, and wine barrels are just some of the available options. Decide what works for you based on aesthetics and the size of the plants you wish to grow. Large vegetables like tomatoes and zucchini need a large container (they do great in wine barrels), while lettuce only needs a four- or five-inch soil depth.

One of the challenges of container gardening is maintaining consistent moisture; they tend to dry out really quickly in hot weather. Small containers and terra-cotta pots are especially susceptible. One tactic to combat this is to mix coconut coir—a growing medium made from coconut husks—into the soil mix to help with water retention, adding roughly one part coconut coir to five parts soil.

SPROUTS & MICROGREENS

Even if you don't have space for a garden, you can grow some of your own fresh produce right in your kitchen. Sprouts and microgreens are great additions to salads and sandwiches, and they're easy to grow at home. (Bonus: Growing your own is much less expensive than buying them at the store, and they're always on hand!) What's the difference between sprouts and microgreens? Sprouts are seeds that, given the right conditions, (surprise!) sprout. Sprouted greens are generally one to two inches long, and you use them along with the seeds. Microgreens are grown in a small amount of soil, and only the greens are edible; clip them off at soil level, then compost the roots and soil.

DIY

Growing Microgreens

Add fresh microgreens to salads, sandwiches, and wraps, or just snack on them plain.

You'll Need:
Shallow container with good drainage (recycled takeout packaging can work)
Potting soil
Seeds: Try organic popcorn, sunflower seeds, peas, and kale

1. Fill a container with potting soil to a 2-inch depth, and scatter seeds thickly over the soil.
2. Cover the seeds with a light layer of potting soil. Thoroughly water newly planted seeds and allow to drain. If you're using a recycled takeout container, close the lid. This helps to retain moisture until the seeds sprout.
3. Place in a sunny window. Water as needed to keep the soil damp but not overly wet. In 2 or 3 days, you'll see tiny sprouts starting to appear. If you're using a lidded container, open the lid to give the sprouts room to grow.
4. When the sprouts are 2 to 3 inches tall, they're ready to harvest. Don't let them get much taller than that, or they'll lose their sweetness. Simply use scissors to snip them off at the base.
5. Some seeds will give a second crop; give it a week to see if you'll get more growth out of the tray before composting it. To keep yourself in fresh microgreens, plant a new tray every 5 days or so for a continual harvest.

DIY

Growing Sprouts

Homegrown sprouts will be ready to eat even more quickly than microgreens. You'll be adding them to your favorite sandwich in just a few days. Expensive specialized sprouting lids are available for purchase, but you can easily make your own and they work just as well.

You'll Need:
Plastic mesh from a craft store or window screen
A 1-quart canning jar with lid and ring
Seeds: Try organic mung beans, radish, broccoli, alfalfa, or clover

1. Make the screened lid: Set the lid on the screen and trace around it with a marker. Use scissors to cut out the circle. Place the mesh or screen circle inside the jar ring.
2. Put about 2 tablespoons seeds into the jar.
3. Fill the jar to the halfway point with filtered water, screw on the screened lid, and let the seeds soak overnight.
4. Turn the jar upside down and allow it to drain the next morning. Rinse the seeds with fresh water and drain again. Maintain the jar at room temperature—storing it on the kitchen counter is fine.

For a gourmet sandwich, try growing sprouts at home; it takes only a few days.

5. Rinse and drain the seeds twice a day for several days. You'll see sprouts begin to emerge from the seeds. When the sprouts are 2 to 3 inches long, they're ready to eat.

6. Give them a final rinse and drain them well. Wrap sprouts in a damp tea towel; this helps manage any remaining excess wetness. They'll keep for several days in the refrigerator.

SOIL IMPROVEMENT

Good garden soil is the key to successful growing. Gardening methods can be very flexible—all gardeners have their own ideas about how to grow the best tomatoes—but one thing that's nonnegotiable is that a garden needs good soil to thrive. The ideal growing medium has a texture that allows roots to grow into it easily. It holds moisture without staying too wet and has airspaces so roots can absorb the oxygen they need. Also important are ample nutrients for plants to utilize as they grow and produce.

Soil is comprised of three components: clay, sand, and silt. Loamy soil, a roughly equal combination of the three, is ideal. Some native soils are close enough to that ideal that they do a good job of supporting garden plants. But when the balance is too far off, plants fail to thrive.

Sandy soil is porous. Sand particles are the largest of the three soil components, making water and nutrient retention poor. Silty soil is a bit powdery. It's fairly fertile, but it becomes compacted and gets waterlogged easily. Clay soil is sticky. When it's wet, it clumps together in the garden bed and sticks to your shoes and generally makes laundry day difficult; when it's dry, it's hard and difficult to dig. The fine clay particles make a very dense, nutritionally deficient soil.

No matter what kind of soil you have, incorporating organic materials is a good plan. It improves aeration in clay soil, water retention in sandy soil, and drainage in silt. Adding manure, compost, or rotted leaves to the garden encourages insects, worms, and bacteria to take up residence, transforming the amendments into nutrients and humus.

Harvesting carrots from the backyard is immensely satisfying.

Humus

Humus (hyüməs) is one component of soil created by the decomposition of leaves and other organic matter.

How best to add those amendments to the garden is a subject of fierce debate among gardeners. For years, the conventional advice has been to rototill amendments into the top six to eight inches of soil. Rototilling a garden bed prior to planting does a great job of handling weeds and leaving loose soil in which to plant, too. But rototilling exposes fertile humus to air, hastening the decomposition of those amendments. This means you'll need to add more amendments to compensate for the loss. Tilling also damages fungal networks, soil organisms, and earthworms living in the soil.

Adopting the No-Till Method

With a "no-till" method, amendments are left on the surface to break down and leach into the soil. No-till allows the structure of the soil (and its beneficial microorganisms) to remain undamaged. Switching to a no-till, deep-mulch method will save work in the long run, though if you're accustomed to rototilling every year, that can be a hard habit to break.

Instead of tilling the weeds in your spring garden, cut them to the ground. Set your vegetable plants in

Incorporating tactics to improve your garden soil will lead to healthier plants and larger harvests.

place *through* the weeds. Dig a planting hole just large enough for each seedling or a narrow trench for planting seeds. Once your seedlings are in place, add a layer of mulch six to eight inches deep all around them. Leave some breathing room between your plants and the mulch, but cover everything else. The deep mulch will hold in moisture and smother weeds, and as it decomposes, add nutrients to the soil. When you notice weeds emerging, add another few inches of mulch. (If you have really persistent weeds, you can put down a layer of cardboard or newspaper first, then add mulch.)

Soil Improvement for Lazy Gardeners

If you find yourself thinking about soil improvement in the fall, skip a lot of labor by heaping manure on your garden beds at the end of the season. Layer it on generously; a two-foot-deep layer of manure is not too much. Let the manure sit through the winter. Rain and melting snow will seep through the manure pile, leaching all that goodness down into the garden beds. Worms and insects will move in, working the manure into the site soil. Come springtime, the manure pile will be substantially smaller and the soil below the manure, much more workable. Plant directly in that layer of rotted manure.

Another lazy way to improve the soil? At the end of the season, toss seeds for cover crops like hairy vetch or red clover onto your garden. These winter hardy legumes capture nitrogen from the atmosphere, and shift it to the soil. In the springtime, cut the tops of your cover crop for a green mulch.

Making Mulch

What to use for mulch in a garden bed? Grass clippings, straw, and leaves are common fare for mulching in the garden. Autumn leaves are great, but don't discount green leaves and plant trimmings. As long as they're not diseased, any remnants from pruning your yard work as mulch, too. This "chop and drop" tactic can easily be adapted to your garden. Newspaper and cardboard are less attractive, but plenty effective in suppressing weeds.

What About Wood Chips?

Using wood chips as mulch is a bit controversial in gardening circles. Given a chance to break down for a year or two before being added to a garden bed, wood chips are great mulch. But "green" chips draw nitrogen from the soil as they break down. Using them can disrupt the soil balance, especially in a vegetable garden where frequent digging and planting allow the chips to be worked into the soil rather than sitting on top. If you choose to use wood chips in the garden, do your best to avoid working them into the soil, and be aware that you might need to supplement with more fertilizer. A better bet? Use wood chips in more permanent garden beds and around trees.

Use Caution When Importing Amendments

Manufactured compost and products labeled as manure might contain biosolids. Made from sludge left over from industrial wastewater or sewage treatment plants, many biosolids are approved by the EPA for use on agricultural crops. Even so, some people will want to opt out of that particular garden amendment. Look for manure labeled 100 percent steer manure or 100 percent chicken manure. If it's not 100 percent, what else is in there? Check the ingredients of compost and potting soil. If you see the word "biosolids," you can certainly cross it off your list; phrases like "inert ingredients" and "enhanced" might be suspect, too.

Lasagna Bed Gardening

A lasagna bed garden implements the idea of layering materials. Instead of tilling and amending a growing area, this method calls for layering a combination of carbon- and nitrogen-rich materials that will break down to create rich soil. Lasagna bed gardening, sometimes called sheet mulching, is essentially a method of slow composting. All the materials added to the bed will break down in time, creating a rich growing medium right where you can use it.

One of the great benefits of a lasagna bed is that you don't have to spend time eradicating grass or weeds. The bedding materials will smother all but the most aggressive weeds, saving you time and effort.

Watch Your Step

Walking on soil compacts it. To avoid this in your garden, designate specific garden bed areas and avoid foot traffic in those areas.

Herbs thrive when grown in good soil and ideal conditions.

When to Test Soil

Oftentimes, simply amending soil with plenty of organic matter is sufficient. If your garden fails to thrive in spite of your efforts, you might consider a soil analysis; these are often available at agricultural colleges or by mail. An analysis can help determine the soil's available plant nutrients and guide you in choosing appropriate soil amendments.

Spring Planting, Fall Prepping

You can take advantage of the benefits of lasagna bed gardening during active gardening season or during your garden's dormant months, but the ideal time to build a lasagna bed is in the fall. Build a lasagna bed as garden season comes to a close, and over the course of the winter months (even if your garden is under snow) it will break down, leaving you with rich soil ready for planting in the spring. You can also start a lasagna bed in the springtime, planting seeds or seedlings directly into the bed. New plants will send roots down into the layered materials, even as they are breaking down.

DIY

Building Your Lasagna Bed

Position your lasagna bed on top of an existing garden bed or in a new area that you want to transform into growing space.

1. Mow the grass or weeds in your chosen spot to make building the bed easier, if necessary.
2. Completely cover the garden bed area with cardboard, two or three layers deep, making sure to overlap the edges. This layer really helps to smother any existing weeds. Choose uncoated cardboard, and remove any plastic tape or labels.
3. Add a layer of nitrogen-rich materials, such as grass clippings or manure, 2 to 3 inches thick over the cardboard.
4. Follow that with a 4- to 6-inch layer of carbon-rich material, such as dry leaves or wood chips.
5. Continue layering material in this fashion until the bed is 2 to 3 feet high. As the pile breaks down, it will shrink.
6. Add a final layer of good topsoil, 2 to 3 inches deep.

Using yard trimmings to create a lasagna bed

Don't worry about being exact—this method is very forgiving—but strive for a roughly 2:1 ratio of carbon to nitrogen materials. The smaller the materials you use, the faster the pile will break down, but you can use bigger items like branches, too. The bottommost layers are the best place to use chunky material that will take longer to break down.

Compost

One of the best ways to improve garden soil is by amending it with decomposed organic matter called compost. That's right—you can turn your kitchen scraps and yard waste into valuable and free soil amendment! Turn to page 232 in the next chapter to create a successful compost pile at home.

Materials for Lasagna Bed Gardening

Nitrogen rich:

- Vegetable scraps
- Grass clippings
- Fresh manure
- Coffee grounds
- Green garden waste
- Weeds (so long as they haven't gone to seed)

Carbon rich:

- Small twigs and branches
- Wood chips
- Shredded cardboard
- Newspaper
- Dry leaves

GREENHOUSE GROWING

Greenhouses can make the difference between garden success and failure in some locales. They're especially useful in northern regions, where the growing season is extremely short. A greenhouse offers a way to extend the season, allowing gardeners to harvest crops that take longer to mature. (Or to experiment with growing fun things like bananas.) Greenhouses aren't just for cold regions, though. Although they certainly offer protection from inclement weather, this style of growing has other merits as well. They're a way for gardeners in wet regions to keep plants dry and to exclude persistent pests; they're also a great place to start seedlings that you'll eventually transplant outdoors. Although the greenhouse's controlled environment can eliminate some gardening pitfalls, it does require some monitoring on your part.

A greenhouse can be a big investment in both time and money. If you've never gardened before, it's probably not the first place you should start. But if you know that your heart is in it? Then a greenhouse just might become your happy place.

A greenhouse extends the growing season.

Building Options

Prefab greenhouses offer an easy-to-install option and come in a wide range of sizes and styles. If you're feeling creative, DIY greenhouse plans can be a less expensive option, depending on local availability and price of materials. You can really cut costs by using upcycled glass windows to create a one-of-a-kind greenhouse. (A quick online search will give you plenty of mesmerizing ideas!) Situate the greenhouse to maximize sun exposure, and make sure you'll have easy access to power and water.

Climate Control

The ideal temperature and humidity in a greenhouse depend on the crops you're growing, but a daytime temperature of 70 to 80°F, dropping by 10 to 20 degrees at night, will support most plants. A passive solar design can achieve this in many regions, but supplemental heat may need to be added in colder areas. Installing a heat system is one way to warm up the interior, but here's another idea: Add animals. At Solviva farm in Massachusetts, goats and chickens are tucked into the greenhouse in the wintertime. The structure shelters them from the elements, and in turn, their residual body heat helps to keep the greenhouse warm.

Be aware that the sunshine helps warm the greenhouse during cold weather but can be the death knell for plants growing inside when the weather warms up. You'll need to monitor the temperature inside the greenhouse. And be sure to install a vent or fan to allow excess heat to escape.

Pollination in a Greenhouse

A greenhouse is great for excluding some garden troubles, especially related to temperature. The downside? Putting up walls prevents pollinators from easily accessing plants. Commercial greenhouse operations are large enough that it makes sense to

A large greenhouse offers space to start seeds in preparation for spring—and a chance to grow tender plants year-round.

A hoop house offers protection from cold weather, allowing gardeners to extend their harvest into the shoulder seasons.

Hand-pollination can be used when bees are not present.

maintain a population of bees inside for pollination purposes, but this often doesn't make sense for a small home version.

Hand-pollinating crops can be tedious. Transferring pollen from the stamen of the male flower to the center of a female blossom with a small, soft paintbrush can result in fruit, but will give you great appreciation for the bees and butterflies that do the job naturally. The easiest way around this? Choose plants for the greenhouse that don't require manual pollination.

Leafy greens, brassicas, root crops, peas, beans, and celery will do just fine in a greenhouse without any extra effort on your part. Although most cucurbits, the gourd and squash family, require pollination, there are some that don't. Parthenocarpic varieties don't make seed and don't require pollination. Try Monika or Carmen if you want to grow cucumbers. Cavili is a light green summer squash; Perfect Pick a dark green zucchini.

Wind-pollinated crops like tomatoes, peppers, eggplant, and corn can produce in a greenhouse, but you'll need to give them a little assist. Shaking the plants a couple times a day will dislodge pollen, sending it out into the air. This is another good reason to provide a method of ventilation to create airflow in the greenhouse. The easiest way to do this is to install a couple of screened windows that can be opened or closed as needed.

DIY

Build a Hoop House

Sometimes called "high tunnels," hoop houses are low-cost alternatives to greenhouses that deliver many of the same perks. In rainy locations, high tunnels keep crops dry. In cool climates, they raise the temperature. Hoop houses can be big or small, semi-permanent or completely portable, depending on how they are constructed.

To build a 6-by-8-foot hoop house, you'll need:

2 (2 × 6-inch) boards, 6 feet long
2 (2 × 6-inch) boards, 8 feet long
6 (15-inch) lengths of rebar
3 (½-inch) PVC pipes, 10 feet long
6 (½-inch) pipe straps
12 (3-inch) deck screws
12 (1-inch) wood screws
10 × 100-foot roll of 2-millimeter clear plastic sheeting
12 (2-inch) spring clamps

1. Set boards upright in a rectangle. Secure each corner using three 3-inch deck screws.
2. Place this rectangular planter on a flat growing area. Pound a piece of rebar into the ground an inch from the end of each 8-foot board on the inside of the box, leaving 6 to 8 inches aboveground. Mark the center point on the two 8-foot boards, and pound rebar into the ground at this point on the inside of the box.
3. Slide an end of a PVC pipe over a piece of rebar, pushing it all the way to the ground so it sticks straight into the air. Secure in place with a pipe strap. Bend the PVC to the opposite side of the box, slide over the rebar, and again secure with a pipe strap. Repeat with remaining lengths of PVC.
4. Cover the entire structure with the plastic sheeting, making sure that there are no gaps. Secure the sheeting in place using the spring clamps. Using spring clamps allows you to easily remove the plastic to work in the garden bed or when the weather is warm.

Tiny Greenhouses

A greenhouse can provide the perfect environment for starting seeds—but you don't always need a full-size outbuilding to take advantage of the concept. Recycle plastic produce and takeout containers to convert into miniature greenhouses. Simply fill the base with potting soil, sprinkle seeds, water well, and close the lid. The closed lid will help retain moisture so your seeds don't accidentally dry out and die. Once seeds are tall enough that they are touching the lid, transplant them to individual containers.

PESTS AND PREDATORS

There's no getting around it: If you have a garden, you're going to have pests. Minuscule insects and wily four-legged critters angling for a share of the harvest may leave you feeling like Elmer Fudd battling Bugs Bunny. Whether you're losing chickens to predators or the snails are decimating the lettuce crop, seeing your hard work disappear almost before your eyes is beyond frustrating. It's safe to assume that there will be some casualties, but you can use a number of tactics to reduce the damage done by marauding critters without resorting to harsh chemicals.

The most important thing to note is that healthy plants tend to have fewer pests because they do a better job of fighting off disease and insect invasions when they do happen. Therefore, choose healthy, sturdy plants when shopping for seedlings; set them—or your seeds—into good-quality soil. But beyond simply keeping your garden as healthy as possible, some other tricks will limit crop damage from large and small pests.

Choose the Right Variety

Opting for plant varieties that thrive in your climate can help eliminate many garden pests and diseases. Planting crops that like hot, dry weather—such as basil, tomatoes, or zucchini—in a cool, wet climate is a sure way to leave plants susceptible to powdery mildew. Choose what grows well in your region and you'll save yourself a lot of frustration.

When shopping for seeds or seedlings, opt for varieties that make it more difficult for trouble to take hold. One option is to choose disease-resistant varieties, and both heirloom and hybrid plants can offer an element of this. Although heirloom plants may have a natural tendency to repel different problems, many hybrids have been bred to resist common viruses and pathogens.

Nurseries and seed companies use a code to indicate specific disease resistance on various crops. For instance, hybrid tomato plants are often marked with the letters V and F. These indicate a resistance to verticillium wilt and fusarium wilt, respectively.

Vine borer moths can wreak havoc in a garden.

Another way to prevent damage from pests is to look for plants with characteristics that will deter common pests naturally. Choosing a long, tightly husked variety of corn, such as Country Gentleman, Staygold, or Silvergent, will deter corn earworms. Butternut squash has a good resistance to squash vine borer, and summer crookneck squash is more resistant to these pests than standard zucchini.

Crop Rotation

The idea of crop rotation may sound like a big endeavor, but you can easily implement it in your garden. Simply put, it means don't plant the same type of crop in the same place year after year. Pests and disease often overwinter in the soil. If vine borers moved in to nosh on the squash, they'll be disappointed to find basil has moved into their favorite dining spot the following year.

Rotating crops helps to prevent soil depletion and the persistence of pests and diseases specific to

Deer may look cute, but if they're not excluded from your garden area, they can decimate it quickly.

certain plants. Group the following plants together in your garden beds, and shift them to a different spot the following year:

- **Allium family:** Chive, garlic, leeks, onions, and shallots
- **Brassica family:** Broccoli, cabbage, cauliflower, collards, kale, kohlrabi, radish, rutabaga, spinach, and turnip
- **Cucurbit family:** Cucumbers, gourds, melons, pumpkin, and squash
- **Legume family:** Beans and peas
- **Solanaceae family:** Eggplant, peppers, potatoes, tomatillo, and tomatoes

Companion Planting for Pest Control

Garden wisdom suggests that some plants do especially well when paired together, with one working to repel a particular pest to which the other is susceptible. Think of it as creating a supportive little community in your garden. Planting a large section of one type of plant creates a monoculture. This can draw pests as they take advantage of having their favorite meal gathered in one easy-to-find place. Interplanting different vegetable crops with flowers and herbs can confuse pests, and some flowers and herbs actually repel them.

Manual Removal

Sometimes the most effective method of pest control is handpicking them. Slugs and snails come out at night, so don a headlamp and start hunting. Use a pair of chopsticks to pick up slugs if you don't want to touch them. Deposit slugs and snails in a container of salty water as you go. Leafhopper larvae congregate on plant stems (they especially like peppers and tomatoes). They tend to scatter when disturbed; quickly smashing them with a gloved hand will reduce their population immediately.

Another way to manually remove pests from your plants is to vacuum them up. This works particularly well with whiteflies; they tend to scatter as soon as

Interplanting flowers and herbs with productive crops can reduce pest damage naturally.

Snails and slugs love to dine on garden greens.

the plants they're feasting on are disturbed. A hand-vacuum with strong suction can pull them right out of the air as they try to escape.

Diatomaceous Earth

As mentioned in Chapter Three, diatomaceous earth—sometimes called DE—is a must-have for naturally repelling household pests. This natural powder made up of fossilized diatoms is also an important addition to your arsenal for tackling garden pests without poisons. When soft-bodied pests crawl across DE, the abrasive powder disturbs the waxy outer layer of exoskeletons and causes dehydration. DE works on pests like aphids, sow bugs (or wood louse), and ants, and can be applied to garden soil or directly on plants. It's most effective when dry; reapply if it gets wet. Just remember that DE can harm beneficial insects as well.

Deterring Wild Visitors

Simply keeping cats or dogs around can dissuade predators from getting too comfortable in your garden. Cats can keep rats, rabbits, and squirrels at bay. Keeping a family dog that has the freedom to roam outside in the garden or orchard can deter deer. Their scent alone will make these pests think twice.

Because a fair number of predators are nocturnal, installing motion sensor lights around your garden can be a deterrent. Motion sensor lights will also alert you to potential marauders so that you can monitor the situation.

Five Beneficial Insects to Encourage in Your Garden

Beneficial insects are the good guys, the ones you want to take up residence in your yard or garden. Pollinators like bees and butterflies are the most obvious beneficial insects, but others are your partners in natural pest control. By creating an environment that is conducive to their survival, you can let nature take the lead.

- **Braconid wasps:** If you have unwanted caterpillars, borers, and beetles in your garden, braconid wasps might help. The adult female injects its eggs into host insects, then the larvae feed inside their hosts, resulting in its demise. Adult braconid wasps are attracted to nectar plants with small flowers. Try dill, parsley, and yarrow.

- **Lacewings:** Lacewings—both adults and their larvae—eat aphids, mealybugs, scales, caterpillars, thrips, and whiteflies. Attract them to your garden by planting angelica, coreopsis, cosmos, and sweet alyssum.

- **Lady beetles:** Call them beetles, call them bugs, but call them to your garden. Ladybugs eat aphids, mites, and mealybugs, and will lay their tiny yellow eggs near infestations. Ladybug larvae are spiny and black and don't resemble their adult counterparts at all—don't mistake them for pests. They're invaluable in controlling aphids. Angelica, coreopsis, dill, fennel, and yarrow attract ladybugs.

- **Praying mantis:** Named for the way it holds its two front legs, the praying mantis is an effective hunter that will eat any insect in its path. Provide plenty of undisturbed cover in which the mantis can hide. There are lots of varieties of praying mantis, but

Garden Friends

These pest-repellent flowers and herbs are easy to add to your garden (and are pretty, too!):

- Lavender deters codling moths under apple trees, as well as a wide variety of flies and beetles.
- Nasturtium acts as a trap plant, drawing aphids away from vegetable crops.
- Grown near carrots, chives repel the carrot rust fly.
- Basil's scent deters mosquitoes, flies, and hornworm caterpillars.
- Marigold is toxic to root nematodes.

Create Barriers

Sometimes the best solution is to make it difficult for pests to reach the plants they're after. Just as a garden fence keeps four-legged marauders out, a barrier around or on individual plants can keep damaging pests from reaching tender seedlings or eating mature crops. The goal here isn't to eliminate the pests (though that's not a bad idea, either) but rather, to prevent them from doing too much damage:

- Place a tin can, opened on both ends, around a tender seedling to prevent cutworms from invading.
- Use a layer of crushed eggshells to deter snails and slugs.
- Place row covers over cabbage to prevent cabbage moths from laying eggs and decimating your crop.
- Slip old panty hose over broccoli or cauliflower heads to protect them.
- Slather a sticky trap product on the stems of trees infested with crawling pests like ants.
- String together shiny objects to flutter in the breeze to help scare away marauding birds.
- Drape bird netting over individual trees or tent it over a berry patch.
- Protect saplings by wrapping their trunks with ½-inch hardware cloth.

they're most commonly tan or green. Establish them in your garden by purchasing egg cases at a nursery or online.

- **Tachinid fly:** The larvae of this little fly burrow themselves into caterpillars, thus killing them. Dill, parsley, and sweet clover attract the adult flies.

Burrowing Critters

If you opt for raised beds, keep underground pests like moles, voles, and gophers from infiltrating them by covering the bottom with half-inch hardware cloth. Without that protection, burrowing pests can invade gardens, orchards, and landscapes. The longer they are left to their own devices, the bigger the problem will become as they breed and multiply. Dropping castor oil pellets into their tunnels can deter them. Running water into their burrows can work, but it is a waste of a precious resource. Arguably the best way to handle an infestation of burrowing pests is to set traps.

Physical barriers can exclude a variety of pests.

Larger Pests

Insects and disease that damage plants are problematic, but there are other pests to consider as well. Squirrels, rats, and rabbits love fresh garden produce almost as much as you do. Many a gardener has walked out to pick that first red tomato, only to find that an uninvited guest got there first. Deer will decimate an entire garden in a night.

Dogs and cats can be good deterrents, but that's not an option for everyone. There are repellents on the market, like predator urine and castor oil; some people swear by scented soap. But these are temporary solutions that must be reapplied regularly. Scare tactics like noisemakers, motion-activated sprinklers, or statues of predators can work, but effectiveness may diminish as pests become familiar with them.

Say "No" to Poison

Poison is certainly a fast and effective way to rid your home and garden of mice, rats, gophers, and other mammals. The trouble is, it may unintentionally harm other animals. Roaming cats and dogs can ingest the poison directly. And predators such as owls, hawks, and foxes who dine on poisoned prey may find themselves victims of accidental poisoning.

Cherries are a favorite of birds; covering trees with protective netting can help keep them at bay.

The very best solution for dealing with these garden marauders? Fencing to exclude them. It's not cheap, but if done right, it will solve the problem permanently. The size and structure of the fenced area and the materials you use will depend on the particular animals you're trying to exclude. To keep rabbits out, you'll need a three-foot fence with mesh no larger than one-inch square. Same for squirrels, but you'll need to add a top, because squirrels will climb up and over. A deer fence is a bigger project. Enclosing individual garden beds works to keep deer at bay, but if you're trying to keep them out of a larger area (say a garden and orchard), you'll need to install a sturdy fence that's at least six feet tall.

• chapter five •
FARM

FARM

CONTENTS

Urban farming is everywhere these days: an inspiring new trend that offers the chance to grow your own food and embrace environmental stewardship right in your backyard. By its very nature, farming creates an awareness of the land—and if you expect that land to nourish *you*, you'll want to nourish it in return. You'll come to see autumn's leaf drop as an opportunity to build soil, rather than as a nuisance to home maintenance. And instead of sending yard clippings off to the green waste facility, you'll keep them for your own compost pile.

A thriving hobby farm will provide personal growth as well as produce; recognizing the rhythms and needs of the crops and animals you're nurturing will become second nature as you go about your chores.

As elements of farming make their way into urban areas by way of rooftop beehives and backyard coops, transformations within the community take shape as well. Instead of buying eggs at the store, you may find yourself trading a basket of apples for your weekly dozen, and calling your neighbors by name. Happily, you won't need a lot of acreage: A suburban lot offers enough space to grow fruit trees, raise poultry, or delve into beekeeping. A half acre opens up the possibilities even further, making small livestock a viable option.

Bringing animals into the equation can help create a closed loop. Instead of purchasing natural fertilizers, chickens and bunnies will devour your kitchen scraps and turn them into a continuous supply of manure (and in the case of chickens, you'll get eggs, too!). Likewise, adding a beehive to your backyard farm will aid in the pollination of your garden, boosting your harvest while supplying you with honey.

Coupled with information from earlier chapters, the skills detailed in the following pages will help you inch closer to a more self-reliant lifestyle. But fair warning: You may need to get some muck boots.

Previous pages: *Chickens in the garden can act as pest control.*
Opposite: *Bees at work*

CREATING AN ORCHARD

Planting fruit trees is an optimistic endeavor, requiring gardeners to take the long view. Unlike a seasonal vegetable garden that can produce bucketloads of food in just a few months, a productive orchard takes a bit more time. Expect to wait three to five years to see a harvest from newly planted trees. Once they hit full production, though, the wait will be worthwhile. Healthy fruit trees produce an annual crop for decades, and they produce abundantly. A semi-dwarf apple tree, for instance, can produce 5 to 10 bushels of fruit. A standard-size tree, 10 to 20 bushels. That's a lot of applesauce!

Fruit Tree Basics

If the word "orchard" makes you think that you need acres and acres of land, think again. Even urban home lots provide enough space to grow some fruit. It's just a matter of deciding what trees are best for your space and climate, and choosing the right growing method.

- **Size:** Fruit trees come in four different sizes: standard, semi-dwarf, dwarf, and, less commonly, super-dwarf or miniature. Standard trees require a fair amount of space and are a good choice if you need a high-branching variety to provide shade. Semi-dwarf trees are great for incorporating into a planting bed; from a landscape design perspective, they provide height for visual interest. If you're an urban gardener, dwarf trees can be planted directly in the ground or in pots. Super-dwarf trees are great for really tight spaces like apartment balconies.

- **Chill hours:** Many fruit trees need cold weather to trigger flowering (and thus fruiting). Some trees need more of these "chill hours" than others. Determine how many chill hours (the average number of hours below 45°F) you get each winter, and use that number when choosing varieties. There are options for most climates, including some specifically bred to work in "low chill" conditions, such as the Dorsett Golden apple variety or Desert Delight nectarine.

Stretch the Harvest

If you have room for more than a few trees, choose varieties that ripen at different times, so you'll have varied harvest times. For instance, to harvest apples for several months, try planting Gravenstein (ripe in August), Golden Delicious (ripe in September), and Rome Beauty (ripe in October).

- **Pollination:** For fruit to set and grow to maturity, blossoms need to be pollinated. Bees carry pollen from one bloom to another, helping to pollinate each. This is why it's so important to invite bees and other pollinators into your garden by planting flowers and creating a hospitable environment free of poisons.

  Fruit trees are sometimes self-fertile, meaning that pollination can happen with just a single tree. This is most common with stone fruit like peaches, nectarines, and apricots; others require cross-pollination between two trees of the same species. Choose trees that bloom at the same time and plant them within 50 feet of each other.

Tiny Orchard Tricks

If you want to add a tree to a patio area or need to be able to move certain

Fruiting trees can be incorporated into many landscapes; they offer shade and structure, as well as fruit.

warm-weather varieties inside for the winter, planting a fruit tree in a container might be the solution. Dwarf and super-dwarf varieties are the best options for growing in containers. The trees stay small and compact.

A 10- to 15-gallon container will work for most dwarf varieties and is a good size if you need to move your tree. A half oak barrel will give the roots a bit more space to spread out but can be heavy to move. Be sure your container has several holes in the bottom so excess water can drain. Choose a good-quality potting soil, and fertilize your potted fruit trees every couple of weeks during the growing season with compost or manure tea.

Another trick for working fruit trees into a small yard? Train them to fit. The art of espalier—and it is an art—is a method of training a tree to grow tightly against a fence or wall. The wall-hugging patterns can be simple or elaborate but take up very little space for urban gardeners. Apples and pears are a common choice for espalier.

Super-dwarf fruit trees can be grown in containers.

Fruiting Trees in the Landscape

Not everyone has the space for a large orchard planted in rows—but that's not to say you cannot grow fruit trees. Many can double as landscape trees, providing shade as well as a fruit crop. When planting a fruiting tree in a landscape, you'll need to consider a few things, beginning with climate. First, know your zone (see the map on page 306). If you want to grow fruit in the northern reaches of the United States (zones 1 through 4), you'll have fewer options than those available in the southern half of the country. Even so, some apple, pear, and plum trees produce fruit in cold climates.

Don't plant a fruit tree in the middle of a bed full of fussy peonies; you'll need to be able to walk under it, use a ladder to harvest fruit, and prune it. Make sure maintaining your fruit tree won't damage the landscape below. You'll also want to think about dropping fruit. If for some reason you cannot harvest the fruit in time, will those plums dropping onto your patio stain the flagstones?

- **Apple *(Malus)*:** The spreading branches of a mature standard-size apple tree are perfect for sitting under. Beautiful white and pink blossoms in the spring are slightly fragrant. Harvest in late summer and autumn.

- **Sweet cherry *(Prunus avium)*:** Nonfruiting or "ornamental" cherry trees are frequently planted in landscapes for their gorgeous blossoms. Opt for a fruiting variety and you'll get more bang for your buck. Harvest in early summer.

- **Tart cherry *(Prunus cerasus)*:** Also called sour cherries, these trees are a bit more cold hardy than the common sweet cherry. Harvest in late summer.

- **Citrus *(Citrus)*:** An evergreen tree for frost-free climates, citrus trees such as orange, tangerine, and lemon are year-round beauties. Harvest in winter.

- **Fig *(Ficus carica)*:** The oversize leaves of a fig tree offer a tropical look to the landscape. Many fig varieties produce two crops a year.

- **Mulberry *(Morus)*:** With large fruit resembling blackberries, a mulberry tree can serve dual purposes in your edible landscape. The fruit is excellent, if a bit hard to harvest. It can also act as a lure to draw birds and squirrels away from other ripening fruit.

- **Nectarine *(Prunus persica nectarina)*:** The dark, slender green leaves of a nectarine tree make it a summertime beauty. Harvest in summer.

■ **Olive *(Olea europaea)*:** An evergreen tree with lustrous silver leaves, olive trees are great landscape plants, and people often plant them for their beauty, rather than the fruit. Olives need to be processed before they are edible. Harvest in late summer.

■ **Peach *(Prunus persica)*:** The fuzzy fruit of a peach tree are tasty reasons to plant one, but the pink springtime blossoms and fall color are another. Harvest in summer.

■ **Pear *(Pyrus)*:** In addition to delicate spring blossoms and a tasty crop, pear trees offer fall color to your yard as well. Harvest in late summer.

■ **Persimmon *(Diospyros)*:** A beautiful tree with spreading branches, persimmons are most noticeable in the fall when the leaves drop and bright orange fruit remains. Harvest in autumn.

■ **Pineapple guava *(Feijoa sellowiana)*:** A small tree or upright shrub, this evergreen produces bluish green fruit. It grows well in cool, coastal locations. Harvest in summer.

■ **Plum *(Prunus domestica)*:** Desirable for their vivid pink spring blossoms, flowering plum trees are used frequently as landscape plants. You can have similar beauty plus a great harvest by choosing a fruiting plum. Harvest in late spring and summer.

RECIPE

Applesauce

Yield: Depends on number of apples used

I was raised in an apple-farming family, so when we made applesauce, we *made applesauce*—hundreds of pounds at a time! You don't need to be that industrious, though. The cool thing about this method is that it makes as much—or as little—as you'd like. In its simplest form, it's just cooked apples, but you can sweeten or spice up the recipe if you like. Use enough apples to fill your chosen pot. (Use a saucepan for a small batch or a stockpot for a large batch.) Once cooked down, their volume will reduce by half. Alternatively, you can make applesauce in a slow cooker: Fill the slow cooker with apple chunks, put about an inch of apple juice in the bottom, and cook on low all day. Store fresh applesauce in a sealed container for up to a week in the refrigerator. Canned applesauce will keep in the pantry for up to two years. (For more on canning, see page 24.)

You'll Need:

Apples (Gravensteins are great for making sauce), peeled, cored, and cut into 1-inch chunks
Apple juice
Sugar (optional)
Cinnamon (optional)

1. Place the chunked apples into a pot with a lid. Add enough apple juice to come up the sides of the pot by an inch (about 2 cups) for a small batch or two inches (about 6 cups) for a large batch.
2. Cover the pot and let cook on low heat, stirring occasionally, until apples become very tender, about 1 to 2 hours, depending on size of pot and number of apples.
3. Use a potato masher to break up the apples until your applesauce reaches desired consistency. Most apples are sweet enough that they don't need extra sugar, but if you like sweeter sauce, add sugar to taste now, along with cinnamon.
4. **Canning directions:** To can, ladle the hot applesauce into jars, leaving ½-inch headspace. Wipe the rims with a damp cloth, set the flats in place on jars, and add the rings. Use your fingertips to screw the rings on firmly, but not too tight. Process pint jars for 15 minutes, quarts for 20 minutes, in a boiling water bath.

Enjoy fresh applesauce warm from the stove with a bit of cinnamon.

Bare Root Fruit

A bare root plant comes just like it sounds—with its roots bare, rather than planted in a potful of soil. Trees (and some perennial fruits and vegetables) are available in bare root form during the late winter, when the plant is dormant and has no leaves. This is a great time to start or expand your home orchard.

Generally speaking, purchasing bare root plants offers a larger selection for buyers. They're less expensive, too. The potted fruit trees stocked at nurseries later in the year are often the varieties that didn't sell during bare root season.

DIY

Planting a Bare Root Tree

Mail-order companies and some quasi-nurseries (like those at home improvement stores) usually sell their bare root plants wrapped in burlap or plastic. If you shop at your local nursery instead, you'll likely find an assortment of fruit trees tucked into loose wood shavings. Choose your tree and pull it from the protection of the wood shavings, roots bared for all to see. Plant these trees—or heel them in—as soon as possible to prevent the roots from drying out:

1. Use hand pruners to trim off any broken or damaged roots.
2. Soak the roots in a bucket of water overnight.
3. Dig a hole two times the width and depth of the tree's root system.
4. Set the roots on the bottom of the hole so that the graft union—where the tree is grafted to the rootstock—is about 4 to 6 inches above ground level. Adjust the bottom of the planting hole to achieve the correct level, slightly mounding soil to create a nice base for the roots.
5. Fan out the roots within the hole, spreading them across the mounded bottom of the hole.
6. Backfill with good-quality soil, slightly compacting soil around the roots.
7. Water deeply, and then water two or three times a week during the tree's first dry season.

Heeling It In

It you don't have the space for your tree quite ready, you'll need to heel in the tree. This is essentially a temporary planting technique that protects the plant and its roots until you're ready to put it in its permanent spot in your yard or home orchard. To do this, dig a hole (or a trench, if you have several trees) that allows you to lay the tree or shrub down at a 45-degree angle, with its roots in the hole. Cover the roots with loose soil, compost, or sawdust. Set the plant in its permanent home before the tree starts leafing out. The earth will not come to a screeching halt if you don't, but it's definitely easier on the tree.

Plant bare root trees in a good-size hole.

Maintaining Your Fruit Trees

The beauty of having a home orchard is that those trees will provide a crop for years with relatively little maintenance. Annual orchard maintenance is done in late winter or early spring, while the trees are dormant.

- **Spraying** Growing an orchard naturally doesn't necessarily mean you'll never spray your fruit trees. An annual dose of a dormant oil spray (available at garden centers) can help reduce the number of pests in an orchard. Although most horticultural oils are derived from petroleum, you can choose from plant-based oils as well. Dormant oil sprays work by

Ripe for Harvest

Ripe fruit should be easy to pick from the tree. Keep the stem attached to the fruit to extend the shelf life before it's ready to eat.

smothering pests that have overwintered on your tree. Apply in late winter or early spring when weather is warming but before trees leaf out.

■ **Fertilizing** Give your fruit trees an annual boost of nitrogen by spreading a two- to three-inch layer of well-aged manure under each tree, out to the edge of the tree's canopy. Cover the manure with a nice layer of mulch to hold in moisture, hold down weeds, and contribute to overall soil health. When adding mulch or fertilizer, be sure to maintain several inches between the tree trunk and the amendments. Raising the soil level at the trunk can cause rot.

■ **Pruning** Pruning fruit trees promotes vigorous growth and should be done annually during a tree's dormant season—late fall, winter, or early spring. Pruning young trees forms their shape over the course of several years. Trim most vigorously in the first year when the new roots are just taking hold and cannot support wide branches. The tactic for shaping trees as you prune depends on the variety of tree. Most stone fruit should be pruned into a vase shape. Apples, pears, and cherries are better pruned into a pyramid shape with a central, upright leader.

To prune a vase-shaped tree (with branches arching upright), select three to five scaffold limbs that grow from the trunk, all pointing in different directions. Scaffold limbs should be between 18 and 36 inches from the ground.

When pruning trees into a pyramidal shape, the central leader should always be the highest point of the tree. This leader is a vigorous branch that grows from the main trunk and should be pruned back every year. Lateral limbs growing out from this central leader should be thinned to four to six inches apart. Choose lateral branches that are equally spaced around the main trunk and more horizontal than vertical, so each lateral branch meets the leader at a wide angle rather than a narrow V.

Regardless of the shape, pruning is a chance to remove weak branches, eliminate crossing branches, and open up the growth of the tree to allow sunlight to filter through.

Pruning trees is a wintertime chore; sharp pruners will assure clean cuts.

POLLINATORS

Pollination is mutually beneficial to both plants and pollinators. When a pollinator such as a honeybee alights on a flower to feed on nectar or to warm in the sun, the pollen on the flower is transferred to their body. When they fly on, that pollen is distributed to the next plant they touch. Spreading pollen in this way is essential for fertilizing plants so they can produce seeds and fruit. It's a win-win situation that developed over millennia of evolution—but now it's a win for gardeners, too! Honeybees are often the first to come to mind when we talk pollinators, but other bees (more than 16,000 species worldwide!), along with butterflies, beetles, and flies, participate in this ritual as well. Some birds and bats also contribute to pollination of certain plants.

A Pollinator's Garden

Planting a flower border around your vegetable garden beds will add color and beauty—but more important, it will bring those pollinators right where you need them. When choosing flowers, incorporate a variety of plants with different bloom times; this will ensure sweet nectar and pollen are available to pollinators throughout the growing season. When planting, set flowering specimens in clumps rather than individually, to better attract pollinators. Plant a wide range of colors and be sure to incorporate some flat-headed flowers like scabiosa and zinnias. These act as landing pads for butterflies.

Butterflies are drawn to flat-headed flowers.

Also, incorporate some native flowering plants in your yard. This will draw in native pollinators, but it's also a great way to support the local ecosystem. A thriving population of native insects will draw birds as they seek food; those birds will in turn feed snakes and small mammals, which then feed foxes, hawks, and owls. It's the food chain right in your backyard, and it all starts with planting flowers.

Stop Spraying!

Spraying pesticides is a quick fix for invasions of garden pests. But insecticides—even natural or organic options—don't differentiate between friend or foe. Spraying your garden or orchard to control pests like aphids, squash bugs, or leafhoppers might do the job, but it disrupts the natural order of things and can harm the good guys. Before you resort to sprays, give Mother Nature a chance to do her thing. You might find that natural predators like birds and bats move in to nibble on the pests that are bugging you.

Opting for natural or organic pesticides is a move in the right direction, but even if you use those, use them sparingly. They can do damage to the beneficial insect population, too.

If you decide the benefits of spraying outweigh the risks, focus on a single trouble spot, rather than spraying the entire garden bed. This will prevent you

Flowers grown near vegetables can help with pests (see page 208)—and they attract pollinators that increase production.

from accidentally killing the bees and butterflies you're trying to encourage.

Provide Water

During the dry summer months, pollinators will be looking for water. Honeybees in particular need this, as the moisture helps them produce honey and cool their hives. A small birdbath works, but be sure to place some stones in the water to give pollinators a place to rest. If you have a faucet that you can set to a very slow drip, place a board beneath it to catch the water.

Provide Caterpillar Food

Offering lots of nectar and pollen for bees and butterflies is great—but you can take it a step further by providing food for the caterpillars that will morph into pollinators, too. In this case, what to plant will depend specifically on what type of butterflies frequent your area. Each variety has a different need for their larval stage. Monarch caterpillars need milkweed. Several varieties of swallowtail caterpillars like dill, parsley, and fennel, while the mourning cloak caterpillar prefers trees like elm, willow, or poplar.

Providing nesting opportunities for mason bees will draw these pollinators to your garden.

DIY

Mason Bee House

Mason bees are excellent pollinators, though they don't provide honey. They live all over North America (with the exception of Alaska and far northern regions of Canada), generally aboveground in narrow spaces such as hollow reeds or holes in trees. One way to encourage them is to retain a bit of wildness in parts of your yard. Keeping your yard pristine interferes with their nesting; if you've raked up all the yard debris, female mason bees will be unable to find suitable cavities in which to lay their eggs. Another way to encourage them is to make a mason bee house.

You'll Need:

A 6-inch deep frame, such as a bird house with an open front or a simple square made from 1 × 6-inch boards

Fine-bladed saw or sharp loppers

Bamboo, ½ to ¾ inch in diameter

1. Cut bamboo into 6-inch lengths using the saw or loppers.
2. Place bamboo into the frame using enough pieces that they fit snugly.
3. Securely mount the mason bee house to a fence, wall, or tree in your yard or garden, making sure that it's protected from rain and won't move around when the wind blows. (An overhanging roof on the bee house is a good idea.) Female bees will lay eggs inside the bamboo in the early spring, sealing each cell with mud.
4. Young bees will emerge the following spring. To prevent the spread of mites and fungus, remove old bamboo and replace with new ones every season.

Drawing in Birds

Birds in the garden can provide beauty, song, and sometimes comic relief. On a more practical note, they and their airborne mammalian counterparts, bats, are a great help in creating a productive food system. They can also control the insect population and contribute to pollinating plants.

Creating a garden that your winged friends want to call home is easy. You'll need to provide food, water, and shelter. Any of these elements will bring birds to your garden for a visit. But providing all three will make them more inclined to take up residence.

Birds control insects and pollinate flower gardens.

Birdie Buffet

Installing a bird feeder might send an unintended invite to the local squirrel population. Choose a squirrel-proof feeder to prevent thievery.

Variety is the spice of life, they say—but it's also the key to creating a desirable bird habitat. Give them plenty of options, so whether they're shopping for a new nesting spot or place to eat, they'll have lots to choose from. Not all birds eat the same thing, and their nesting habits vary.

Trees and shrubs offer hiding places and materials for nests. You can double down by choosing trees and shrubs that produce nontoxic berries, making them food sources as well. Cavity-dwelling birds are harder to accommodate naturally, but offering birdhouses will go a long way toward giving them safe spaces in which to nest. Natural food sources come in the form of berries, weed seeds, and insects, but you can supplement with a bird feeder, too. Just be sure to clean it regularly to prevent mold and transmitting illness. A birdbath provides a water source for birds, but you don't need anything fancy. A heavy bowl placed under a faucet works, too.

Plant These for the Bees

With plentiful flowers that are particularly enticing to bees, these perennials are great for tucking into edges near your vegetable garden, drawing pollinators and boosting the pollination process in your garden.

- **Aster *(Aster)*:** There are many, many varieties of aster to choose from. The star-shaped flowers come in purples, pinks, and whites. They often bloom in the fall, providing a great nectar source when many springtime flowers are past their prime.

- **Cranesbill geranium *(Geranium sanguineum)*:** This is not the neon-bright geranium your grandma grew. Cranesbill geraniums are delicate-looking, low-growing perennials that flower in the pink and purple range.

- **Purple coneflower *(Echinacea purpurea)*:** Commonly known as coneflower, echinacea may also be familiar as a health supplement, made from this plant that sports gorgeous pink blossoms.

- **Lavender *(Lavandula)*:** Known for its fragrance, lavender is beloved by bees for its flowers (which differ in shape from variety to variety). Lavender is also considered a culinary herb, and can be used to flavor some of your kitchen creations (try it stirred into homemade ice cream or fresh lemonade!).

- **Mint *(Mentha)*:** Although humans are generally more interested in mint's leaves, bees love its flowers. Mint species can be invasive, though, so be sure to plant it in an area where its aggressiveness won't take over your yard. Alternatively, contain it in a pot and grow it on your patio.

- **Bee balm *(Monarda)*:** Bee balm is a member of the mint family. In addition to attracting pollinators to your garden, it's good for flavoring drinks, and is used medicinally as well. Bee balm comes in both annual and perennial varieties, with many different types of flowers.

- **Salvia *(Salvia)*:** There are both annual and perennial varieties of salvia. They're all great for attracting bees, but if you choose a perennial variety, you'll enjoy the benefits for many seasons.

- **Pincushion flower *(Scabiosa)*:** This low-growing perennial attracts pollinators with purple or pink flowers that seem to float above the leaves on long stems. They're great cut flowers, too—just be sure to leave some for the bees and butterflies.

- **Thyme *(Thymus)*:** You may know thyme as a go-to herb in your spice cupboard, but its small flowers are very attractive to bees. As a rule, it grows low; try the Mother of Thyme variety for a great ground cover that will make the bees happy (and be useful to you as well).

- **Yarrow *(Achillea millefolium)*:** Grown for its many medicinal benefits, including soothing digestion and menstrual pain, the flat flower clusters of yarrow are favorite landing spots for butterflies as well as bees. Yarrow is a low-maintenance perennial that tolerates heat and drought well, too.

BEEKEEPING 

You might want to delve into beekeeping for a couple reasons—not the least of which is the honey. Sweet goodness produced right in your backyard! Hard to go wrong with that. Having a beehive at your place improves fruiting, too; as the bees move from blossom to blossom gathering nectar, they also move pollen, assisting the pollination process. Interested in the idea of beekeeping? The world of bees is fascinating and complex, so you'll need to understand some of the basics before you head out to get a hive. It's a good idea to join a beekeeping association or find a mentor to help as you get started. Keeping bees requires a certain amount of time and knowledge to manage a hive well.

Colony Basics

Honeybees are social insects that live together as a colony in a structured system; they communicate with one another and work together efficiently to maintain and defend the hive. Each colony consists of tens of thousands of bees, made up of three varieties of adults:

The **queen bee** is the only sexually developed bee in each colony; her primary function is reproduction. A single queen can produce as many as 250,000 eggs in a year, primarily during the spring and summer months. Not all of those eggs are fertile, though. In addition to reproduction, the queen has a secondary function: She produces pheromones. Without getting too scientific, these pheromones give the colony its identity. No two queens produce the same pheromones.

Queens can live up to five years, but two to three years is average. There are three different times a queen bee is produced in the hive: when an older queen stops being fully productive, in the event of an accidental death, or when the hive swarms. The colony produces new queens from fertilized eggs or young worker bee larvae.

Drones are male bees and the largest bees in the colony. Their primary function is to mate with the queen, after which they die immediately.

Worker bees are the lifeblood of the hive. These sexually undeveloped females make up the majority of the bees in the colony. And they do most of the work. These are the bees you see buzzing around your garden. They also work inside the hive feeding the brood, caring for the queen, maintaining the hive, and building beeswax combs.

Choosing a Hive

The behavior of honeybee colonies is entirely dependent upon the climate where they live. Choose when to start your hive based on your local conditions, but spring is generally the best season.

A hive is the container in which your bees will house their colony. They come in a number of styles. Upright beehives—most commonly the Langstroth—are often used in fruit orchards. By design, these hives can be expanded in size to accommodate a larger swarm. They are essentially topless, bottomless wooden boxes, called supers, filled with square wood frames; the bees build their honeycombs within these frames. Generally, the lower supers are the main hive where the bees live, with smaller supers on top, from which honey is harvested. This style of hive can be heavy, but they're easy to move as the parts can be stacked and unstacked.

Top bar hives can be a bit easier for beekeepers to use. This variety allows beekeepers to remove individ-

A beehive is a bustling center of action during the warmer months.

ual frames, rather than having to lift the entire super. They are also fairly easy to build, so the cost of getting set up is less than with an upright hive.

Bees can more easily control the temperature of Langstroth hives than the top bar variety, and Langstroths are designed to maximize honey production. But a top bar hive is easy to maintain with minimal disruption of the colony. Each style has its pros and cons; you'll need to decide which makes the most sense for your setup. No matter which type of hive you choose, position it to get morning sunlight and shade in the heat of the afternoon.

Populating the Hive

Once the hive is set up, you'll want bees to start living in it. Unfortunately, they're unlikely to see the vacancy sign and just move in. You can buy a package of bees or a "nuc" hive, short for nucleus hive. A package consists of several thousand bees and a queen. A nuc comes with several frames of established brood and honey, along with bees and a queen.

Another option is to rescue a swarming hive. Honeybees tend to swarm and split off from their mother colony in the springtime. In their search for a new home, these clusters of bees land on structures while scouts look for a more permanent location. At this stage, beekeepers can capture a swarm. If possible, talk to local beekeepers and let them know that you have a hive in need of residents.

Backyard beehives require regular care and maintenance.

An uncapping tool removes wax to expose the honey.

Protective Gear

Honeybees only sting when threatened. Disturbing their hive to check on them may feel like a threat. Although some extremely experienced beekeepers will work a hive sans protective gear, it's not recommended.

At the very minimum, you'll want a veil. This is a wide-brimmed hat with netting attached to prevent honeybees from stinging your tender face or scalp, or even trying to enter your ears or nostrils.

A beekeeper's suit will protect your body. These suits offer head-to-toe coverage and are bright white. There's disagreement in the beekeeping world about why white is the preferred color. Some think that bees tend to act more aggressively when approached by darker colors. If you don't want to invest in a suit, long pants and a long-sleeved shirt are a good idea.

Top it all off with a pair of leather gloves. Beekeeper gloves extend up to the elbow. If you opt for simpler leather garden gloves, use duct tape to secure the wrist opening to your shirt.

Extracting Honey

When—and how much—honey to harvest depends on many variables. Generally speaking, though, honey is harvested when nectar production in the surrounding area has tapered off substantially and 80 percent or more of the honey is capped and cured. This is often late summer. A new beekeeper may only harvest a small amount of honey the first year, as the colony is still building its population.

Beekeepers all have their favorite method for separating honey from the beeswax. An extractor is a mechanical device that uses centrifugal force, and can be powered manually or by an electric motor. The honey spins free and collects for you to strain.

To get to the honey, you'll need to cut the caps from the beeswax; the bees will have sealed each cell. Place an entire frame in the extractor and spin the honey out of the comb. If you are only seeking honey, try to keep the wax as intact as possible because the bees will use it as a base to rebuild.

If you are harvesting wax as well as honey, a more simplistic method of extraction is the crush and strain method. The only specialized equipment you'll need is mosquito netting.

Start by cutting the wax and honey from the frame and placing it in a bowl. Use a potato masher to crush it into a blob of waxy honey. You can strain it in a couple of ways: Simply line a colander with mosquito netting and strain into another bowl. Or strain it straight into the jar.

To do this, fill a quart-size canning jar with the waxy honey. Tighten on a ring without the lid. Cut a 10- to 12-inch circle of mosquito netting and place it over the opening of a second quart-size jar. Push the netting into the jar with your fingers to create a kind of "strainer" of netting. Screw on a second ring to hold

Five Must-Have Beekeeping Tools

Smoker: A portable contraption that allows you to burn wood chips, pine needles, or leaves to create smoke. Smoke calms the bees so you can access the hive more easily.

Hive tool: Bees glue parts of a hive together with their propolis. This aptly named multipurpose tool is used to pry open the seal, detach the combs from the hive, and pry frames apart.

Bee brush: This soft-bristled brush gently moves bees out of the way when harvesting honey.

Uncapping tool: These are used to remove the caps from the beeswax. Heated knives and uncapping combs make quick work of this task.

Protective gear: When opening the hive, you'll be up close and personal with the bees. You'll want to protect yourself with a bee suit, gloves, and a hat with a veil to cover the face.

it in place. Upend the empty jar over the full jar and duct tape the two necks together. Invert, and allow to sit for a few hours. Gravity will cause the honey to flow downward, through the netting, and into the bottom jar.

RECIPE

Herb-Infused Honey

Makes varying amounts depending on how much honey you use

It's easy to infuse honey with a variety of flavors. Herbs like lavender, cinnamon, rosemary, or lemon balm are good options for helping honey go gourmet. If you're lucky enough to have access to truffles, you can even make an Italian specialty, *miele al tartufo,* or truffle honey. Infused honey makes great gifts! Store infused honey in a cool, dry place for up to two years, and serve it with biscuits and butter, stirred into tea or lemonade, or in salad dressings.

You'll Need:
Fresh or dried herbs of choice
Honey

1. Fill a glass jar halfway with fresh herbs. If you're using dried herbs, fill the jar a quarter of the way.
2. Cover the herbs with honey, and seal the jar with a tight-fitting lid.
3. Set the honey on a sunny windowsill, and invert the jar daily for about a week. If the herbs have swelled and are not submerged, add a bit more honey to the jar.
4. Strain out and discard the herbs, return the honey to the jar, and enjoy.

RECIPE

Fruit Mead

Makes about 1 gallon

Making mead—also known as honey wine or melomel—is one of the easier methods for brewing adult beverages at home and a fun way to use some of your honey harvest. The flavor of mead varies based on the honey and fruit you choose, of course, but the yeast is also a deciding factor in flavor. You can pick up yeast at a home brew store or order it online. Making mead offers endless opportunity for experimentation, as evidenced by the sheer number of mead recipes you'll find with a quick internet search. This is a good, basic one to start with. Store sealed mead in a cool dry place indefinitely.

Infusing honey with herbs takes its flavor to new heights.

You'll Need:
8 cups filtered (unchlorinated) water
1 quart honey
½ packet (1 teaspoon) Champagne yeast
1 cup fruit of choice, mashed
Special equipment: 2 (gallon-size) glass jugs with a narrow neck, 1 air lock with a rubber stopper, funnel, thermometer, sanitizer (specifically for brewing), a bottling tool, mini auto-siphon with tubing, swing-top bottles

1. Sanitize 1 glass jug, the air lock, funnel, and thermometer.
2. Pour the filtered water into a large stainless steel pot. Heat the water over medium-high heat to 150°F.
3. Stir in the honey. To pasteurize, hold the mixture at 150°F for 5 minutes.
4. Using the funnel, pour the sweetened water into one of the glass jugs; add the fruit. This liquid mixture is called the "must."
5. Add enough cold water to the jug of must to bring the water level to within 3 inches of the top.
6. Cap the jug, and shake it gently to mix everything together.
7. When the liquid has cooled to 75°F or less, add the half packet of Champagne yeast.
8. Cap the jug again. Shake it vigorously for 2 minutes to combine the ingredients and hydrate the yeast.
9. Fill the air lock with water to the marked line, and push the rubber stopper (with air lock attached) into the top of your jug.
10. Set the jug in a pan or tray to catch any accidental overflow. The mead will be pretty active for the first 24 hours or so. If it foams and overflows, rinse the jar and the air lock and put it back in place.
11. Store the jug in a cool, dark place until bubbling ceases—about 4 weeks, depending on ambient temperature; warm weather means faster fermentation.

■ **Racking the mead:** The process of "racking" is simply moving the liquid via siphon from one container to another, leaving the sediment behind. To rack your mead, sanitize the auto-siphon and the second jug before transferring the must. Do your best to avoid disturbing the sediment as you move the mead from one container to another. Racking the mead generally kicks off a second ferment that lasts a week or two. Set the air lock in place, and keep an eye on the mead. During this stage, the liquid will begin to clear. When the mead stops bubbling, it's time to bottle.

■ **Bottling the mead:** Sanitize everything that will come in contact with the liquid (including the individual bottles). Set the jug of mead on a table or countertop with the bottles at a lower level. Attach the bottling tool to the auto-siphon, then press it to the bottom of each bottle to release the mead into the bottles, leaving about an inch of headspace. (Lifting it will stop the flow.) Seal the bottles and store them in a cool, dark place. You can drink the mead at this stage, but it will only improve with age, becoming smoother and less "green" tasting. For more on mead making and bottling mead, visit *www.growforagecookferment.com.*

DIY

Rendering Beeswax

Beeswax is a valuable by-product of honey extraction. It can be used to make candles (see page 74), as an ingredient in personal care items (see page 118), and to make beeswax wraps, an eco-friendly replacement for plastic wrap (see page 92). The saucepan will be ruined, so perhaps keep one just for this purpose, or use a coffee can.

You'll Need:
Honeycomb remaining after extraction
Cheesecloth
Saucepan
Tongs and a knife

1. Wrap the sticky honeycomb in a couple layers of cheesecloth and place it in a saucepan.
2. Fill the saucepan with enough water to cover the cheesecloth bundle; allow at least 3 inches between the water level and the top of the pan. Bring to a simmer. The wax will melt and seep from the cheesecloth, leaving behind any undesirable bits.
3. Simmer for 30 minutes, moving the bundle around in the hot water every 5 minutes or so. Remove from the heat. Use tongs to lift the cheesecloth from the water.
4. Cool slightly, then squeeze as much liquid from the cheesecloth as possible before discarding it.

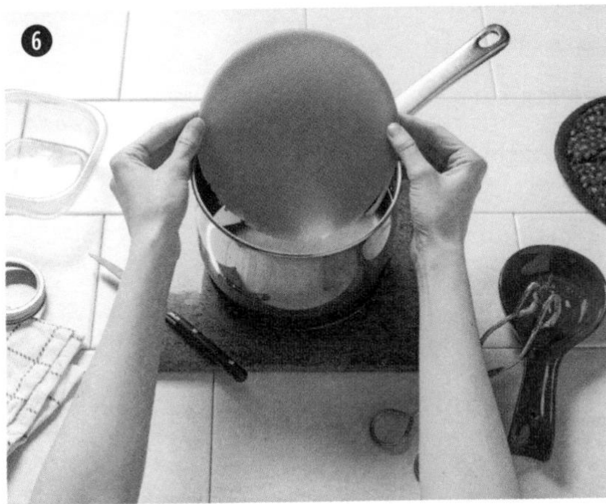

You'll see a sheen of liquid wax on top of the water.

5. Allow the water in the saucepan to cool overnight. The beeswax will harden as it cools, resulting in a round disk of wax floating on top of the water (much like beef fat hardens atop a pot full of broth as it cools).

6. Loosen the wax from the edge of the pot with a knife, lift the hardened beeswax disk from the water and drain. Store in an airtight container.

NOTE: Avoid letting the water boil. Beeswax is flammable, and an accidental boilover can cause fire and injury.

COMPOSTING

Compost is essentially decayed organic material. In the wild, the decomposition process takes place naturally in forests. Leaves drift to the ground, rain falls, and worms and insects break down the waste into smaller bits. Without anyone doing any special work, the forest floor becomes a bed of naturally decayed, nutrient-rich material called humus. Gardeners embrace compost for its ability to fertilize gardens naturally (and they tend to be a lot more impatient than Mother Nature!). Thank goodness, savvy planters can do plenty to mimic the natural process of creating compost.

Active and Passive Compost

Home gardeners can make their own compost using yard waste, kitchen scraps, and other assorted compostable items. There are—basically—two ways to do this, although all gardeners will tell you that their method is the best! No matter how you opt to compost, the benefits are twofold: You'll end up with free fertilizer for the garden, plus you'll divert lots of waste from the landfill.

The easiest way to compost takes a cue from nature and doesn't require much help. **Passive composting** is a matter of piling material in one place and letting it break down in its own time. It can take a couple of years, but it doesn't get much easier than that. Just try to avoid putting weeds with mature seedpods in a passive compost pile.

Kitchen and yard waste will break down into compost.

Active composting is often referred to as "hot composting," because the pile becomes quite warm. This heat kills weed seeds and any diseases present, and also assures a fast breakdown of materials. Maintaining a hot compost pile requires more effort as explained in the following.

Whether your compost pile is active or passive, you can simply build it in a corner of your yard or in a contained space. (Lots of people utilize pallets to create an inexpensive composting bin.) With the appropriate combination of materials, a compost pile generates very little odor. One method is no better than another as far as the final product goes—but if you have critters that might get into it, a covered compost bin is a good idea.

DIY

Making an Active Compost Pile

The internal temperature of an active compost pile can reach temperatures of 120° to 150°F, and the compost will be ready to use in four to six weeks. See page 237 for suggested carbon and nitrogen materials you can throw in the pile:

1. Start with materials that are chopped into small pieces for the fastest results.
2. Add carbon and nitrogen materials to a pile in a roughly 2:1 ratio—two pitchforks of carbon, one of nitrogen—and repeat.
3. Sprinkle the pile with water as you build it; the pile should be moist but not wet.

When combined with carbon materials, lawn clippings make an excellent addition to a compost pile.

4. Make sure that the pile is a minimum of one cubic yard in size to maintain heat.
5. Once a week, use a pitchfork to turn the pile. The easiest way to do this is to shift the pile over. Pitchfork the material from the top of the pile so that it's adjacent to the first pile, and continue dismantling the old pile and building a new one right next to it. Sprinkle with water to maintain moisture, if necessary.

Trench Composting

There are some natural items that should not be added to a standard compost pile. (Synthetic items should never be added.) That's not to say they won't break down, but they could generate problems. Adding meat and dairy products sparingly won't hurt the compost; what it can do is draw animals. And stink. A better alternative would be to bury those items as part of a trench composting system. As you might

The trench composting method puts organic materials directly in the soil, where they will break down.

expect, this entails digging a long trench, often alongside an actively growing crop. Add items directly to the trench, covering it with soil as you go. The buried items will decompose right in place, feeding the roots of nearby plants.

Using Manure

Some people consider animal manure a "waste product" when, in fact, it's a valuable commodity that adds nutrients and organic matter to the soil. Manure from cows, horses, pigs, chickens, goats, sheep, rabbits, and even llamas and alpacas is safe to use in your garden or orchard. (Don't use cat or dog poop.)

Fresh manure is very high in nitrogen (especially so for chicken manure). However, it's not a good idea to spread it on an actively growing garden, as it can damage the plants. Fresh manure can also carry pathogens; placing it where you're harvesting fresh fruits or vegetables can spread those pathogens. It's better to use it on fallow garden beds at least three months prior to planting time. This way, the manure will leach down into the soil while it sits, improving the quality while allowing the nitrogen levels to mellow out a bit.

One drawback to fresh manure is that it may come with seeds. If animals have been eating weed seeds, those can pass right through their system and still remain viable.

Composting manure using the hot compost method will kill weed seeds and pathogens, making it safe to use directly on food crops. If you're using manure harvested from inside a coop or barn that's mixed with bedding like straw or wood shavings, pretty much all you have to do is pile it up and let it cook. You won't need to add anything to it, because

Using Finished Compost

- Add a scoop of finished compost to planting holes.
- Use it as a side dressing while your garden is growing.
- Mix some into potting soil when planting in containers.
- Fill an old sock with one to two cups of compost and soak in a five-gallon bucket of water to make compost tea, a natural liquid fertilizer.

the combination of manure and bedding is a nice balance of carbon and nitrogen materials.

If you don't have your own animals, you can still get in on the goodness of manure. Of course, it's available for purchase at nurseries and home centers, but you might be able to find it for free by seeking out a local ranch, horse stable, or dairy. These places often have a glut of the stuff, and they'll happily send you off with as much as you'd like. If they don't have a tractor with a bucket for loading, you might have to shovel it yourself and transport it in a sealed container.

DIY

Vermicomposter

Vermicomposting allows you to turn kitchen waste into a rich garden amendment. A worm bin—a layered unit that houses worms that will eat your garbage—doesn't take up much space, it doesn't stink, and the worm castings are very high in nutrients. Keep one under your kitchen sink, in the garage, or outside in the shade.

You'll Need:
2 nesting 5-gallon buckets
1 bucket lid
A drill fit with ⅛-inch bit
Kitchen scraps
Red wigglers
Newspaper

1. Drill 10 to 15 holes in the bottom of one of the buckets. This allows excess liquid to drain.
2. Add several handfuls of kitchen scraps to the bucket.
3. Place the red wigglers on top of the kitchen scraps.
4. Shred newspaper. Thoroughly wet the shredded newspaper; allow it to drain for a moment, then place it atop the worms to a depth of about 6 inches.
5. Put the bucket with the worms inside the second bucket, and put on the lid. The bottom bucket serves the purpose of catching any liquid that leaches from the active bin.
6. Add a handful of scraps every 2 to 3 weeks, tucking them under the newspaper. As the worm colony grows, they can process more scraps. Add more when the worms have eaten through most of the scraps in the bin. The worms will multiply based on how much food is made available to them.
7. When there's a substantial amount of dark brown worm castings, it's time to harvest. Stop adding new scraps for a few weeks. Dump the entire contents of the worm bucket onto a piece of cardboard and expose it to sunshine. The worms dislike light and will crawl to the bottom of the pile. Carefully remove castings from the top of the pile, repeating this several times until you've harvested most of it.
8. Put the worms back into the bucket, and start anew.

A worm bin of this size is best suited to a single person or couple. You can use the same method with large plastic storage containers for a larger household. Or make a large-scale outdoor vermicomposting system in a recycled wooden shipping crate or 55-gallon drum. Drill drainage holes and set the container up on blocks to allow liquid to escape. Add food scraps, leaves, and shredded newspaper as described. When the container is full, let it sit for a month or so to allow the worms to finish processing the material, then harvest the castings.

A vermicomposting system is easy to make with buckets.

PRESORTED
FIRST-CLASS MAIL
U.S. POSTAGE PAID
PERSHING LLC. A
BNY MELLON COMPANY

WHAT YOU CAN COMPOST

Composting the waste your home generates is one way to reduce the amount of trash you send to the landfill. Kitchen scraps are perhaps the most obvious item to compost, but a closer look at what you're tossing out will likely reveal a windfall of surprising items that can be diverted to the compost pile. Might as well turn that trash into garden treasure!

NITROGEN MATERIALS
(sometimes referred to as "green")

- Grass clippings
- Weeds (avoid weed seeds in a passive pile)
- Fruit and vegetable scraps
- Eggshells
- Coffee grounds (along with paper filters)
- Tea bags and loose-leaf tea
- Stale or spoiled food
- Green leaves and garden trimmings
- Feathers
- Manure from chickens, goats, cows, and horses

CARBON MATERIALS
(sometimes referred to as "brown")

- Dry leaves
- Wood chips
- Sawdust
- Cornstalks
- Straw
- Paper
- Newspapers
- Used paper plates, napkins, and paper towels
- Junk mail and envelopes (remove the plastic window)
- Nonplastic egg cartons
- Cardboard and paperboard containers, including paper towel rolls and toilet paper tubes
- Cotton swabs
- Dryer lint (from 100 percent natural fabrics only)
- Fabric scraps and old clothing (made from natural materials like cotton and wool)

RAISING CHICKENS

Chickens are one of the easiest barnyard animals to integrate into your backyard farm. If you have 10 extra minutes a day, you have time for chickens. Raising chickens might seem like a huge undertaking, but in fact, adult chickens require very little effort. Adopting newly hatched chicks does take a bit of extra work, as you'll need to keep them warm, fed, and watered. If that's a deal breaker for you, seek out young hens (called pullets).

How many hens you start with depends upon the amount of space you have available. Hens in their prime lay one egg almost daily; knowing how many eggs you use in a week will help you determine the ideal number of hens you need to skip the supermarket egg cartons.

Starting With Chicks

Unbelievable as it might seem, it's possible to shop for baby chicks online and have them delivered right to your door. (Newly hatched chicks can survive up to 72 hours without food or water.) The benefit of going this route is that you'll have a much broader selection of breeds than you will by picking up chicks at your local farm supply store. That's not to say the basic breeds that your farm supply store carries aren't worthwhile. But it's hard to deny the comical draw of a frizzle-headed or feather-legged flock.

In their early days, young chicks require a heat lamp.

Tiny, freshly hatched chicks will steal your heart with their fuzzy cuteness. At this stage, they don't need a lot of space. A cardboard box or storage tote can suffice, depending upon how many chicks you decide to bring home.

They will outgrow this first brooder quickly, though. At about the time they do, you'll notice that they've begun to stink quite a bit. For this reason, you'll want to keep them somewhere that prevents you from having to constantly smell the unpleasant odor. Keep them in a secure, warm space outside that predators (even rats are an issue) won't breach, if possible. If not, utilize your garage, laundry room, or extra bathroom. Move them up to a larger enclosure that has sides at least 15 inches high to prevent them from flying out. A kiddie pool works great at this stage, as does a large cardboard box from an appliance store. Provide a perch that's a couple inches off the ground, and the chicks will begin roosting on it when they're ready.

Keep an eye on their bums for signs of "pasty butt." If soft droppings accumulate, they can harden and block their vent. If this happens, use a warm cloth to soften and remove the hardened poop; chicks can die from this.

It's essential that chicks are kept warm until they're entirely feathered out. That fuzzy down is cute, but it's not so great at keeping them warm. Without mom to tuck them under her wing, you'll need a heat source. Choose from brooders that use radiant heat or a simple clamp-on brooder light equipped with an infrared heat emitter. No matter which you choose, make sure that the heat source is far enough from any flammable material.

Hens provide eggs, of course—but they can also help keep weeds down.

Feeding Chicks

Keep food in the brooder at all times. Starter crumble (which you can purchase at feed stores) is generally recommended for chicks and is often medicated to help prevent health issues. Organic crumble without medication is also available. Choose a feeder that prevents the chicks from climbing into the food.

To prevent chicks from getting wet, choose a waterer they cannot climb into. If you don't want to purchase a waterer, you can fill a recycled container with marbles then add water. The marbles won't interfere with their drinking, but they will prevent the chicks from going for a swim. Chicks can drown in deeper water.

Moving Into the Coop

Once the chicks are feathered out, they can be moved to a permanent outdoor coop. At this point they shouldn't need heat unless temperatures are really low, and you can change your order at the feed store to introduce larger pellets and some scratch or cracked corn if you like. You can feed and water the chickens in the run or in the coop, whichever works best for you. (See page 248 for more on feeding chickens.)

When the weather is fine, chickens don't require much in the way of a coop for their own comfort; a perch and a roof over their heads is all they need to be happy. The larger purpose of a chicken coop is to protect the birds from predators. For this, the coop needs to be completely secure; snakes or rats can squeeze in through chicken wire. A better, longer lasting option is to use steel wire (sometimes called hardware cloth or aviary netting). Overlap the wire as you construct the coop, preventing any gaps (or predators like skunks, bobcats, and raccoons will work their way in). Aim for two to three square feet of space for each chicken to give them enough room when they're on lockdown at night or crowd in during inclement weather.

In the Chicken Run

Your girls will spend most of their time in the chicken run. Ten square feet per hen is sufficient, but if you've got room, more is always better. A larger space provides more opportunity for scratching and pecking for bugs.

You might consider implementing a couple of ideas in your chicken run if it's big enough. If you expect to have chickens in this space for a number of years, plant a few fruiting trees like mulberry or elderberry inside the premises. As fruit ripens and falls, the chickens will gobble it up. Vegetation inside the coop offers cover from aerial predators as well.

The chicken run is also a great place to set up a compost pile. The hens will work it as they seek out bugs and other edible tidbits. Using a simple square of 12-inch-diameter logs will allow the chickens to jump up and scratch for bugs and worms and yet keep the pile contained. When it's full, move the logs and start anew. The larger the pile, the more foraging your flock will be able to do—and the less you'll need to supplement with expensive feed.

Free-Ranging Hens

If you've got plenty of space and you're not concerned about chickens scratching up your garden beds, you can forgo the chicken run entirely and let them free-range. This does come with the risk of daytime predators like wandering dogs and hawks. The idea of giving chickens free range to roam their surroundings and naturally forage for bugs appeals to a lot of people, and they consider it worth the risk.

Monitor chickens in the garden to prevent damage.

Depending upon breed, chicken eggs come in a variety of hues, including white, brown, chocolate brown, blue, and green.

A good compromise is to keep the hens locked inside the chicken run during the day, but allow them out in the late afternoon. Chickens will naturally return home to roost every evening, but you can encourage their return by tossing out a bit of scratch inside their run while you call them. They'll come running for the scratch they know goes with your call.

Nesting Boxes

At roughly six months of age, your hens will start laying. Although it's a good idea to provide nesting boxes, hens will produce eggs whether or not you do. Nesting boxes can be made from any number of recycled materials; square buckets, milk crates, and even old tires set directly on the ground will give hens a place to lay their eggs. If your hens use a nesting box, you'll always know right where to look to find the eggs. (Not so if they seek out a private spot under a shrub.) Plus, a nesting box full of clean shavings helps to keep eggs clean. (Yes, you might get one with a little poop on it now and again, but that's normal.)

A couple of nesting boxes for a small flock will suffice; you certainly don't need one for every hen. Hens tend to become fond of one nesting box, laying their eggs in the same one. Two (or three!) hens might even cram themselves together into one favored box,

Bathing Chickens

Hens do a good job of keeping themselves clean and bug free, so long as they have access to a dust bath. They'll scratch up a dry patch of dirt to create one, but you can make an area for dust bathing in a low tub or even a shallow hole in the ground; it just needs to be protected from rain. Boost the efficacy of the dust bath by adding a cup or so of diatomaceous earth or a small bucketful of ash. The hens will jump in and throw the dry dust up on themselves, working it into their feathers.

while others sit empty. To encourage your hens to lay eggs inside the box, place a fake egg (or even a golf ball) in the nest as they near laying age.

Roosters

A common concern from those considering chickens is the noise a rooster makes. Well, yes. They do make a bit of a racket, and that can be a problem for urban residents. They crow throughout the day, not just at the crack of dawn. But here's the good news: You don't have to have a rooster to maintain a successful egg-laying flock. That's right. Hens lay eggs whether or not there's a rooster around. Roosters are only necessary if your goal is to have fertile eggs to increase the size of your flock.

If noise isn't a factor, there are some good arguments for keeping a rooster as part of the flock, the strongest of which is safety. Roosters are wired to protect the flock; his presence can deter small predators, and his call when danger lurks warns his girls to seek cover. The comedic relief a rooster provides in interacting with his hens is a plus, too.

On the other hand, in their ongoing efforts to keep their flock safe, roosters can be mean to humans. The surest way to prevent this is to handle the rooster regularly from the time it's young. If he sees you as friend rather than foe, he'll be a lot less likely to jump you when you walk into the pen.

Roosters are optional members of the flock.

Good Breeds for Egg Laying

Some chickens are better egg layers than others. Choosing a breed that lays consistently will make your efforts and feed expenses more worthwhile. Another thing to consider when choosing your flock is egg color. Sure, they all taste the same, but there is just something wonderful about gathering a basketful of light brown, dark brown, white, blue, and green eggs from your own hens.

- **Araucanas** have little poofs of feathers at the sides of their head. They're the "Easter egg" chicken, laying eggs that range from blue to green in color.
- **Hybridized white leghorns** are used in commercial egg-laying operations, but the heritage breed is available to consumers. They lay white eggs.
- **Orpingtons** come in several colors, but Buff Orpingtons are the most common. These large birds lay brown eggs.
- **Plymouth Rocks** (or Barred Rocks) are black-and white-striped and lay brown eggs.
- **Black and White Marans** look similar to Plymouth Rocks, but are less common. They lay a dark chocolate brown egg.
- **Rhode Island Reds** are common and a good dual-purpose bird, meaning they're good egg layers and also a good size for meat birds. They lay brown eggs.
- **Black Stars and Red Stars** are sex-link chickens, which means they can be "sexed" upon hatching. In chicken parlance, this means it's possible to identify males and females upon hatching because they're different colors. Both varieties lay brown eggs.

Broody Hens

A reference to a "broody hen" describes a chicken that's intent on hatching chicks. Hens will go broody even without a rooster around to create fertile eggs; it's just their instinct. If you want chicks and have access to fertile eggs (or have a rooster on the premises), letting a momma hen raise babies is the easiest way to grow your flock. She does all the work. If you don't want her to hatch eggs for you, gather eggs daily and be sure to check under her. It's not unheard of for another hen to climb in with the broody hen to lay an egg, which the broody hen will then slide under her body.

Considering the End of Eggs

Although it does vary, you can expect to get about three years of good egg production from a hen, with diminishing numbers in the following years. Chickens can live to be more than 10 years old; some will even live close to 20 years.

This is where the tough decisions come in. What will you do when the cost of feed outweighs the return in eggs? Serious backyard homesteaders turn their flocks over every year, bringing new hens in and butchering hens with reduced production. Others opt to let their hens live out their natural lives. You'll have to decide which method is best for you, but it's worth some consideration. Adding more hens every few years to maintain egg production can quickly result in a flock that costs a pretty penny to maintain without providing much return on that investment.

Raising Meat Birds

All chickens are edible. That said, if you're going to do the work of butchering, it makes sense to raise birds that will reach a decent size and provide a substantial amount of meat. Some breeds are considered "dual purpose" in that they are good egg layers that grow to good broiler size. People who go this route will typically order "straight run" chicks that are not sexed. The hens become egg layers, the roosters, dinner.

If you opt to go with strictly meat birds, you'll have to choose between heirloom breeds and hybrids. The big difference between the two is time. Hybrids reach ideal weight more quickly and are quite heavily breasted. This means they yield more meat, but a hybrid flock needs careful management. Their rapid growth can cause bone ailments or heart failure. Timing the butchering for when they reach target weight is crucial.

Heritage birds take longer to reach target weight, but they tend to be good at foraging independently for food. Heritage breeds are also less prone to health issues and have richer-flavored meat than fast-growing hybrids.

A portable tractor allows you to move chickens onto new ground at regular intervals.

Here are some breeds to consider:

- **White Cornish hybrids** are generally ready to harvest in six to seven weeks. They don't do well with high temperatures and prefer to be housed indoors. Their edible meat at harvest is about 75 percent of live weight.

- **Colored hybrids** like Freedom Ranger, Red Broiler, Rosambro, and Silver Cross take about 11 weeks to mature. Raise them on pasture; their colored feathers make them more difficult for predators to spot. Their edible meat at harvest is about 70 percent of live weight.

- **Heritage breeds**—Delaware, New Hampshire, Plymouth Rock, Wyandotte—need a full 16 weeks to mature. Their edible meat at harvest is about 65 percent of live weight.

Housing Broilers

Broilers can be housed in a manner similar to egg layers, though it's common to see them kept in a more confined space. A chicken tractor—a small, lightweight cage, often on wheels so it's easy to move—works well to provide the birds with fresh ground on a daily basis. If kept confined like this, use a large piece of cardboard to round off the inside corners of the pen. Without the cardboard, the unlucky few who get stuck in the corner will be smashed and likely die.

Feeding Broilers

To make raising broilers as cost effective as possible, most growers do their best to fatten them up quickly and get them into the freezer. Specially formulated broiler feeds provide 20 to 22 percent protein—higher than what you're feeding your egg layers. If you're not concerned with how quickly your broilers reach target weight, they can certainly eat the same diet as your egg layers.

Butchering Chickens

When we began harvesting some of our flock to fill the freezer, we had a friend walk us through the process. I highly recommend this if you can at all manage it. Butchering chickens takes mettle and a certain amount of knowledge. Having an expert guide for some of the intricacies of using the right tools and cutting *just so* can make all the difference for making the process safe for the humans and humane for the animal.

Although every butcher has a favored technique for making the kill, some steps must be followed closely to retain the quality of the meat; a mentor can help you learn the process, start to finish.

DIY

How to Cut Up a Chicken

Butchering a chicken, start to finish—complete with feathers and feet and innards—might be more than you want to tackle. But learning to cut up a whole chicken is a valuable skill. Buying a whole chicken from a local butcher or farm nets two legs, two thighs, two wings, two breasts, and a bonus, the backbone. Use the backbone for making soup or broth! (See page 29 for how to make broth.)

You'll Need:
A whole chicken
Cutting board
Sharp knife
Kitchen shears (optional, but useful)

1. Set the chicken on a cutting board, back down.
2. Remove the legs: Make a slice in the skin between the leg and the breast, where the thigh connects. Bend the leg away from the body. This will reveal the thighbone. Find the joint and cut through it and the adjacent meat, severing the leg from the body. Repeat on the other side.
3. Separate the drumstick and thigh: Place a leg skin side down. Look for a visible line of fat where the thigh and drumstick meet. The joint is located below this. Make a cut right through that joint and the meat. Repeat.
4. Remove the wings: Lift a wing away from the body and use your fingers to locate the joint. Use a knife to cut through the joint, severing the wing from the body. Repeat on the other side.
5. Cut off the backbone: This part can be done with a knife as well, but using kitchen shears is a bit easier. Again, look for a line of fat that runs from the front to the back of the body. Use that as a guide, cutting across that line of fat. You'll encounter rib bones here; just cut through those. Repeat on the opposite side until the back is almost free.
6. At this point, you may need to use your hands to break the back free. Cut through any skin or meat that is still attached.

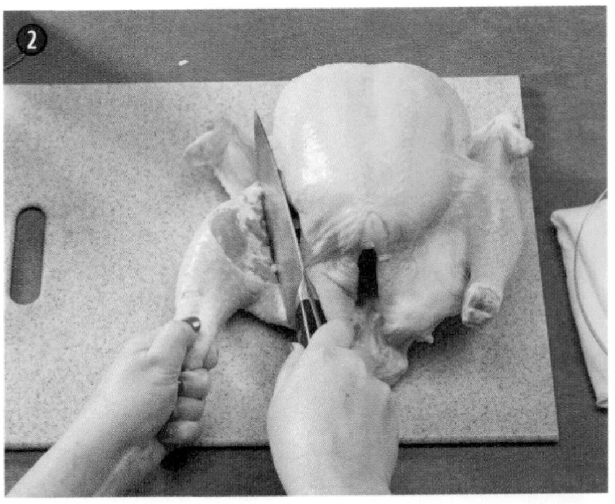

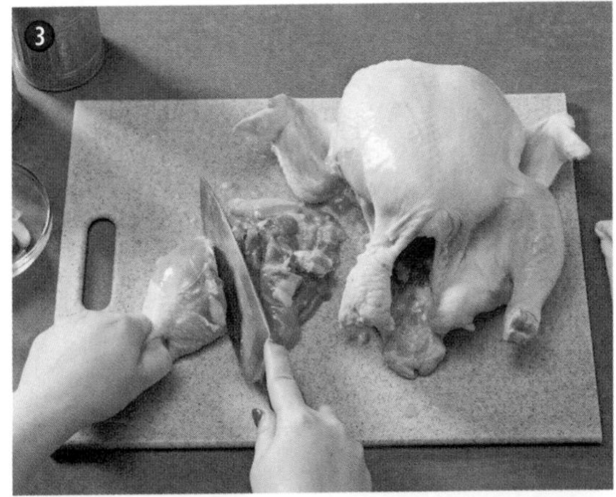

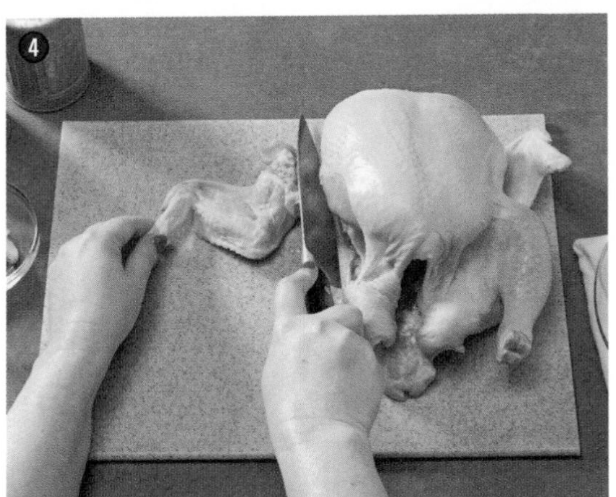

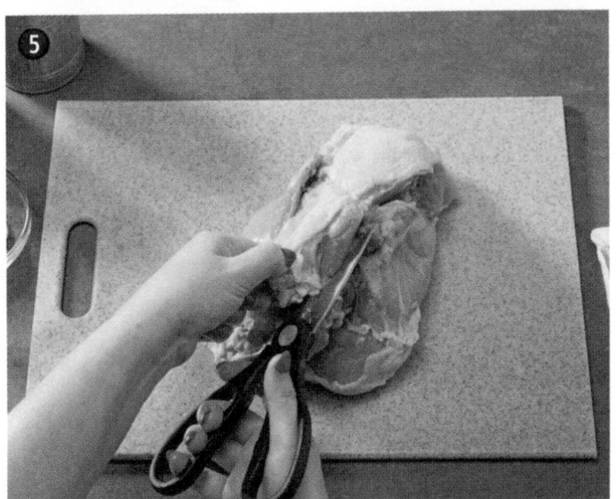

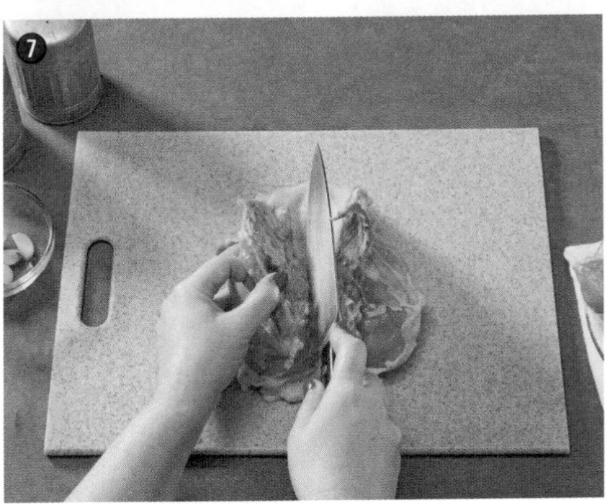

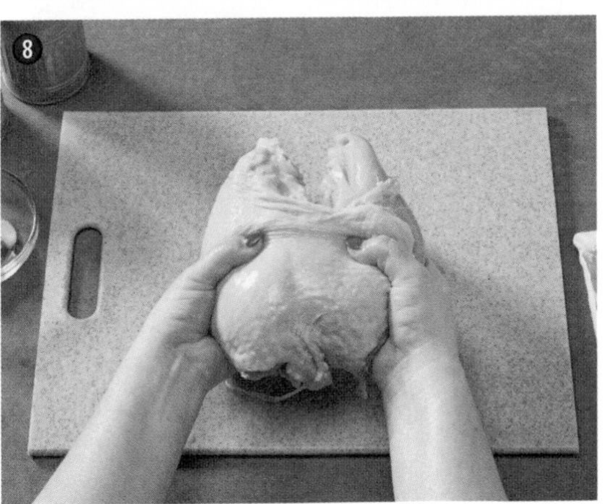

7. Divide the breasts: Place the breasts skin side down, and use a knife to make a shallow cut down the breastbone.
8. Flip the breasts over and use your hands to crack the breastbone further along the shallow cut. Place the breastbone on the cutting board (skin side up), and make a cut down the middle, between the two meaty breasts. Your knife will encounter the breastbone, but because you've already broken it, it will be easy to cut through.
9. Cook chicken immediately or package for freezing.

BEYOND CHICKENS

Although raising chickens—even in the suburbs—has become a way for many people to embrace food production on a small scale, chickens are by no means the only type of poultry to consider. Ducks, turkeys, and even quail can be excellent sources of eggs or meat for intrepid urban homesteaders, and the requirements for raising these unique breeds of fowl are simpler than you may think.

Raising Ducks

If the idea of a reproductive flock in your backyard is appealing, but a crowing rooster is less so, ducks might be a good alternative. Male ducks—drakes—make substantially less noise than roosters. An ideal flock of ducks has one drake to six hens.

Ducks can be excellent egg layers, producing eggs on par with the number a chicken would lay, but roughly 50 percent larger.

It's important to note that ducks need water to swallow their food. At the very least, provide a bowl of water next to their food dish. They can get by without a pond, but they'll be happier if you can provide them with a container of water that's large enough for them to bathe in. Make sure the container either has a drainage hole or is small enough that you can turn it over for cleaning. Ducks will turn even a small bucket full of water into a muddy mess in no time.

Provide your ducks with a secure, fenced space where they'll be safe from predators. Unlike chickens, ducks don't roost. Give them a place to tuck in and stay warm—a large doghouse works—but don't be surprised to find them happily hanging out in the rain. They are excellent foragers, and they'll do so around the clock in mild weather. They'll even sound the alarm if intruders near. In winter, you'll want to move them into a coop and provide extra bedding for warmth.

Ducks provide excellent slug control.

Duck Breeds for Egg Laying

Khaki Campbells tend to be excellent layers, but they can be a bit skittish. **Cayuga** and **Pekin** varieties lay well and are known to be calm. Breeders often have their own hybrid birds that they've bred specifically to be good egg layers.

Talking Turkey

Turkey eggs are edible, but raising turkeys for eggs isn't exactly cost efficient. They only lay about two eggs a week. Turkeys are generally raised as meat birds. Commercially produced turkeys are oh, so cheap during the holiday season, but raising your own allows you to control what the birds eat and assures a much more humane method of care and butchering.

Turkeys can be surprisingly more delicate than other varieties of poultry. Keep poults—newly hatched chicks—under a heat lamp for

What Constitutes a Heritage Turkey?

If you opt to raise heritage birds, you'll help with the conservation of biodiversity. There are a few requirements:

Natural mating. The birds must reproduce naturally with a 70 to 80 percent fertility rate.

Long, productive outdoor life span. That's five to seven years for hens and three to five years for toms.

Slow growth. Modern commercial hybrids hurry the meat process. Heritage turkeys grow to full size in 28 weeks, developing a strong skeletal structure and healthy organs before putting on muscle mass.

the first four to five weeks of their life. Aim for a temperature of about 90°F on the floor of the brooder; decrease that temperature by five degrees each week. Provide a roost in the brooder; turkeys will begin to roost at about 14 days.

Turkey poults need 14 hours of light daily to eat well and thrive. Feed them a high-protein (28 percent) diet for the first six weeks.

Poults are susceptible to soil-borne pathogens and should not be allowed onto pasture until they reach 8 to 12 weeks of age. To give them access to the outdoors, create a raised open area adjacent to the brooder. Be sure to keep them out of the rain, as their feathers are not oily enough to repel water. A shelter with at least three square feet per bird is critical.

Coturnix Quail

Quail require less food and space than other poultry. They can even be raised indoors, which makes them a great alternative for urban homesteaders. Coturnix quail—also known as Jumbo Japanese quail—are commonly raised for egg and meat production.

Caged quail require only 40 to 50 square inches of ground per bird if you're raising them for eggs. Provide meat birds a full square foot of ground per bird. Quail prefer a long, narrow cage as opposed to a square, and they don't need much in the way of headspace. A 12-inch-high ceiling is sufficient. Build or choose a cage with a wire mesh bottom to prevent the birds from standing in or eating their manure, which can spread disease.

Quail require 21 to 25 percent protein in their feed. This can be achieved by feeding them turkey or wild game feed or supplementing layer feed with bugs and grains.

Quail begin laying eggs at six to eight weeks of age. Their eggs are small; you'll need about five or six to replace a single chicken egg. Provide a nesting box lined with shavings or sand, but don't be surprised if you regularly find eggs outside the box. If you're raising quail for meat, plan to butcher them between 8 to 12 weeks of age. A dressed quail will weigh about six ounces.

An ideal option for urban farming, quail can be raised for both eggs and meat, and require minimal space.

POULTRY FEED

Chicken folks talk a lot about feeding chickens the "right" foods. Of course, you'll want your flock to be full and happy. But what if the recommendations for a perfectly balanced diet are skewed to focus on what commercial farmers need to feed to get the highest egg yield? Sensible for them, because it's their livelihood. Backyard farmers and urban chicken keepers probably have a bit more flexibility, though. Instead of feeding only commercial feed—often imported from a substantial distance—delve into some alternatives to help supplement your flock's diet. As a chicken owner, you certainly have some things to consider when it comes to feeding your chickens, but there's not one "right" way to do it.

What Do Chickens Eat?

Let's get this straight, right off the bat: Chickens are not vegetarians. They are omnivores. "Vegetarian fed" listed as an asset on egg cartons does not equal vegetarian chickens. They *like* meat. They'll even eat a mouse if one wanders too close to the coop. Whether or not to actually feed chickens meat is perhaps one of the biggest debates in backyard chicken circles. The question is mostly an ethical one. If you're comfortable with it, your flock will devour raw or cooked meat scraps and pick soup bones clean.

The average chicken eats four to five ounces of feed a day, though that can increase a bit during peak production or in cold weather. Their total diet should be roughly 20 percent protein. Chickens with the ability to range free, or those that have a large run, will naturally supplement their diet by seeking out sources of protein like bugs, grubs, and worms. They'll eat what they need to round out what you provide.

Purchasing Feed

Commercial poultry feed comes in a variety of options and is sold under myriad names. You can offer your flock essentially two products: feed that is formulated to be nutritionally balanced, providing the 20 percent protein requirement, and scratch. Feed comes in pellet form or in crumbles and can contain "extras" like probiotics or medication (common in starter feed given to chicks). Scratch is to chickens as chocolate is to humans. They love the mixture of cracked corn and seeds, but it doesn't provide complete nutrition.

You'll need to decide whether you want to purchase feed made with conventionally raised crops or those produced organically. Chicken feeds are heavily dependent upon soy and corn—two crops that are genetically engineered to survive being sprayed with herbicide. There's no way to know if the corn and soy in poultry feed are from farms that embrace GMO crops. By law, organic feed cannot include genetically engineered products. People who are concerned about potential health risks to their chickens or the possibility of eggs retaining traces of the herbicide glyphosate can choose organic feed to avoid the GMO ingredients.

Feed These to Your Hens Instead of Throwing Them Away

Hens have a fairly flexible diet, so it makes sense to use resources you have on hand, including waste from the kitchen:

- Grains from your cupboard, for instance, that have a bug infestation
- Excess kombucha SCOBY (cut in pieces) (see page 40)
- Stale food like chips and crackers
- Cooked potato peels
- Leftovers and vegetable scraps
- Crushed eggshells
- Cheese rinds

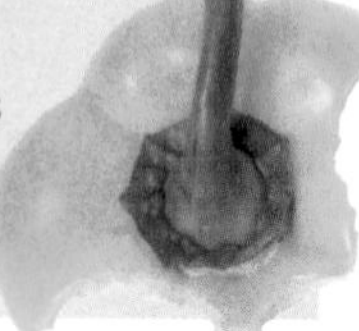

Chickens will eat a wide range of food, including many of the scraps produced in your kitchen.

Although commercial chicken feed is the easiest way to feed a flock, it's not the cheapest—especially if you opt for organic. You can cut your feed budget in numerous ways, and if you're really passionate about it and have enough space, you might be able to eliminate feed costs altogether.

Grow a Chicken Garden

If you have space, growing a garden full of foods that chickens love can help you cut feed costs. Grow extra as part of your family garden, or set aside an area specifically for the flock so that you can give them access to it for a short amount of time each day. They will eat the tops of radishes and beets and save the roots for you!

Even when space is limited, you can plant a few containers with cut and come again greens like lettuce, kale, spinach, and collards, and rotate them in and out of the run so you always have something fresh. Swiss chard is good for this. After the chickens nibble the leaves down to nothing, pull the planter from their run and more leaves will grow. Chickens also like sunflowers, buckwheat, amaranth, tomatoes, and melons.

SMALL LIVESTOCK

Small livestock can earn their keep on your little homestead by producing fiber, dairy, meat, and even manure to build soil. But before you get too excited about a barnyard full of animals, take time to consider the needs of those animals. For instance, although goats are fun and offer a bright spot of comic relief in the barnyard, they are social creatures that need the companionship of other goats. Do you have space to provide that for them? Likewise, although milking does not hurt dairy animals, and in fact lightens their burden, it does need to be done on a regular basis. Does your schedule allow for that? Raising small livestock requires a commitment to their care.

When acquiring livestock, seek out a breeder who provides animals with excellent care, access to fresh air and plenty of space, and protection from inclement weather.

You'll also need to check local zoning laws. There may be limitations on the types and quantity of livestock you can have in your community.

Rabbits

Rabbits are often listed as allowable as "pets," making them a bit of a loophole to those zoning ordinances when it comes to raising livestock in suburban settings. Angora rabbits are raised for their fiber. Both rabbits and fur can fetch a good price on the market. Other breeds are raised for their meat. Rabbits are hard to beat as a high-protein source of calories that doesn't take up much space. Their prolific nature when it comes to breeding makes them a reliable source of meat.

- **Housing:** Whether elevated above the ground or in small cages with wire on the bottom that allows them access to green grass without the ability to tunnel (and escape), rabbit hutches are standard housing. Male rabbits—called bucks—each need their own space. Females—does—can share a space unless they are raising young. Be sure your cages are protected from rain and harsh sun. Rabbits dislike fluctuating temperatures.

- **Feed:** Most breeders feed their rabbits pelleted food, but grass clippings, vegetable tops, and root vegetables can supplement this. Clean water is essential.

- **Breeding:** It depends somewhat on their breed, but generally speaking, rabbits are sexually mature at about six months of age. Once reaching this milestone, does are fertile almost continuously. If a doe begins to display signs of restlessness, move her into a hutch with a buck. (Never move a buck into a doe's cage, as she might feel threatened and attack.) When a rabbit gives birth, the process is called "kindling" and occurs 31 days after conception. Provide a pregnant doe with a nesting box full of straw a few days before birth. Once she's given birth, check the babies

Rabbit manure is a valuable by-product for gardeners.

Dairy goats are a good option for small-scale urban farmers; just be certain that they're securely fenced in.

and remove any that didn't survive. Start feeding the new mom a high-protein diet to prevent her from killing her babies. Kits can be separated from their mom at about eight weeks; males and females should be separated from each other at this time, too, to prevent unplanned breeding.

Goats

Dairy goats are available in two convenient sizes: large and small. Full-size goats, like Nubians and Saanens, can weigh in at about 200 pounds; Nigerian dwarf goats stay well under 100 pounds. A full-size goat produces three to four quarts of milk a day; a dwarf, one to two quarts a day. Female goats—does—produce milk after they've birthed. The easiest way to get started with dairy goats is to purchase a milking doe, one that's recently given birth.

- **Housing:** A goat barn should be kept cool and dry, provide a draft-free sleeping area, and offer access to an outside fenced area. Goats are known escape artists, so be sure that the fencing is sturdily supported and a minimum of four feet high. Make sure the goats have access to fresh water, and expect to refill the trough often.

- **Feed:** Goats love to forage. Provide a pasture area that includes a variety of leaves, branches, and weeds. (Be sure nothing could be poisonous to them!) If pasturing is not possible, or if you need to supplement, provide well-cured hay in a rack; they won't eat hay off the ground. Lactating does will need more protein. Supplement their diet with two to four pounds of grains a day. Goats can overeat, and too much grain can cause bloat. To avoid this, feed grain only after they've had a good amount of hay or forage.

■ **Milking:** Determine where you'll milk your doe. A concrete floor that can be kept very clean is ideal. This can be built into the goat barn or as a separate unit from their living quarters. You'll need a milking stand with a stanchion, or locking head gate, to hold the doe in place while you milk. Always clean the udder before you milk, wiping away any dirt or debris with a warm, wet rag to prevent it from falling into the bucket as you milk. It's a good idea to use a clean rag for each doe.

Milking goats requires some hand strength and a bit of practice. The space between your thumb and first finger is the key to successful milking. You should never pull downward on the teat, as that will cause damage. Grasp the teat near the udder between your thumb and forefinger, squeezing slightly to trap the milk in the teat canal. (If you didn't do this, any further squeezing of the teat would send the milk back up into the udder.) Close the remaining fingers on the teat in top to bottom order, pushing the milk down the teat canal. Squirt each teat once or twice into a waste pail to clear any blockage. Give it a quick look, checking for blood or clumps that might indicate mastitis. If the milk is clear, continue milking into a sanitized milking bucket. Repeat until the udder is completely empty and slack.

RECIPE

Ricotta Cheese

Makes 3 to 4 cups

This soft cheese is easy to make at home with fresh goat's milk, but you can also use store-bought goat or cow milk. For the best results, opt for milk that hasn't been ultra-pasteurized. Add garlic and herbs to make a spread for fresh bread, or use it in your favorite lasagna recipe. Store leftover ricotta covered in the refrigerator for up to a week.

You'll Need:
3 quarts whole milk
1 teaspoon salt
3 tablespoons lemon juice
Special equipment: cheesecloth

When goat milk is plentiful, make ricotta cheese!

1. Mix the milk and salt in a stockpot. Cook over medium-high heat, stirring every few minutes, until the milk reaches 185°F on a candy thermometer. (If you don't have a candy thermometer, bring the milk to a simmer but do not let it boil.)
2. Stir in the lemon juice, turn the heat down to medium, and let the mixture sit for 1 minute; you'll see the milk start to curdle and separate.
3. Gently stir again, and turn off the heat. Let the milk sit, without stirring, for 10 minutes.
4. Meanwhile, line a colander with several layers of cheesecloth. Place the colander in a bowl to catch the whey (the liquid by-product of making cheese).
5. Pour the contents of the pot into the colander. Pull opposite corners of the cheesecloth together and tie a knot. Repeat with remaining corners.
6. Slide a wooden spoon between the knots, and suspend the bag over the now empty pot to catch any drips. Let drain for 2 hours, then transfer to a storage container.

Safe Handling of Raw Milk

Keep it clean, and keep it cold. Those are the tenets of handling raw milk. Start with the cleanliness of your animals and the milking area. Cleaning your goat's teats thoroughly before milking will reduce the risks of contamination. Fresh milk should be cooled immediately. Moving it from field to fridge quickly prevents the bacteria count from rising. Store fresh milk in sanitized glass containers, and get it into the refrigerator immediately.

DIY

Udder Balm

Milking twice a day can irritate and dry out a goat's teats and udder. This balm will keep her skin soft and supple.

You'll Need:
½ cup coconut oil
½ cup shea butter
1 tablespoon honey
20 drops tea tree essential oil
Melt-and-pour container (see page 74)
Wooden chopstick
Small containers

1. Combine the oil and shea butter in a melt-and-pour container. Place the tin can in a saucepan filled with 2 to 3 inches of water to create an improvised double boiler. Be sure you don't get any water in the oil.
2. Set the saucepan over medium heat until the shea butter is melted, stirring the liquid with the chopstick to combine.
3. Remove from heat, and stir in the honey and essential oil.
4. Pour the balm into a sealed container.
5. Apply the udder balm after milking.

Swine

Pigs are raised primarily for their meat, though they can be useful, too. Put a portable pigpen in an area that you need turned over and pigs will make quick work of it. They'll use their strong snouts to root up hearty weeds, all while tilling their manure into the soil. Unlike most livestock, pigs don't mind living alone.

Unless you're interested in creating a reproductive swine herd, opting for a weaner pig or two is your best bet. These are young pigs, six to eight weeks old, recently weaned from mom's teat.

Housing: You'll need good, strong fencing. It doesn't have to be high; pigs can't really jump, but they'll root a weak post out of the ground in no time. Full-grown pigs are strong, and they'll have no qualms about using that strength to escape from whatever method of confinement you've devised. Provide a covered area where pigs can get out of the rain or hot sun.

Feed: Pigs eat a lot. Keeping them on pasture will allow them to forage some of their own food, but it won't suffice by itself. It's not cheap to buy pig food. If you're trying to raise pigs in a cost-effective manner, it's a good idea to plan for a surplus of garden produce like pumpkins, corn, and melons. You can also reach out to restaurants and grocery stores to see if you can pick up their nonmeat food waste. Collect it all in a bucket and it becomes what you've heard referred to as "slop."

Pigs can be smelly, so try to raise them away from neighbors.

• chapter six •

TREK

TREK

For most of human history, people had an innate sense of the weather, seasons, and cycle of nature. Why? Back then, being outside was part of the daily routine. Farmers and mariners knew the signs of potential crop loss or dangerous seas without aid of the nightly news. Herbalists knew the best times of year to forage for different specimens, and trappers looked for signs of animal activity to find the best places for their snares.

Although this kind of knowledge is still true for some professions, many of us have fallen into the trap of spending more time indoors than out. As a result, our observation skills and awareness of nature's rhythm have suffered. (I suspect plenty of people simply wouldn't notice if the sun rose one day in the west and set in the east.)

The good news? We can take back nature by simply getting back to nature. Whether you're heading to a regional park for a short hike or camping in wilderness, focusing on your surroundings and learning to thrive in the open air offers up lessons we can all embrace.

Psychologists are just starting to gather data on the therapeutic benefits of wilderness, but it is something we already know in our bones. We get a centering sense of awe from standing in pounding surf on a beach, and a cathartic sense of accomplishment from cresting a mountain peak. Another consideration? Bushcraft skills are really good practice for dealing with short-term emergency situations like hurricanes or earthquakes. If the power fails, the experience that comes from spending a weekend camping off-grid will be immensely useful. You'll know how to prepare meals, wash dishes, and deal with a multitude of other tasks when the grid is down.

Although these kinds of tasks may feel unnatural at first, in no time you'll begin to wonder why you didn't do them sooner.

• CONTENTS •

Previous pages: *Whittling is a natural activity when enjoying the outdoors.* **Opposite:** *Forage for mushrooms only if you're sure they're safely edible.*

VENTURE OUT

Isn't it high time to step away from technology and household chores to spend some time enjoying the great outdoors? No matter where you live, you likely have a hiking trail or park or greenbelt that would make a great place to reintroduce yourself to Mother Nature and hone your skills as a naturalist. Start with some short trail loops, work up to a full-day hike, and before you know it, you'll be ready to camp overnight.

Packing a Day Bag

No matter the length of your hike, it's a good idea to take a lightweight pack along, so you'll have necessities along with some handy items in case of injury. To maintain maximum mobility while you're out, opt for a pack with a narrow profile, and choose one that's appropriately sized to your needs. Backpacks are sized in liters based on the volume each will hold. A 10-liter pack allows enough room for a lightweight jacket and a few energy bars, whereas one twice that size allows for a more substantial lunch or extras like a field guide and camera.

When packing, place soft items in the area that will be pressing against your back, and heavier items toward the base of the pack. Although you want to be as prepared as possible, you'll also want to make certain that the pack remains light. Opt for the lightest versions of these essentials, and pack with comfort in mind.

- **Water:** Developed trails often provide access to potable water along the way, but check to be sure. I'm a big fan of "hydration packs" with a bladder and drinking tube for easy access. Alternately, carry a leakproof water bottle for each person, and refill it as you can. Even if water from a stream looks clear, do not drink from it without adding iodine tablets or running it through a purifier purchased from an outfitter. Hot weather means you'll crave more water, but remember to drink plenty even in cold weather—you're still exercising!

- **Food:** What you'll need in the way of food will depend on the length of your hike and your personal weight. You'll need to pack enough calories to keep you fueled throughout your hike. Depending upon weight, hikers burn between 400 to 500 calories an hour. Pack snacks like beef jerky, apple slices with peanut butter, dried fruits, and nuts for day trips. If you're heading out for just a couple of hours, high-protein bars are a good snack option. Keep your pack light by portioning only what you need, such as one granola bar each rather than the full box.

- **Sunscreen and insect repellent:** Even on cool days, the sun can pack a punch. Apply sunscreen before you head out, and be sure to reapply as the day progresses. Sunglasses and a hat are good ideas, too. Depending on conditions, mosquitoes and other insects might be a problem. Pack a small container of repellent just in case.

- **Light:** Pack a headlamp or flashlight along with extra batteries, even if you intend to be back well before dark, just in case.

- **Multifunction tool or knife:** Used for creating wood shavings to start a fire, sawing a small tree branch, or gutting fish, a multifunction tool has a knife blade plus numerous extra gadgets. See page 272 for discussion of knife blade styles.

- **First aid:** There are plenty of small ready-made first aid kits to choose from. At the very

Glorious vistas await backpackers and explorers who venture off the beaten path.

least, bandages are essential in case of injury, but they're also useful for protecting and treating blisters.

- **Personal hygiene:** When you've gotta go, you've gotta go. Pack a small trowel or foldable shovel to bury your waste, and a small amount of toilet paper (that you'll pack back out in your trash bag). Include feminine hygiene products, if necessary. Hand sanitizer is a good idea, too, if you're not hiking near a water source.

- **A trash bag:** Always pack out your litter to leave nothing but footprints behind.

- **Miscellaneous**: Does your pack have some extra room? Pack a camera or journal and pen to remember your journey. Pack a whistle for emergency use—to alert rescuers, even if your voice is tapped out. A bandanna has multiple uses and is easy to tuck into a pack. Use it as a sweatband, dust mask, or makeshift knapsack.

What to Wear

We're not talking fashion, here, but hiking function. First rule: Don't wear cotton. It absorbs moisture and takes a long time to dry. Instead, opt for clothing that is good at wicking moisture away from your body. You're bound to work up a sweat while hiking; clothing that allows moisture to evaporate prevents you from getting cold and also helps with chafing. Merino wool (it's not scratchy!) is an excellent natural material to choose.

If you're venturing out during the warm summer months, a lightweight long-sleeved shirt can help protect you from the sun and bugs. Choose pants or shorts that dry quickly (or pick up a pair of pants with zip-off legs for dual-purpose use). If you're in an area with ticks, wear long pants and tuck them into your socks—yes, it looks as dorky as you expect. Round out your outfit with a wide-brimmed hat to protect your face and neck from the sun.

Shoes, of course, should have good traction, provide some ankle support, and be comfortable. For easy hikes, a comfortable pair of tennis or walking shoes should work fine, but if you're crossing rough terrain, opt for hiking boots with ankle support. Wear wool hiking socks even in summer to help you avoid blisters and to wick moisture. The folks at Darn Tough have a good selection of socks, and offer a lifetime replacement warranty.

> **Packing Tip**
>
> Duct tape has myriad uses. Wind a small amount around your water bottle and peel off as needed—that way you can leave the full heavy roll at home.

It might seem like an extravagance to outfit yourself with gear that you'll only wear occasionally. Nothing is stopping you from hiking in everyday gym clothes, but good-quality gear will last you for years if it's cared for properly. And it will be a lot easier to enjoy your adventure if you're not feeling cold or uncomfortable.

Stay Warm and Dry

If you're unexpectedly stuck spending the night in the wilderness, a fire will help keep you warm (and act as a signal to rescuers). Take along a lighter or matches in a watertight container as well as fire-starting material. Bring a warm layer and hat in your pack if the weather may turn cool or wet. Although I generally try to avoid disposable plastic, a garbage bag or some zip-top baggies will protect your valuables if you get caught in the rain.

Navigation

Even popular routes can be missing trail markers or unmaintained, creating the real possibility that you could lose your way. A phone or GPS device can be useful, but you could easily lose service. Therefore, be sure to pack a map of the local area showing trails and topography. Mark the location of your car on the map. Out in the wild, a compass is probably more trustworthy—take some time to learn how to use it. It's always a good idea to leave a copy of your planned route in your vehicle or with a friend, in case it becomes necessary to track you down.

Understanding a Compass

A compass with a tiny magnetized metal needle that spins freely accurately locates north, south, east, and west. Earth's magnetic field causes the compass needle to move so that one end is pointed to magnetic north, and the other

A clear compass set over an area map makes orienting yourself easy in the wild.

south. If you're heading north, it's easy enough to simply walk in the direction the needle is pointing. However, if you're heading west, you'll need to walk in the direction that puts the compass needle pointing to your right.

A compass will help you get back on track if you lose your way—for example, navigating a rocky surface that lacks the clear direction provided by a dirt path, paddling across a lake, or locating a backcountry campsite. Compasses made of clear plastic can be set on a map so you can get your bearings relative to visible landmarks and your destination. Navigating by compass, sometimes called "orienteering," is an art form and fun hobby in its own right.

DIY

Neem Seed Mosquito Repellent

Heading into the woods means you're likely to be faced with mosquitoes. This homemade mosquito repellent is an effective alternative to DEET, the active ingredient in many commercial bug repellents. Although the EPA says DEET is safe to use if directions are followed, deaths and hospitalizations have been linked to the improper use of products made with this ingredient. I prefer not to risk it, and use a more natural option. Neem is a naturally occurring pesticide found in the seeds of the neem tree.

You'll Need:

2 tablespoons neem seed oil
1 tablespoon olive oil
1 tablespoon coconut oil
10 to 15 drops citronella essential oil

1. If necessary, melt coconut oil. (Most coconut oil solidifies at room temperature.)
2. Mix all ingredients together.
3. Store in a small jar or roller ball dispenser.
4. To use, rub onto exposed skin.

NOTE: You should not use neem seed oil if you are pregnant or trying to get pregnant, as it is a possible abortifacient.

BUILDING A FIRE

Maybe it's a primal instinct to gather around the flames or maybe it's the smoke-scented air, but sitting around a crackling fire provides an unrivaled sense of fulfillment and relaxation. Sipping a mug of coffee by a fire and listening to songbirds herald the arrival of the sun is the best way to start a day at camp. In the evening, a campfire is the hub of a campsite, drawing people together around the glowing embers. Knowing how to start a campfire might make you the most popular person in camp when it's time to roast marshmallows or on a chilly night when campers gather close for warmth.

The Necessity of Caution

Whether you're building a backyard bonfire or camping out overnight, there are some safety measures to consider. Most developed campsites have strict rules about campfires. (During the driest months, when forest fires are a real risk, these safety measures might even prohibit them.) You'll need to use your own judgment and an abundance of common sense when building a fire in rustic campsites—or even in your backyard.

Consider the season and fire danger before lighting up. Hot, dry conditions are risk factors, and if the weather calls for wind, rethink your plan. Remember, even if your fire is well contained, hot embers float and can ignite dry grass or leaves very quickly. If you see cause for concern, water down the area around your fire and always reserve enough water to douse the fire.

Choose a location devoid of overhanging branches and clear of dry grass. Using a shovel, dig a fire pit about six inches deep and two feet across. As you dig, pile the loose dirt on the outside of the circle for containment.

Required Materials

It's tempting to jump right in and start lighting up. But one key to a good fire is to patiently gather all your materials ahead of time. The small bits you use to start a fire will burn especially quickly. You don't want to run out and have to start all over again from the beginning.

You'll need tinder, kindling, and fuel wood to get your fire going.

Tinder materials burn fast and hot; it's crucial to have dry tinder to start a fire. Look for moss, dry leaves, grass, pine needles, or small bits of bark that will catch fire easily, or use a knife to slice wood shavings from one of your logs. When camping, it's not a bad idea to pack along some of your own dry tinder material or fire starters, especially if there's a chance that everything will be wet. Newspaper, cardboard boxes, toilet paper rolls, egg cartons, dryer lint, or jute twine are easy options. Fire-starter packets are always nice to have on hand, too.

Kindling is a bit more substantial than tinder—maybe the width of a pencil—and will burn longer. Dry twigs and small branches make good natural kindling. Again, if you have an ax or large knife, you can use it to create slivers from a dry log. Pine, in particular, catches fire easily. Green wood will bend but not snap—don't use that, as it will smoke but not catch fire.

Be prepared with dry material for starting campfires.

Airflow and dry materials are critical to successfully start a fire.

Fuel wood (ideally three to six inches in diameter) is what keeps the fire burning. Once these catch fire, courtesy of the kindling, these small logs will burn for some time. Fallen branches that are dry enough to break will catch fire readily, but it's less critical for fuel wood to be completely dry. A little dampness won't prevent the fire from taking off, though damp wood does tend to burn with more smoke.

Pick out a long, sturdy poker stick, or cut down a thin branch to tend your fire and rearrange burning logs from a safe distance.

How to Build a Fire

Ask a hundred people the best way to stack the materials to start a fire and you'll get a hundred different answers. People can be a bit passionate about their fire-starting methods—you've probably heard about the "log cabin," "tepee," or "lean-to" methods. Those are solid strategies, but they all have the same objective: Ignite little stuff to catch the bigger stuff on fire. Before getting caught up in construction plans, follow this foolproof system for campfire success.

A fire needs oxygen to burn. Piling all your fire materials tightly prevents oxygen flow. Instead, stack the materials in a way that allows channels of air.

Make a small pile of tinder, and position the kindling in a pyramid over the tinder. The gaps between the kindling sticks allow oxygen to enter. Place fuel logs nearby; they can help block the wind if necessary.

Once you've built a base of coals, larger logs will easily catch fire as you add them.

Now you can light the tinder—even in a few different places. Hold up a windscreen (anything flat will do) if a breeze is making it too difficult to sustain your lighter or the tinder. As the first kindling catches, keep adding more from the pile you've gathered, starting with small pieces. Once this is burning well, integrate some larger pieces. A good method is to put each new stick perpendicular to another to grow the area on fire. Use these as a bridge to guide the flame onto the large fuel logs. Once those are burning, you're pretty good to go. Keep adding fuel logs and smaller branches to continue building a crackling fire.

Maintaining the Fire

Until you have a bed of coals, you'll need to actively participate in the process. Blow or fan your smoldering kindling so it can grow into flames. As the kindling burns and the fuel wood catches fire, the wood will begin to collapse. As fuel wood burns down, continue adding more logs, remembering to maintain the airflow. Try to place them so they don't smash the burning wood, reducing oxygen flow. Save one long stick to use as a poker to keep your distance from the hot flames.

Dousing the Fire

Put out the fire before leaving the area or heading off to bed. Pour water on the fire, stirring it around to make sure that the coals are thoroughly drenched.

DIY

Tuna Can Stove

Sometimes—say, when you're in a no-fire zone, your firewood is wet or unavailable, or the power goes out at home—you'll need a way to warm food without the benefit of a campfire. A backpackers' trick is to make a few of these tuna can stoves to keep on hand for emergencies or to tuck into your backpack for hot coffee on the trail.

You'll Need:

Recycled corrugated cardboard
Empty tuna can (or other shallow tin can)
Wax (any wax will do, but beeswax burns longest)
Melt-and-pour container (see page 74)

1. Cutting across the grain, trim cardboard into strips the same height as the tuna can.
2. Coil the strips of cardboard, placing them in the

tuna can. Add more strips until the tuna can is filled with cardboard.

3. Put wax in the melt-and-pour container. Set in a saucepan and add water to reach halfway up the can. Cook over medium heat for 10 to 15 minutes or until wax is melted.
4. Pour melted wax into the tuna can, leaving about ⅛ inch of cardboard visible above the wax. You can use it immediately or allow the wax to cool.
5. To light the stove, hold a match or lighter to the exposed cardboard until it catches fire.
6. To use for cooking, find three level rocks slightly taller than the tuna can. Set in a triangle with the tuna can stove at the center. Place a light cooking pan on the three rocks and use just like a single-burner Sterno stove. Elevating the pan on rocks allows air to flow to the fire, but prop up a windscreen if there is a breeze.

For warming a meal on the go, pack one (or two) of these tuna can stoves for a quick heat source.

OUTDOOR COOKING

Cooking in the great outdoors—whether for a backyard campout or a weeklong sojourn into the woods—requires a different skill set than preparing meals at home. Packing along a propane burner means that frying eggs for breakfast or whipping up a batch of chili for dinner is easy enough. But there are certainly other ways to cook food and produce a hot meal while you're enjoying the fresh air and wide-open spaces. Weenie roasts and s'mores are just a gateway to the potentially gourmet world of campfire cuisine that you can enjoy with just a little extra planning before you head out.

Campfire Cookery

The area directly above a campfire is quite hot. If you plan to grill over the open flames, build your fire off to one side of the fire ring. Set your grill in place on the opposite side of the ring and rake coals under the grill to achieve desired heat.

You'll also want to be certain to have cooking equipment that's well suited to the open flames. Cast iron is the best cookware (see page 274), and you'll need long-handled metal utensils, like a spatula and tongs. Stainless steel is also safe, but don't use nonstick pans over a campfire—the high heat of an open flame can cause the chemical coating to degrade. Remember to pack pot holders and a trivet for handling hot dishes. If you cook over open flames on a regular basis, you might want to invest in a pair of welders' gloves. Unconventional, sure—but they work.

Your campfire pots are bound to get sooty so bring a designated storage sack for packing them home without getting soot on the rest of your gear. A Boy Scout trick is to coat the outside of the pot with liquid soap before using. It's hard to sterilize your cookware and dishes thoroughly while outdoors so always rewash at home when you unpack from a trip.

Portioning Is a Camper's Best Friend

Before leaving home, measure out exactly how much food you'll need into a small cloth bag or plastic baggie, rather than bringing the entire box. It will reduce the weight or your pack, as well as the waste you'll need to pack out:

- Pull out a few granola bars and oatmeal packets.
- Get single-serving hot chocolate packets or instant coffee.
- Measure a serving of dry pasta into a smaller container or baggie.
- Grate cheese at home and carry in a baggie so you don't need a grater on trail.
- Save mini-jars and bottles to reuse for portioning: A washed-out hot sauce bottle can be perfect for a portion of olive oil, vinegar, or maple syrup.

DIY

Roll-Up Utensil Wrap

Taking along a lightweight set of utensils makes sense for camping out, picnics, and hiking. Tucking one into a purse or your car's glove compartment means you can skip the disposable plasticware when you find yourself grabbing meals on the run, too. This easy project starts with a thrift store place mat, but you could also use a similarly sized hemmed piece of fabric.

You'll Need:

Lightweight fabric place mat
18-inch length of wide ribbon
Straight pin
Sewing machine with thread to match place mat

1. Set the place mat in front of you, wrong side up. Fold the place mat in thirds, then unfold the top

This easy wrap makes it easy to take real utensils along on your adventures.

layer. You've created a pocket along the bottom.

2. Place the ribbon behind the place mat with 9 inches extending out past the right edge and 9 inches under. Align so that it sits just below the folded over edge. Use a straight pin to secure the ribbon in place at the right edge. This will be the tie for the utensil wrap.
3. Use a straight stitch (see page 84) to sew the right and left sides of the pocket together. You'll sew the ribbon in place at this step, too.
4. Mark four pencil lines about an inch and a half apart, starting at (and parallel to) the left side of the place mat.
5. Use a straight stitch to sew along these lines from the bottom of the pocket to the top edge.

Keep Your Cooler Extra Cool

When it's hot out, ice can melt quickly in a cooler. To slow the process, cover the cooler with a reflective windshield shade. Freezing ice blocks in milk cartons will keep melt water contained so it doesn't make your produce soggy.

6. Slip utensils into each slot (bamboo utensils are lightweight and good for hiking), and roll up lengthwise. Tie closed with the ribbon.

RECIPE

Make-Ahead Breakfast Burritos

Makes 8 burritos

Make these breakfast burritos at home for an easy hot breakfast at camp. The prep work takes place at home, but tuck the foil-wrapped packets among the coals at the outer part of the fire and they'll be warm in no time. Refrigerated, these burritos will keep for several days.

You'll Need:

8 flour tortillas
1 tablespoon olive oil
½ cup diced onion
½ cup diced bell pepper
12 eggs
1 cup diced ham
2 cups shredded cheddar cheese
½ teaspoon salt
½ teaspoon pepper

1. To make the tortillas easier to roll, wrap them in aluminum foil and place in a 350°F oven for 15 minutes.
2. Meanwhile, heat the oil in a skillet. Add the onion and bell pepper, and cook over medium-high heat until soft.
3. Crack the eggs into a bowl and whisk to combine.
4. Add the eggs and ham to the skillet. Cook, stirring occasionally, until the eggs are set. Stir in the cheese, salt, and pepper.
5. Divide the scrambled eggs between the warmed tortillas.
6. Roll up and wrap the breakfast burritos in heavy-duty aluminum foil. Refrigerate, then transport in a cooler when you head out to camp.
7. To warm breakfast burritos at camp, set them on mature, grayish coals in a single layer. Cook for 10 to 15 minutes, turning once with tongs during cooking time.

What Can You Cook on a Stick?

Obviously, marshmallows and hot dogs. But there are other fun options as well. Just be sure to wait until your fire dies down to glowing coals, rather than cooking over roaring flames that may incinerate your meal:

- Bring along a batch of homemade pizza dough (or two, if you plan to make pizza!) to make curly bread sticks. Pull off pieces of dough, roll them into long skinny pieces, then wrap them around the end of your stick. Hold over the flames until nicely browned.
- Skewer chunks of pineapple and peaches for a grilled fruit salad.
- Thread cherry tomatoes and fresh basil onto a stick for the beginnings of a roasted caprese salad (just add mozzarella).
- Thread a piece of bacon onto your roasting stick and cook it to crispy perfection.

Food on a Stick

Perhaps the easiest (and most fun) way to cook over a campfire is dangling food directly over the flames, à la roasted marshmallows. To safely cook food in this manner, you'll need a good, long stick to get the food close to the heat without burning yourself. Seek out green wood to prevent the stick from catching fire. Whittle one end to be pointy and free of bark.

You can cook more than just marshmallows on a stick!

Tinfoil Meals

Once your campfire has a nice bed of coals, you can cook some dishes directly on them. Wrap individual vegetables like potatoes or corn on the cob in heavy-duty aluminum foil, and tuck them into coals that are hot but no longer flaming. Cook corn for 10 minutes or so. Potatoes will take longer; give them a squeeze to test for doneness. Use tongs to turn them a couple times while cooking.

Tinfoil packet meals are another option for cooking directly in the fire, and the options are endless. Cut meat and vegetables into similar sizes to assure that everything will be done at the same time. Season as desired, and wrap individual servings in heavy-duty aluminum foil. Place packets on mature coals, and cook until done. This is variable and will depend on the heat of your coals and the meal you're cooking. Think about how long it would take to cook a similar meal on the stove top and use that as your guide.

Apples, Brie cheese, and honey combine to make a deliciously decadent campfire sandwich.

Campfire Sandwiches

Sandwiches are an easy camp lunch, but you can up your game with hot varieties. The possibilities are endless and can include sweet or savory options, making them good choices for breakfast and dinner, too. Campfire sandwiches are also a great way to use up leftovers.

To warm the sandwiches, brush the outside with a bit of olive oil or butter and wrap in foil. Set a grate two to three inches above glowing coals and cook the sandwiches for about five minutes on each side. Try these combinations between two slices of bread or ready-made waffles:

- Peanut butter with sliced bananas and a drizzle of honey
- Thinly sliced apples and raisins with cinnamon and honey
- Ricotta cheese and your favorite homemade jam
- Brie cheese and thinly sliced apples or blueberries (or both!)
- Pepperoni, sliced olives, and mozzarella cheese with a light spread of pizza sauce
- Cheddar cheese, crispy bacon, and shredded chicken
- Tomato slices, pesto, mozzarella, and shredded chicken
- Goat cheese and grilled veggies
- Apricot jam, Brie cheese, and crumbled bacon
- Scrambled eggs, ham, bell pepper, and cheddar cheese

DIY

Cleaning a Fish

If the fish you're making for dinner is fresh out of a lake or stream, you'll probably want to gut it in preparation for cooking. Although some small fish are cooked whole, most people prefer to remove the icky bits before putting them on the grill. This also makes for faster cooking fish.

Fish Skin and Scales

Some fish have hard scales that will need to be removed before you cook dinner. A good rule of thumb is that if scales come off in your hands while handling the fish, you should descale it. Use a spoon to scrape the scales from the fish. Do this outside, as scales tend to scatter when you do this. You don't want to be picking scales off the ceiling. Fish can be cooked with the skin on, or the skin can be removed.

A sharp knife is a must for cleaning fresh fish.

You'll Need:
A cutting board on a sturdy surface
A sharp knife

1. Set the fish flat on the cutting board. Removing the head is optional.
2. Insert a knife into the fish's belly near the anal opening, with the blade facing the head. Cutting shallowly (to avoid the intestines), move the knife up the body toward the head.
3. Spread the fish open, and slide your finger along the backbone to remove the entrails. You'll notice that these are still attached at the anus. Use the knife to cut a V shape around the anus to remove them.
4. If there's a kidney attached to the backbone (some fish have one), use a spoon to remove this.
5. Thoroughly rinse the fish, inside and out.
6. Store the fish on ice until you're ready to cook it.

RECIPE

Fresh Fish Foil Packet

Makes 4 foil packets

For this recipe, use fresh fillets, or if you've been lucky on the lake, whole, small trout works well, too; you'll just have to avoid the bones in the cooked fish, and you may need to cook the fish slightly longer.

You'll Need:
2 medium zucchini
1 medium yellow onion
1 red bell pepper
3 lemons
4 fish fillets
4 tablespoons olive oil
Salt and pepper
Herbs such as thyme (optional)

1. Slice the zucchini, onion, red pepper, and 2 lemons into ¼-inch-thick rounds; set aside.
2. Lay out four sheets of aluminum foil (each about 12 × 15 inches). Divide the lemon rounds between the foil, placing them near the center.
3. Set the fish fillets on top of the lemon slices. (In addition to flavoring the fish, this helps prevent it from sticking to the foil.)
4. Drizzle the fish fillets with olive oil, and generously sprinkle with salt and pepper.
5. Set the sliced vegetables and herbs on top of the fish, dividing them between the four packets.
6. Halve the third lemon and squeeze its juice over the vegetables.
7. Fold up the edges of the aluminum foil, crimping them securely so no steam can escape.
8. Grill over glowing coals; cook for 15 minutes.

Sealing fish along with vegetables and a squeeze of lemon in tin foil makes a flavorful and easy camp meal.

BUSHCRAFT KNIVES

From harvesting plants, to shaving wood kindling, to gutting your fresh-caught fish, a good, well-sharpened blade can become outdoorsmen's or -women's favorite tool. A multitool like a Leatherman certainly provides a lot of options—but will you really use all those foldout gadgets? A larger fixed-blade knife is safer and can also be incredibly versatile. Quality blades are long-lasting tools you can pass down through the generations.

❶ **Drop point:** This versatile knife with a strong tip resists breaking. Favored by hunters as a skinning knife, the more subtle point is not good for piercing. This is a good option for cleaning fish.

❷ **Clip point:** With a sharper and thinner tip than a drop point blade, the clip point is better for piercing but also more susceptible to breaking. A clip point blade is good for slicing and controlled cuts.

❸ **Sheepsfoot:** The flat blade and rounded tip of a sheepsfoot knife minimizes the risk of accidental punctures. It's a good choice for camp cooking. Sailors favor this blade style for cutting through ropes and rigging without piercing their sails.

❹ **Serrated:** A serrated blade might be handy if you expect to saw through trees or rope, but they're not as versatile. A big drawback: They're difficult to sharpen. Fortunately, many bushcraft knives have a serrated portion of the blade.

❺ **Foraging knife:** If foraging for wild edibles and medicinals is your thing, you may want to invest in a knife specifically designed for that purpose. With a smooth, curved blade on one side and a serrated portion on the other, this knife covers all the bases. The brush will gently sweep away debris or insects.

4 Serrated
OPINEL
INOX
OPINEL
SAVOIE FRANCE
5 Foraging knife
ELSALVADOR
1 Drop point
3 Sheepsfoot
OLD TIMER
SCHRADE
Clip point 2

CAST-IRON COOKERY

One of the greatest investments you can make as a cook is a collection of cast-iron cookware. If you care for it well, cast iron will last generations. It's the very best option for cooking over an open fire and a great asset in the homestead kitchen as well.

A well-seasoned cast-iron pan has a great nonstick surface. We fry eggs in our cast-iron frying pan; with just a bit of oil, eggs are easy to flip, and cleanup is a breeze. Is it *equally* as nonstick as Teflon or ceramic surfaces? Probably not. But a cast-iron nonstick surface doesn't have a chemical coating, it can go from stove top to oven, and can even be used over open flames, which makes it a favorite option for camping (or at least, car camping). You can pick up a new, preseasoned pan or salvage an old pan. Thrift stores and yard sales often have cast-iron pans for a bargain price. Steel wool and elbow grease can get rust out of used cast iron, or you can contact an auto body shop and arrange to have your piece sandblasted.

How to Season Cast Iron

The "seasoning" on cast iron is what protects the metal from the elements and what, in time, will provide its nonstick quality. You don't need to season the pan every time you use it. Think of it as a way to resuscitate a piece when it's a bit weak, a pan that's been sitting in the cupboard for a long while, or one that's been exposed to soapy water. Cast iron works best when it's used regularly!

To season your piece, start with a clean, rust-free surface. Use a rag to spread a very thin layer of cooking oil over the entire surface. Line the bottom rack of the oven with aluminum foil. Place the pan upside down on the rack above the foil. This prevents the oil from puddling inside the pan. Turn the oven to 350°F, and bake for an hour. Turn off the oven, allowing the pan to cool inside. Once cooled, it's ready for use.

How to Clean Cast Iron

Proper care of cast iron is a surprisingly hot topic. People are passionate about how they clean their cast iron. Some use soap; some do not. Some people prevent their cast iron from ever having contact with water. Certainly, you don't want to let it sit in water, but a little rinse to clean it won't hurt it. (Don't put it in the dishwasher, though!)

Rinse with water while the pan is still hot then sprinkle in one to two tablespoons of coarse salt. Use a scrubber brush to scrub away any remnants of food or cooked-on bits and rinse again. Dry thoroughly by placing the pan back on the stove over low heat for a few minutes until it's dry. Reapply a very light layer of cooking oil before storing it away.

Cast iron loves oil and grease! It's what creates and maintains its nonstick surface. Grandma knew what she was doing when she wiped the bacon grease from the pan and set it back on the stove without washing it. If you're offended by the idea of skipping soap, you can still use it. But know that it will be harder to acquire that lovely cast-iron seasoning.

Using Dutch Ovens Outdoors

In the popular *Little House on the Prairie* books, Ma cooked dinner for her family in something called a "spider." It was essentially a deep skillet with three legs, used for cooking directly over coals. Elevating the pot above the coals (rather than sitting directly on them) helps provide a more even cooking temperature and

A cast-iron Dutch oven offers up many open-air culinary possibilities.

prevents burning on the bottom, but a flat-bottomed Dutch oven can still achieve great results. Lodge is a very recognizable—and durable—brand of cast iron to look for.

To bake over an open fire, you'll need to surround the Dutch oven with heat to mimic the heat of a kitchen oven. Placing hot coals under the oven and on top of the lid serves this purpose.

Most Dutch oven baking recipes call for charcoal briquettes. The best way to prepare these is with a specialized tube of aluminum called a chimney, just like starting coals for a barbecue. Place the chimney on a fireproof surface, put some crumpled paper in the bottom, and add the number of coals you'll need. Light the paper and let the coals heat just until they stop flaming. You can also use coals from a campfire. Choose red-hot coals similar in size to charcoal briquettes.

DIY

Baking in a Dutch Oven

Cake, brownies, fruit crumbles, and even sourdough bread can be cooked in a Dutch oven, though it can take some practice to get just right. Cooking outside has more variables than using a calibrated oven in the kitchen, but it's a fun activity for camping (and in case of emergency power outages, the skill could serve you well).

1. Choose an area clear of flammable materials in which to cook. Rake away any dry leaves or pine needles that might catch fire.
2. Fill the Dutch oven with your prepared recipe, such as the following campfire pizza recipe, and cover with the lid.
3. To maintain a temperature of about 350°F inside the Dutch oven, place 7 or 8 (2-inch) coals in the

cleared cooking area as the base. Set the Dutch oven on top of these coals.

4. Using tongs, place 10 to 12 (2-inch) hot coals on the lid.
5. Bake for the required length of time. If you're converting a recipe for the Dutch oven, baking time should be similar to that required in a standard recipe, but test for doneness before you discard the coals.

NOTE: To maintain the oven's heat for more than 40 minutes or so, you'll need to replace the old coals with hotter ones. Start a new chimney full of coals about 20 minutes after you initially started cooking, or pull fresh coals from the campfire.

RECIPE

Campout Pizza

There's only one rule for assembling pizza to be cooked in a Dutch oven: Go easy on the moisture. You might normally opt for extra sauce, but in this case, lots of sauce will create steam inside the oven, leading to a soggy crust. Therefore, go light on the sauce, as well as on veggies like mushrooms and peppers, which have a high moisture content. If you like to use lots of veggies, sauté them first to remove some of the moisture. To make this pizza in the great outdoors, make the dough at home in advance.

You'll Need:

Prepared raw pizza dough (use Family Favorite Pizza Dough on page 52)
Pizza sauce
Mozzarella cheese
Toppings
Special equipment: 30 coals for a 10-inch oven or 33 coals for a 12-inch oven (or more if making multiple pizzas), parchment paper, 3 metal skewers, long-handled pliers for lifting the lid, tongs for lifting coals

■ **At home:** Make the pizza dough, seal the ball in a zip-top bag with a bit of olive oil, and freeze. Keep in a cooler until you're ready to cook it. Before using the dough, transfer it to a bowl and allow it to come to air temperature.

■ **At camp:**

1. Prepare the coals (see previous page). Begin cooking when they are red hot and the flames begin to die down.
2. Preheat the empty Dutch oven by spreading 10 of the red-hot coals under the oven and 20 red-hot coals around the rim of the lid (11 coals under and 22 coals on top for a larger oven).
3. Roll out the pizza dough on parchment paper. (No rolling pin at the campsite? Your water bottle or a sauce jar works in a pinch!) Shape the dough into a round that will fit easily into the bottom of the Dutch oven.
4. Spread a thin layer of pizza sauce on the dough; add cheese and toppings as desired.
5. Use pliers to lift the lid.
6. Lift the uncooked pizza by the parchment paper and lower it into the Dutch oven, including the parchment paper.
7. To allow some steam to escape without losing a lot of heat during cooking, set the metal skewers across the open oven, then set the lid on top of them.
8. Bake until the crust is browned, 15 to 20 minutes.
9. If you're cooking more than 1 pizza, refresh the coals between each.

RECIPE

Campfire Corn Bread

If you're planning to make this corn bread on a camping trip, mix together the dry ingredients (with the exception of the sugar) at home. It will make the preparation more streamlined once you reach camp.

You'll Need:

⅔ cup butter, softened, plus 1 tablespoon for cooking
¾ cup sugar
3 eggs
1⅔ cups milk
2 cups unbleached all-purpose flour
1⅓ cups cornmeal
1½ tablespoons baking powder
½ teaspoon salt
Special equipment: 24 coals for a 10-inch oven or 27 coals for a 12-inch oven, long-handled pliers for lifting the lid, tongs for lifting coals

1. Prepare the coals (see previous page).
2. In a mixing bowl, cream the ⅔ cup butter and the sugar with a wooden spoon.
3. Add the eggs and milk, and stir until well combined.

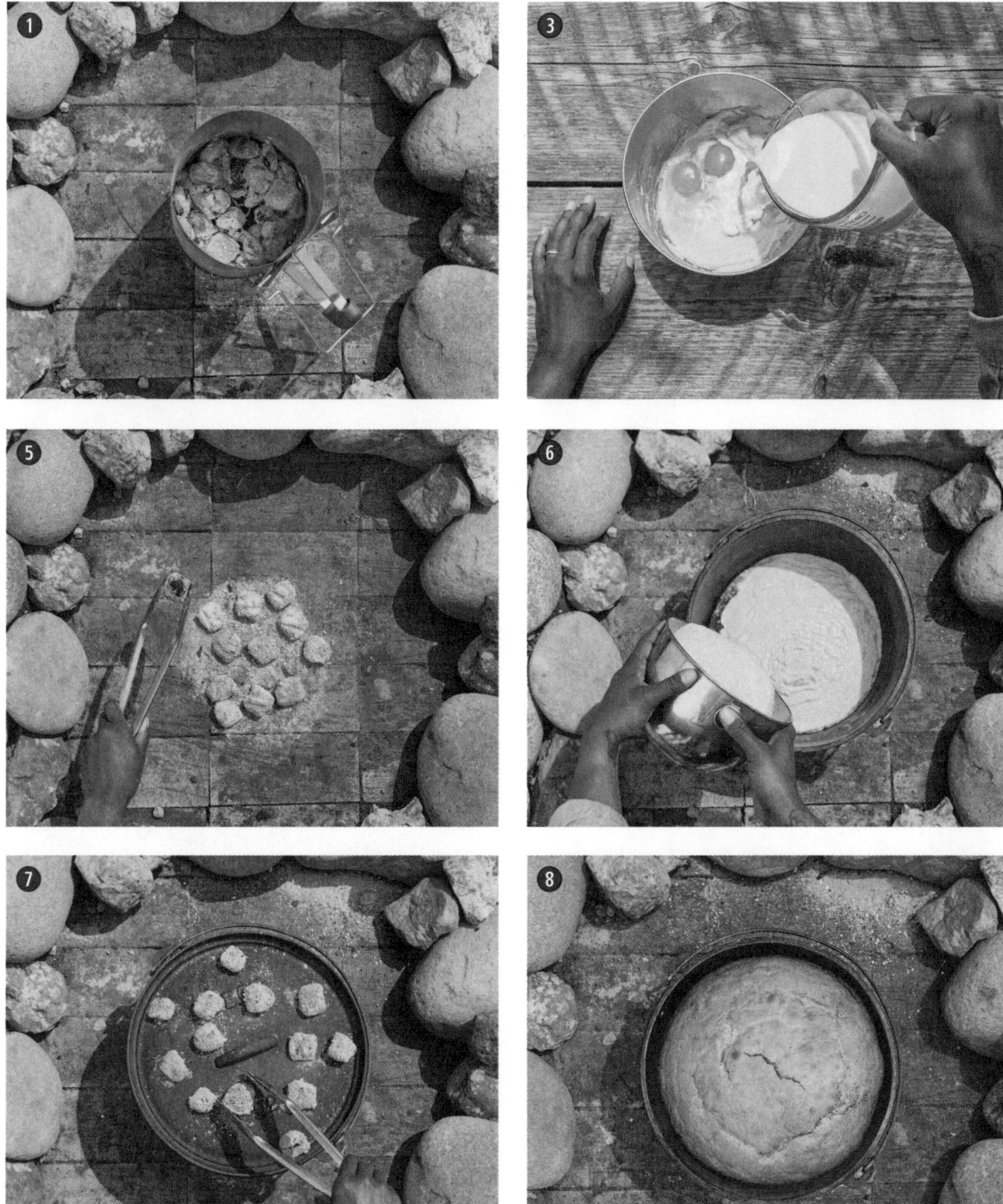

4. In a bowl, combine the flour, cornmeal, baking powder, and salt, then stir them into the wet ingredients.
5. Set out 8 to 10 red-hot coals, and place the Dutch oven on top to warm.
6. Drop the remaining tablespoon of butter into the Dutch oven to melt, swirling it to coat the bottom and up the sides. Pour the batter into the oven and cover.
7. Place the remaining hot coals on the lid.
8. Cook until a knife inserted in the center of the corn bread comes out clean, 25 to 30 minutes.

NATURAL SHELTERS

Long before REI gear and pop-up tents became the norm, spending time out of doors meant knowing how to create a shelter with whatever was on hand if the need arose. From shade and wind protection to shelter from an unexpected storm, building shelter is still a valuable skill for resourceful folks who prefer natural materials. These green structures are fun to build and can be surprisingly cozy.

Leaf Hut

Stand a dozen or so tall, straight branches upright, leaning them together following a clockwise pattern. Tie the poles together at the top with rope or long grasses. Push the bases of the poles into the ground to secure them, adjusting each until the structure stands solidly. Lean leafy branches over the gaps to provide protection from sun and wind. You can also build a structure like this using a tree as a support post in the center. It means a little less space inside, but that might be a good trade-off—this method can be easier to build, especially if you're working alone.

Lean-To for Rain

One of the easiest types of shelter to make, a lean-to utilizes a natural formation such as a large deadfall, big boulder, or bank as one "wall" of the structure. Lean several long branches against the solid "wall," then secure several more long branches horizontally, to create a grid. Create a solid cover by adding leafy branches, large leaves, or even long grasses, overlapping the layers as you move toward the top, much like house shingles are installed. By doing so, you'll encourage the rain to flow from the top layer to the next until it reaches the ground, instead of seeping through.

A hammock is perfect for sleeping or relaxing the day away.

A Trusty Tarp

For most emergency shelters, a tarp is your best bet—this multipurpose item should be in everyone's car or camping kit. Tie it overhead for shade or a rain shelter, string it into an A-frame shape for an improvised tent, hang it as a hammock, or stake it out as a lean-to windscreen.

Triangle Hut

Gather branches (about three feet long) and sort them into similar lengths, progressing from shortest to longest. (Using forked branches can help lock the structure together as you build it.) Beginning with the shortest lengths, set two branches together into a peak or upside-down V shape. Match this V shape with two more branches. Continue in this manner until the hut is long enough for you to lie down in. Keep the shelter low—no more than three feet high—to help retain body heat. The base of the structure should be wide enough to accommodate one or two people in a prone position. Once the structure is complete, you can add a thick layer of dry leaves, twigs, and other nearby detritus to help insulate it from wind and cold.

Leaning downed limbs against a sturdy tree trunk provides a foundation for reducing exposure to inclement weather.

OBSERVING NATURE

If your time outdoors is typically spent barbecuing in the backyard, you might need a refresher course in the signs that nature provides for us. The 20th-century writer, biologist, and conservationist Rachel Carson wrote that "it is not half so important to *know* as to *feel*. If facts are the seeds that later produce knowledge and wisdom, then the emotions and the impressions of the senses are the fertile soil in which the seeds must grow."

Gaining the expertise of a naturalist takes practice, but it all starts with paying attention and knowing what to look for.

An awareness of the surrounding area—trees! blue sky! wildflowers!—is, first and foremost, awe-inspiring. But taking time to really look at the world around gives us a chance to read nature. We begin to notice things like the coarseness of a tree's bark, the surface of rocks and stones along a path, and the level of water in streams.

These observations can help you explore a new environment and understand the interconnected web of life you're stepping into. Spotting an incoming storm or rising stream could even be lifesaving. If you're lucky enough to return to the same destination several times a year, you can track the changes you see, noting differences like the lay of the land, leaf color, water flow, and animal behavior. Perceiving nature like this is an interesting endeavor in its own right, but practicing your observation skills can benefit other efforts. For instance, gardeners who are keenly aware of changes in their environment might notice minor damage to tomato plants and find the tomato hornworm *before* it decimates the entire crop.

Keeping a Field Journal

Maintaining a record of your observations will help you remember specimens you find, but also give you a chance to assess how one sighting compares to another to detect patterns and rhythms. (See pages 102-103 for how to make a leather journal.) Whether tracking flora or fauna, include these good points of information:

- Location
- Date
- Time of day
- Temperature
- Current weather conditions (make note of wind, rain, clouds, or sunny skies)
- Earlier weather conditions
- Soil conditions
- Size of the organism you're observing
- Proximity to other organisms
- Behavior notes

For plants

- Condition and color of leaves
- Flowers
- Seeds

For insects

- Describe behavior
- Interaction (are they mating or fighting?)

Natural Weather Forecasting

Although numerous folk sayings foretell weather, some hold up to scientific scrutiny. Take these, for example:

- **Pinecones seal up with damp weather.** As the reproductive part of the tree, the seeds within the cone must remain viable. In dry weather, the outer part of the cone dries more rapidly than the inner part, causing the cone to open. When those scales absorb moisture during wet weather, they close up to protect the seed.

Taking notes or sketching nature is even more fun using a hand-crafted journal.

■ **Ring around the moon, 'twill rain soon.** Those halos ringing the moon (or sun) are caused by light reflecting off the millions of ice crystals in high-altitude cirrus clouds. Although the skies may appear clear, a halo is an indicator that clouds are forming 20,000 feet up, and that rain may be on the way.

■ **When hawks fly low, prepare for a blow.** Low-flying birds are an indicator that bad weather is brewing. Here's why: When air pressure drops before a storm, the air gets heavier, making it harder for birds to fly. They compensate by flying lower. *Hawks flying high means a clear sky.*

Making Waves

It's easy to bask in the beauty when you're near a body of water. But wave patterns shift and change from season to season or day to day.

Ocean tides shift from low to high twice a day on a pretty regular schedule. If you'll be spending time at the seaside, pick up a tide chart for the area; these list the time of high and low tides. Tide pools are accessible during low tide and great for exploring, but keeping track of the incoming waves will help you avoid getting stranded in an area that's underwater when the tide is high.

Tidal rivers, estuaries, and streams surprisingly far inland may rise and fall several feet over the course of a day. Take note of the level of a stream when you arrive by choosing a few recognizable rocks as markers. If you notice the rocks becoming more submerged, it can mean the water level is rising. In an area that's prone to flash flooding, tracking the water level can help you avoid a dangerous situation. Running water like streams, rivers, or brooks will also have a current that will lead you back to the source.

Spending the day at the lake? If you look closely, you might be able to see a "waterline." Receding water levels leave behind a band of earth with no vegetation. In severe drought, the waterline can be vast. If a waterline is not visible, the lake is at capacity.

Coastal tide pools teem with life.

Check the Hot Spots

Earth is teeming with life, but narrowing your search to habitat hot spots will give the best chance at witnessing wildlife "at large." All these ventures require stealth and patience—as well as a good bit of luck—on behalf of wildlife watchers!

The seashore is big, but narrow your search to a tidal pool and you may be rewarded with hermit crabs, sea stars, algae, barnacles, mussels, and other fascinating marine life in the shallows. Water recedes from tidal marshes at low tide, offering the best chance to see crabs, mollusks, wetland birds, and turtles.

In the forest, look for a downed tree—its slow decay supports a wide variety or organisms. Fungi and plants will grow quickly, bringing birds to feed off insects or fruit; deer mice may nest in the stump, and salamanders and newts may inhabit the log's damp recess.

Finding a water source, whether a creek in a dry canyon or a pond on the prairie, allows an opportunity to see a variety of mammals as they come by to hydrate.

Birdsong

Animal behavior ebbs and flows with the seasons. In springtime, birds build nests and hatch their young. Wild ducks and geese are probably the most visible example of this, as ducklings and goslings parade across ponds and lakes. Although songbirds hide their nests well, birds of prey often build their enormous nests at the top of dead trees—or even telephone poles. If you spot one, keep your eyes on the nest and you may be lucky enough to see its residents. (Binoculars can help with this.)

An estimated five billion birds migrate across North America. Spring and fall are the traffic seasons for migratory birds—the ones you often see stitch the sky in a V as they relocate to their seasonal home. Birds navigate along a relatively fixed path called a flyway, which always runs north to south and back again. Find out if your home is on a flyway, and check the forecast of birdlife coming your way; ornithologists report this information in a similar manner to meteorologists who forecast the weather on television. During peak migration, hundreds or even thousands of birds will pass overhead both day and night. You'll have the best chance of observing birds at a "stop-over point" on the flyway, usually a wildlife refuge or park. Similar to pit stops humans make on a road trip, these locations are rich in water and food that help birds refuel for the journey ahead.

Find the North Star

Otherwise known as the North Star, Polaris is situated over the North Pole, and unlike other stars in the sky, it remains in a relatively fixed position. Polaris is visible from anywhere in the Northern Hemisphere. But famous though it may be, it is not the brightest object in the night sky. Finding it takes a little skill and practice; it helps to check a dark sky free from city light pollution or even the glare of your house lights.

We all know the Big Dipper, right? We can use that as a guide to help us find Polaris. The two stars on the "front" of the Dipper (opposite the handle) are sometimes called the Guardians of the Pole. Connect the dots between those two stars, starting at the base of the Dipper, and follow that line up to Polaris. Check

Identifying Stars

If gazing at the universe enthralls you, there's an app for that. Download Star Chart, and point your phone at stars in the sky; the app will tell you what you're looking at. There are 88 official constellations that you can learn to identify!

Escaping bright city lights makes the stars in our night sky far more visible.

your work with a compass—are you pointing north?

Polaris is a fixed star: As seasons pass, the various constellations shift, slowly spinning around it. The sky you see in springtime will differ from what you see in fall or winter.

Flying Nightlife

Moths of all colors and sizes come out after dark. You can take a closer look by creating a moth trap. (Don't worry; none will be harmed!)

As you know, moths are attracted to light, so it's not difficult to draw them to a viewing area where you can easily see their markings and antennae. Simply hang a white sheet on a clothesline and set a couple of flashlights so that they shine against the white fabric. The brightness will attract moths, and you'll be able to observe them up close. This would be a great time to get out your sketchbook to capture the patterns on their wings or the shape of their antennae.

One caveat: The surrounding area needs to be dark. In a backyard, that means turning out all household lights; at a campsite, turn off the lanterns.

TRAIL SIGNS AND TRACKING

When you're out exploring all that nature has to offer, it's important to remember that you're sharing space with the wild creatures that live there. From tiny mites to great whales, animals vastly outnumber human beings on planet Earth—but it doesn't feel that way when you're searching for a glimpse through your binoculars. The lucky few among us have witnessed a bison herd on the prairie, a migrating flock of birds, or a whirlwind of bats exiting their roost. However, knowing how to spot some simple signs to clue you in on the resident critters can both satisfy your curiosity and help avoid a potentially dangerous encounter. Hunters use these clues as well as they track their prey.

Footprints

Clear tracks, if you're lucky enough to find them, are a great way to deduce what types of animals might be nearby. Not surprisingly, wild felines like mountain lions and bobcats leave prints that are quite similar to their domesticated cat cousins. Likewise, coyote and fox tracks will appear similar to a dog's. It's fairly easy to discern between mammalian tracks and bird tracks, but avian tracks can differ quite a bit between bird species. Webbed tracks, for instance, might clue you in to the presence of geese, ducks, or gulls. Hoofed tracks are common throughout North America; they are more likely to be deer but could also be moose or elk, depending on your location. Use a field guide to familiarize yourself with which species are in range.

Here are the questions to answer to help identify animal tracks:

- **Size:** Taking note of the print's size is easy if you carry a ruler on naturalist expeditions, and can help you tell the difference between two similar animals. Keep in mind, though, that a small print could belong to a young animal.

- **Number of toes:** This will help narrow down what group of animals the tracks belong to. Bears have five toes; canines and felines have four.

- **Weight of indentation:** A heavier animal will make a deeper print, but this can also indicate that an animal was running or jumping when it made the print.

- **Nails or webbing:** Nails are not always visible on a print, but generally speaking, canine nails are more visible than feline. (Cats' nails are usually retracted when walking.) A webbed print is a clue that your animal is aquatic.

- **Gait:** The stride and straddle of prints can also help you narrow down an animal's identity. Stride is the distance between the heel of one print to the heel of the other print (on the same side). Straddle is the width between the outside of the left and right prints.

- **Front versus rear:** There may be a difference in size and shape between front and rear feet. This can be subtle, or obvious, such as a raccoon's small, front C-shaped heel pad compared to its elongated rear heel pad.

Trailing Along and Bedding Down

That narrow trail cut through the underbrush is likely a path carved by the passage of a variety of wild animals. If you opt for this well-worn route, be aware—they may still be close by! Although your scent and the noise you make will likely scare away any nearby animals, be cautious just in case. If you find a trampled depression in vegetation, you've probably found a spot where deer bed down for the night. These could be out in the open in a meadow, or tucked into a more protected area—but they are generally used only once.

If you know what you're looking for, animal tracks offer clues about the critters that left them behind.

Scratching an Itch

Keep an eye on the trees. Areas with bark worn off or visible score marks could indicate that animals are using the tree as a scratching post. Male deer—bucks—rub their antlers on small trees in an effort to rub off the velvet, a hairy layer that covers antlers during their spring and summer growth. When antlers stop growing for the season, the velvet sheds. Bucks help the process along, giving us clues to their presence along the way.

Cougars and other wildcats, as well as bears, often score marks in tree bark with their claws. Chunks of bark completely pulled away from a tree can indicate a bite, which bears use to mark their turf. Bears will also remove bark from a tree to use as nesting material. Tree bark that appears to have been smoothed over time is likely a favorite back rubbing spot.

Animal Scat

Most people recognize cat and dog poop, but wild animal poop—called scat—is distinctive, too. The size of the scat and any recognizable contents can help you narrow down from whom it came. Deer droppings are usually little round pebbles. Bear scat is good sized and can have visible remnants of trash if they've been dumpster diving. Smallish scat peppered with berry seeds sitting on top of a rock is likely the work of a fox. (There are trail guides for scat identification, in case you're really intrigued!) In winter, yellow snow is an obvious clue that wildlife has passed nearby.

PLANT IDENTIFICATION

Spending time out in the fresh air among wild plants, whether trees or wildflowers or even desert shrubs, is a window into the wildly diverse array of vegetation on Earth. Learning to identify a few common plant species out in the wild is a stepping-stone to recognizing more. As you learn to look at flower shapes and leaf groupings, you'll hone your observer's eye and be well on your way to becoming a knowledgeable naturalist.

Keen Observations

Identifying plants is a bit like detective work. Learning to notice specific details can help you determine what you're looking at. Take, for example, these two different observations:

1. That's a plant with a yellow flower. Well, that could be a number of things, couldn't it? Daisies, gladiolas, daffodils, and sunflowers are all yellow flowers, but they are remarkably different in their growth habits.

2. The plant has a yellow flower with a multitude of petals. Each petal is somewhat rectangular in shape, and slightly jagged on the end. Each flower sits individually on a stem that's four to six inches long. The stems emerge from a flat rosette of leaves that clings to the ground. The leaves are a bit hairy and irregular. In addition to the yellow flowers, some stems have a white puffball where a flower has gone to seed.

Focusing on Identification

When attempting to identify a particular specimen in the wild, answering these questions will help you narrow down the possibilities:

- Is the plant woody or nonwoody?
- Is it a shrub or tree? How tall?
- Are the leaves smooth or serrated?
- Are the leaflets alternate or opposite?
- Are there flowers or seedpods or cones?
- What color are the leaves? The flowers?
- Is the specimen growing in sun or shade?

That's a lot more specific! (Did you recognize this description as a dandelion?)

Keen observation, coupled with a good guidebook, will have you well on the way to recognizing and identifying the shrubs and trees you encounter on your wilderness adventures and even around town.

Classifying Trees and Shrubs

A good plant guide focused on your region (or the region you plan to visit) is a must-have resource if you're interested in learning more about specific vegetation. That said, you'll come across some basic and easily recognizable categories of plant materials in your adventures. Learning to identify these is a good place to start.

Deciduous Versus Evergreen Trees and Shrubs

Deciduous trees and shrubs lose their leaves all at once every year. This process is called abscission, and gives us the vivid show that occurs in autumn as leaves change from green to shades of yellow and red before they drop.

Evergreens also lose their leaves, but they don't do it all at once. Newer green leaves (or needles) remain, while the old ones fall. These specimens are never bare-branched as deciduous trees and shrubs are during much of the winter, giving them their "evergreen" descriptor.

Broad-Leaved Versus Coniferous Trees

Coniferous trees and shrubs—also known as gymnosperms—bear their seeds in cones and sport needles

Keen observation skills can help you identify trees and plants in the surrounding area.

of varying sizes. Conifers include pine, fir, yew, cypress, and redwoods.

Broad-leaved trees (such as maple and magnolia) have relatively flat leaves, but the shape and style can vary from single leaves to compound leaves, where more than one leaflet is joined to a single stem.

Most broad-leaved specimens are deciduous, and conifers are generally evergreen, though there are a few exceptions.

Characteristics of Leaves

Now that you've given some thought to the different types of trees and shrubs you might encounter in your adventures, let's dig in and consider the leaves of broad-leaved trees and shrubs. Leaves are distinctive, even from plant to plant within a species, and will help you identify specimens.

You'll need to know some simple terms to start identifying leaves. The "petiole" attaches the leaf to the plant and can extend into some leaves, dividing them directly in half. When this central stem becomes part of the leaf, it's called a "midrib" and divides the leaf into two blades, one on each side of the midrib. The stem end of a leaf is considered the "base"; the tip of the leaf is called the "apex." The edges of a leaf are called the "margin." The place where the petiole attaches to the plant stem is called a "node."

The following are some of the more commonly found shapes and styles of broad leaves. Observe these characteristics to identify the species.

■ Broad-leaved shapes

There are dozens of leaf shapes. Here are a few of the most common:

Deltoid: Triangular, with rounded corners and a pointed apex
Elliptical: Elongated, symmetrical leaves that are somewhat rounded at each end
Lanceolate: Elongated, symmetrical leaves that taper narrowly—sometimes to a point—at each end
Linear: Long, thin leaves, often the same width at both ends
Ovate: Egg-shaped, broader at the leaf base
Obovate: Egg-shaped, broader at the leaf tip

■ Leaf venation

Veins carry nutrients and water into the leaves.
Palmate: Veins feather out in approximately parallel lines from one central vein that runs to the terminal of the leaf.
Pinnate: Three to seven primary veins extend like a fan from the same point where the base of the leaf meets the stalk.

■ Leaf edge

The margin of a leaf comes in many textures. Here are some examples:
Smooth: Also called "entire," these leaves have a smooth edge with no texture.
Toothed: Observe the type of ridged teeth—they may be irregular, spiny, or just slightly evident.
Undulate: Wavy margins that move in and out of the plane of the leaves

■ Leaf attachment

Observe if the stalk has a single leaf or a compound of multiple leaflets.
Alternate: A single leaf emerging from each node, alternating from side to side with nothing across from it
Opposite: Two leaves at each node directly across from each other
Basal: Leaves in a cluster, forming a rosette pattern
Whorled: Multiple leaves emerging from one node to form a circular pattern

Toxic Leaves

Some plants can cause an itchy, painful rash when they come in contact with human skin—an unfortunate reminder of your outdoor excursion. Although not the only plants that can cause allergic reaction, poison ivy, poison oak, and poison sumac are the most common. These three plants are related, and all contain an oil called urushiol. Brushing against the leaves or stems

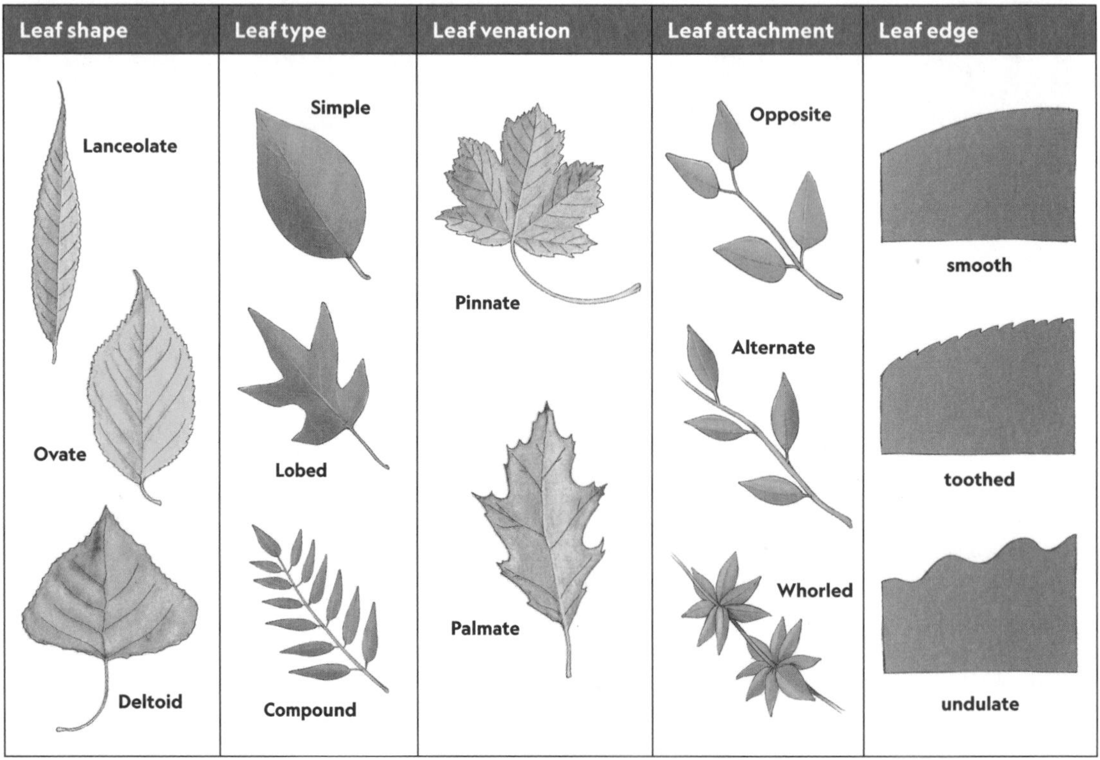

transfers this oil to your skin, resulting in a painful, itchy rash that appears 12 to 72 hours after contact. Know what to look for when you head outside—even if you're just exploring a local park or trail.

Poison ivy has three almond-shaped leaflets.

■ **Poison ivy:** Found throughout the United States, with the exception of California, Alaska, and Hawaii, poison ivy grows in leaflets of three. The leaflets are almond-shaped and situated at the end of a branch. Poison ivy grows low, as a ground cover, or as a taller shrub or even a vine, making it hard to distinguish by shape alone. The leaves are green, turning to reddish brown in the fall before they drop. The bare branches are harder to identify, but you'll still find yourself with a rash if you come in contact with them. Small yellowish white or yellowish green flowers grow in clusters in spring.

Poison oak's scalloped leaves turn deep red in the fall.

■ **Poison oak:** Similar to poison ivy, poison oak has leaflets of three that are (not surprisingly) scalloped like many oak leaves. The leaves of poison oak are shiny and can range from green and yellow to pink and red, depending on the time of year. Like poison ivy, it can grow as ground cover, shrubs, or vines. You'll find poison oak in fields, thickets, oak woodlands, and Douglas fir forests, across much of the continental United States. It also grows in cultivated areas, so you might encounter it in the suburbs along paths, trails, or even the edge of your yard. The bare branches can cause a rash too.

Poison sumac thrives in wet, swampy conditions.

■ **Poison sumac:** With a preference for swampy, wet areas, poison sumac is less widespread than poison oak and poison ivy. It's no less vicious in causing a rash, though. Poison sumac is a small tree with opposite leaflets, plus one at the tip of the stem. The stems are red in springtime, changing to brown as the seasons progress. Poison sumac sprouts have blossoms in early summer and the leaves turn orange or red in fall. This plant is found in the eastern United States and Canada, as well as Texas.

Botanist Tip

"Leaflets three, let it be" is a good phrase to remember, and applies to both poison oak and poison ivy. Of course, it applies to other plants as well, but if you're unsure what you're looking at, it's best to use caution.

FORAGING

Wild food is free food. And as someone who grew up foraging for wild blackberries every summer, I can assure you that wild food is good food, too. But whether gathering berries for homemade jam or snacking on the trail, safety is paramount. Although there are plenty of edible and medicinal plants in the wild, you'll need to know what to look for and apply common sense. Be certain that a berry or leaf is edible before popping it in your mouth.

Edible Plant Identification

If you head out intending to harvest wild edibles, you need to be sure that what you find is safe to eat. This is especially important when gathering mushrooms, as some deadly varieties can look convincingly like edible mushrooms. If you're not 100 percent sure that it's safe, don't eat it.

You have a couple ways to boost your ability to recognize safe-to-eat foods in the wild. The first, and arguably best, is to find a mentor, someone who can walk the trails with you, pointing out safe edibles and comparing them to those that are not. Take note of special characteristics that can help you make positive identification of wild edibles. Learning the common dangerous plants in your area is a good idea, too.

Thumbing through photos in a plant identification book or carrying flash cards is another good way to get to know wild edibles. Comparing images with a plant found on the trail allows you to focus on the traits of individual plants in your range, solidifying your ability to recognize specimens.

Still not sure? Snap a photo or press a leaf, and ask at your local cooperative extension office or nursery.

Latin Names

Learning and using the Latin names for the plants you harvest can prevent confusion. Morel mushrooms are commonly foraged, but that name is aligned with both "true" morels (edible) and "false" morels (poisonous). Ditto with hemlock; though one is poisonous, *Tsuga canadensis* (the eastern hemlock tree) has edible leaf tips. As well, *Conium maculatum*, a root that resembles the edible wild carrot, is poisonous. Using correct Latin names will eliminate misunderstandings and prevent accidental ingestion of the wrong plant.

Ethical Foraging

Wild edibles are free for the taking, but that doesn't mean you should wantonly harvest what you find. First of all, take only what you need; anything more is simply wasteful. And no matter how much you think you need, be mindful of overharvesting. A good rule of thumb is to harvest only 10 percent of what's growing. This allows a clump of plants to continue to thrive, and leaves enough for animals who don't have the option to shop at a supermarket.

Be courteous, too. If plants you desire are on private property, ask permission before barging in to harvest.

Choose Your Spot

Be aware of contaminants that might have impacted plants you're planning to harvest. Roadside plants have been exposed to vehicle exhaust, runoff, and possibly poisonous weed killers. The water that bog plants are growing in can be contaminated as well. As tempting as it is to pluck straight from the bush, rinse well before consuming.

Five Common Plants to Know

These five species are easy to identify and commonly found throughout most of North America, making them great for novice naturalists to begin foraging for wild edibles or medicinals.

Plantain is a common weed that has multiple uses, both medicinally and as a food source.

■ **Cattail *(Typha latifolia)***

Leaves: Erect, bladelike leaves emerge from the base of each plant.

Flowers: The cattail flower is brown and sits singly atop a sturdy stalk, though it doesn't look much like a flower. The slender protuberance emerging from the cigar-shaped female flower is (not surprisingly) the male portion of the flower. In fall, fluffy seeds emerge from the brown flower heads. A swamp full of cattails looks not unlike a field of corn dogs.

Height: 3 to 6 feet tall

Habitat: Wetlands, swamps, ditches, and marshes

Uses: Young shoots of cattail can be cooked like asparagus. The roots can be dried and ground into flour.

■ **American black elderberry *(Sambucus canadensis)***

Leaves: Compound leaves have 5 to 9 dark green leaflets with serrated edges.

Flowers: Tiny, five-petaled white flowers are borne in masses in an umbrella-like cluster, 5 to 8 inches across.

Fruit: Small (⅛-inch) dark purple berries ripen into somewhat sagging clusters in late summer.

Height: 5 to 12 feet. The bark of an elderberry is smooth to the touch, with bumps dotting its gray-brown surface.

Habitat: Prefers full sun and moist soil. Look for it in gulches, field edges, thickets, and roadsides.

Uses: Elderberry syrup is used to boost immunity. Flowers are edible, too.

■ **Mullein *(Verbascum thapsus)***

Leaves: Grayish green leaves are velvety and grow close to the ground in a rosette. A tall, erect stalk emerges from the center of this rosette, making mullein recognizable at a distance, but it only emerges in a plant's second year.

Flowers: Five-petaled yellow flowers are ¾ inch across and borne on an erect stalk that emerges from the center of the rosette of leaves. Flowers bloom a few at a time during summer, over a period of about 6 weeks. As flowers are spent, they're replaced by roundish seedpods that contain tiny seeds.

Height: The flower stalk can reach about 5 feet in height.

Habitat: Dry sunny fields, roadsides, desert shrublands, and open areas

Uses: The leaves and flowers are edible, commonly used as a tea to treat respiratory congestion. Infuse mullein flowers in oil for an herbal earache remedy. Traditionally, the highly flammable dried flower spikes were dipped in wax and lit as torches.

■ **Stinging nettle *(Urtica dioica)***

Leaves: Finely serrated, spade-shaped leaves, 2 to 6 inches long. The entire plant is covered with tiny hairs that pierce the skin and cause itching and burning.

Flowers: Male and female flowers appear on different plants. The male flowers are a grayish yellow with four stamens and yellow anthers. Female flowers are grayish green and somewhat hairy. The entire flower head is small, less than three inches.

Height: 3 to 6 feet

Habitat: Riparian zones (wetlands near streams and rivers) and along partially shaded trails, especially where the ground has been disturbed

Uses: Beneficial for urinary tract issues and joint pain, these leaves can be made into a tea or added to recipes that call for greens, or even used to top pizza.

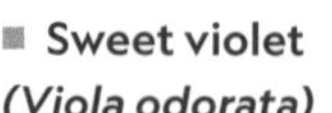

■ **Sweet violet *(Viola odorata)***

Leaves: Somewhat heart-shaped, the 1- to 2-inch leaves of the wild violet cup slightly upward. Leaf margins are serrated.

Flowers: Generally in the blue and purple range, wild violet flowers also appear in yellow and white. Wild violets have a bit of white at the center that droops a bit and five petals.

Height: No taller than 12 inches

Habitat: Shady, moist areas like forests and stream banks, though you may see them in sunnier spots as well

Uses: The leaves

and mild-flavored flowers are both edible and a fun addition to salads and for decorating cakes.

Give Weeds a Chance

What some people consider weeds can actually make a nice addition to the dinner table. Take these common backyard plants, for instance:

- **Plantain *(Plantago)*:** This weed comes in a broad-leaved or narrow-leaved variety. Traditionally used as treatment for ailments like urinary tract infection, jaundice, and bronchitis, the young green leaves can also be added to a salad. **Range:** Throughout most of the United States and Canada.

- **Dandelion *(Taraxacum)*:** All parts of the dandelion are edible. The dried roots make a passable herbal substitute for coffee. The leaves can be used as you would any green. And the flowers can be battered and fried or turned into dandelion wine. **Range:** Throughout most of the United States and Canada.

- **Sweet clover *(Melilotus)*:** Although the entire plant is technically edible, the young blossoms are tasty fresh or dried for tea. The rest of the plant is considered a famine food, eaten only in desperate times. It should be eaten in limited quantities. **Range:** Throughout most of the United States and Canada.

- **Kudzu *(Pueraria)*:** Sometimes called "the vine that ate the South," kudzu grows aggressively. The leaves, vine tips, flowers, and roots are all edible. The potatolike tubers can be pulverized and dried, then used to thicken soups or coat foods for frying. **Range:** Southeastern United States and the Pacific Northwest.

- **Miner's lettuce *(Claytonia)*:** This light green, slightly spongy leaf pops up in springtime and makes a good addition to salads. The leaves are high in vitamin C. **Range:** Western United States and Canada.

- **Ramp *(Allium tricoccum)*:** Thriving on moist forest floors and riverbanks, pungent ramps are a type of wild leek favored by chefs. Try making ramp soup, sautéing the spicy bulbs, or blending the leaves into dressing or pesto. This fragrant perennial is protected in some states due to overharvesting, so check regulations before you pluck. Regardless, never take more than 10 percent of a patch, and leave the flowering females. There is only a short window in March or April to gather ramps. **Range:** Eastern United States and Canada.

A common lawn weed, dandelion has many uses.

Seasonal Studies

Plants, shrubs, and trees can change in appearance over the course of a year. Think of a deciduous tree lush with leaves in the summer, dropping its colorful leaves in the fall, and standing bare through the winter months.

Winter Foraging

Although warm weather makes for prime foraging, some wild edibles can be found during the winter months. Bright orange or red rose hips hang on dormant rosebushes and can be used in teas for a dose of vitamin C. Juniper berries have a unique flavor and are used for flavoring. And evergreen pine offers edible needles as well as delicious pine nuts.

Ramps are a favorite of foragers, offering a mild onion flavor in early spring before gardens have begun to produce.

Learning to identify a specimen during one season is a good start—but if you only recognize a walnut tree when the tree is in full drop mode, the squirrels might beat you to the nuts. If you learn to recognize a walnut tree in spring and summer, you can keep your eyes on it to begin harvesting as soon as the walnuts are ready. (Of course, you'll want to leave some behind for the squirrels, too!)

Likewise, if a plant is best harvested when the leaves are new and tender, but you only recognize the plant when it's full grown, you'll miss the chance to fill your basket with that particular specimen.

Grow Some Weeds

It might sound counterintuitive, but instead of pulling weeds, consider planting some. Many catalogs offer seeds of plants that are valuable and yet often considered weeds. Check *rareseeds.com* for options like dandelion, plantain, mullein, stinging nettle, and purslane. Be sure to check in with your local extension office before planting varieties that are not already thriving nearby. You don't want to be the person who imports terribly invasive weeds to your area! Depending on the conditions in your backyard, you might be able to successfully transplant some of your favorite wild edibles so you have them close at hand, too. This is especially true if your yard has some ungroomed, wild edges where they'll thrive.

Down by the Sea

When you think "foraging," you likely imagine woodlands and meadows. If you live in a coastal region, however, the ocean offers up a chance to forage for fresh food. Rocks covered with mussels and limpets—in their little cone-shaped shells—are a common sight, but they're often overlooked as a food source. Seaweed, too, is a relatively untapped opportunity. No saltwater coastal seaweed has been found to be poisonous (though admittedly, some is tastier than others).

If you love sushi, you're probably familiar with nori, though its natural state looks a bit different than the dried sheets used to wrap your favorite roll. Tasty seaweeds to look for include sea lettuces (which resemble the lettuce you'd put in your salad), kombu, and laver. Like many landlocked plants, seaweed can be used as both a source of food or as a medicinal. It also makes a great addition to the garden as a fertilizer.

The best time to harvest seaweed is at low tide, when tide pools are easier to access. (Just keep an eye on the ocean for safety's sake. When the tide begins to come in, it's time for you to head inland.) Avoid loose seaweed, as there's really no way to know how fresh it is. Instead, harvest seaweed that's still attached to rocks. Small specimens can be lifted in their entirety. Use scissors to snip off what you need from larger specimens. Rinse seaweed before adding it to salads and sandwiches. To store for later use, dry it much as you would herbs (see page 22).

Seaweed

"Seaweed" is the term commonly used to describe a large number of marine plants and algae. These can be grouped into several categories, with numerous species in each:

Brown algae include kelps and wracks. If you've ever been treated with the natural remedy bladder wrack, it started as seaweed.

Red algae encompass dulse, carrageenan, and nori. Carrageenan is used as a thickening agent in many processed foods.

Green algae are the smallest of the groups. Here's where you'll find the sea lettuces and spongeweed.

Edible varieties of seaweed include sea lettuce, dulse, wakame, thongweed, and kombu.

COLLECTING WILDFLOWERS

If you've ever found yourself in a meadow of wildflowers during peak season, you'll know what a riot of color Mother Nature can produce. Gazing into the distance across a vast expanse of blossoms, you'll see colors flow across the landscape. But get up close and personal with the flowers that make up that image and you'll see that every variety has a different color and shape. From the flat, pale blue flowers of chicory to bright orange California poppies, the differences are noteworthy—but each is beautiful in its own right.

A wildflower meadow is its own little ecosystem, supporting pollinators like native bees and butterflies. In fact, when integrated with agricultural crops, wildflowers can boost yield and reduce pests (and therefore, pesticides). Human development has been hard on some wildflower species, though, as we pave over their preferred habitat. Before plucking a flower, check with the landowner or organization if the plant is on private land, or consult local regulations if you are foraging on public land or parkland.

California poppies can light up a meadow with their color.

Saving Seeds

If you like the idea of helping wildflower populations thrive, you might want to plant native wildflowers in your yard or neighborhood. Native species that are already growing well in your region are good options, because they will probably also thrive near your home. When you find a particular bloom that suits your fancy, you can gather some seeds to help spread the wildflower love.

The first rule of thumb when gathering wildflower seeds? Don't be greedy. If a given area has only a few of a certain species, don't harvest seeds; leaving seed heads in place will allow the plant to establish there. When seed heads are in abundance, take some, but leave more.

Timing the seed harvest is important. Flower heads transform into seed heads as the plant moves through its life cycle. For seeds to be viable, they need a chance to completely mature. Look for seedpods that are already drying out and a bit crumbly to the touch. For plants like poppies that store seeds inside the flower head, shake them a bit. If you hear the seeds rattle inside the head, they're ready.

Gathering Seeds

Avoid using a plastic bag for gathering seeds; moisture can accumulate inside the plastic and inhibit drying or result in mold. A reusable cloth produce bag works well (see pages 86–87).

Harvest seed heads of individual flower species, collecting them into their own cloth bag and making note of the variety. This will help you recognize plants when they begin growing in springtime. Use scissors to trim off mature seed heads, or just pull them off with your hands.

To save seeds for a later planting, dry the seed heads completely by placing them on a sheet of newspaper in a cool place with plenty of airflow to prevent molding. When they are completely dry, use your hands to crush the flower heads. You'll have a combination of seeds and dried flower petals. You can remove the dried flower bits, but you don't have to be too particular about it. Store the seeds in a cotton bag or a paper envelope in the refrigerator until you're ready to plant.

RECIPE

Pickled Nasturtium Seeds

Makes about ½ cup

This recipe uses a fermentation method (see page 36) to transform nasturtium seeds into a crunchy condiment somewhat reminiscent of capers. The pickled seeds will keep, refrigerated, for up to six months.

You'll Need:

½ cup freshly harvested young green nasturtium seedpods
1 cup distilled water
2 teaspoons sea salt

1. Wash the nasturtium seeds thoroughly, remove any remaining stems, and break the seedpods apart. (They grow in bundles of three.) Place the seeds in the jar.
2. Dissolve the salt in the distilled water to make a brine; pour the brine over the nasturtium seeds to cover. Refrigerate any remaining brine.
3. Place a weight on top of the seeds to prevent them from floating; they need to remain submerged.
4. Place the lid on the jar. Loosen the lid daily to release built-up gases. Let sit at room temperature for 3 days.
5. Open the jar; you will likely smell a bit of a sulfur odor. Drain the seeds, cover them again with the reserved brine, and seal the jar again. Let the jar sit at room temperature for another 3 days or so, then transfer to the refrigerator.

Nasturtium seeds offer an unexpected pop of flavor.

Growing Wildflowers

They key to growing wildflowers is remembering that they are wild. They are perfect for beautifying grassy margins, but not a good choice for groomed areas. For wildflowers to thrive, they need to be—ready for this?—left alone. Mowing an area where you've planted wildflower seeds will defeat the purpose.

When to sow wildflower seeds depends a bit on what you're planting and what your climate is like. Your best bet is to choose wildflowers native to your region. To plant in springtime, do so after the soil has warmed and the risk of frost has passed. With fall planting, some seeds will germinate and the roots will winter over. Others do better planted at a temperature that allows the seeds to remain dormant until spring frost. Ask at your local nursery about the best time to plant different seeds in your region.

To sow wildflower seeds, you can simply scatter them on the ground. After all, that's how Mother Nature does it. You'll have better luck with germination, though, if you do some soil preparation in advance. Remove competing weeds and grasses and loosen the soil (or even rototill). Seeds need moisture to germinate; you could water them in, or you can time your planting to coincide with a rainstorm.

DIY

Mini-Flower Press

Pressing flowers is a good way to keep mementos of a trip, but is also useful for plant identification purposes. Bringing home pressed flowers (or leaves) from a mystery plant allows you to look it up once you're home or ask a mentor. Basswood is a lightweight wood that comes in thin sheets, making it a good option for a portable flower press. Craft stores should have all the supplies for this project. You may need to cut the basswood to the appropriate size; it's easy to do with an X-acto or box knife.

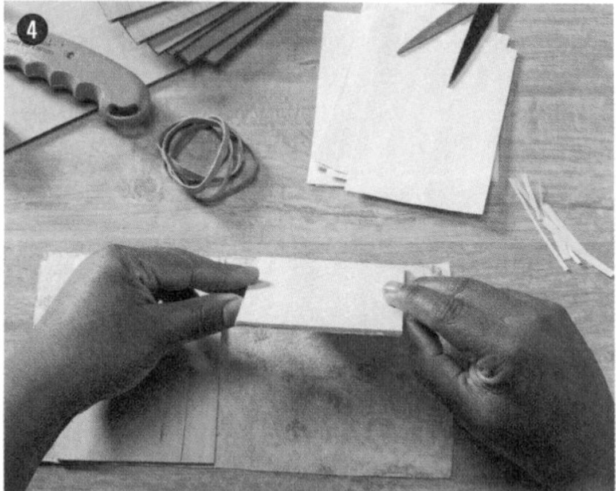

You'll Need:
2 pieces of basswood, 4 × 6 inches
Fabric, 6 × 11 inches
Glue
Paintbrush
6 to 8 sheets of corrugated cardboard, 4 × 6 inches
18 pieces of newsprint, 4 × 6 inches
Several large rubber bands

1. With the wrong side of the fabric facing up, measure and mark 5 inches in from each end.
2. Position basswood pieces on the fabric side by side on those marks, aligning the top and bottom of the wood with the top and bottom of the fabric. Leave a 1-inch gap between the basswood and an inch of fabric extending beyond each end.
3. Dilute about 2 tablespoons glue with a bit of water, just enough that it's easily spreadable. Dip the paintbrush in the glue and spread it on the basswood where it sits, covering the entire thing.
4. Now flip over the basswood, putting the glue side down in exactly the same position.
5. Spread more glue on each of the fabric ends, along with a bead of undiluted glue for extra security.
6. Fold ends over, pressing the fabric onto the basswood. Allow the flower press to dry.
7. Stack newsprint and cardboard, beginning with two sheets of newsprint, followed by one piece of cardboard, then repeat. You'll end with two sheets of newsprint.
8. Insert the stacked newsprint and cardboard between the front and back covers. The quantity of cardboard pieces required will depend on the thickness of the cardboard you use.
9. Place plant material between two sheets of newsprint. (The newsprint helps absorb moisture and will need to be replaced after a couple of uses.)
10. Secure the flower press closed with rubber bands, and leave for 2 to 4 weeks.

Wonderful Wildflowers

As you pick your way through a meadow harvesting colorful blooms, be mindful that they might be considered invasive in your area. If they've developed seed heads, be careful that you don't spread seeds of invasive plants.

DIY

Mounting Wildflowers

Blooms from a wedding bouquet, pressed wildflowers, or the leaves of elegant ferns can become a memento of your explorations or a special occasion. Mounting them allows you to appreciate their beauty more than once! Pressed leaves or flowers can be framed and hung on the wall, or can be used to make cards or laminated bookmarks. Cut the card stock in a size to suit your desired end product, such as the measurement of the frame. Another option is to glue right onto the glass of the frame.

You'll Need:
Pressed flowers
Heavy card stock in the color of your choice
Glue (Elmer's works well)
Small disposable dish (such as a recycled plastic lid)
Toothpicks
Tweezers (optional but helpful)

1. Begin by arranging the pressed flowers in a pattern that pleases you and fits the size of your project.
2. Pour a teaspoon or so of glue onto the dish.
3. Dip one end of a toothpick into the glue and dab a small dot on the back side of a flower in several places. If your design has overlapping flowers, start by gluing the bottom layer in place first.
4. Use tweezers to turn the flower over and set in place. Gently press the flower to the paper and hold for a few seconds to secure it in place. Repeat with remaining flowers and allow it to dry.

Pressed flowers can be framed or used to make note cards.

TAPPING TREES FOR SYRUP

Pancakes for breakfast are a rare treat around here. Topping them with real maple syrup, even more so. Every single bite reminds me of the incredible journey of that syrup, from beneath the bark of a maple tree to the end of my fork. Bundled up against the crisp cold air, snow crunching underfoot, hobbyists and maple syrup producers alike closely watch the mercury in the thermometer, eagerly monitoring the temperature until the time comes to kick off a new season in the sugar bush.

Maple syrup production requires extracting the sap of a maple tree and cooking it down into a rich, thick syrup. As a general rule, it takes 40 gallons of sap to make a single gallon of syrup, though it can be more or less, depending on the sugar content of the sap. It's no wonder real maple syrup is such a point of pride for the people who make it!

All About the Taste

Although the sugar maple *(Acer saccharum)* is traditionally tapped, other maples can be good options for tapping as well. The sugar content of their sap is not as high, though, so the syrup yield is much lower. Even non-maple species can be tapped for syrup. The flavor profile will vary between maple tree varieties, and even more so with sap derived from uncommon tree sources. Birch sap, for example, is a little more acidic, and it takes much more to make syrup, but it's fun to try this slightly spicy sweetener if you are lucky enough to have a stand of birches nearby. Tapping trees you have readily available in your region means a more localized source of sweetener.

Sugaring Season

With tapping, it's all about the timing, and that part's up to Mother Nature. Temperatures that fluctuate between freezing and thawing cause the sap to flow. A thaw of 40 degrees during the day but a dip back to freezing temperatures at night creates the ideal conditions for sap to drip into your bucket. The time frame for this depends on your location and can vary from year to year, but plan on tapping sometime between mid-February and mid-April.

Surprising Trees to Tap for Sap

Although sugar maples are the most familiar tree for tapping, all varieties of maple can be tapped. No maple tree? No problem! The flavors and tapping season varies, but you can experiment with sap from a number of other trees:

Butternut, white walnut *(Juglans cinerea)*
Black walnut *(Juglans nigra)*
Heartnut *(Juglans ailantifolia)*
English walnut *(Juglans regia)*
Paper birch *(Betula papyrifera)*
Yellow birch *(Betula alleghaniensis)*
Black birch *(Betula lenta)*
River birch *(Betula nigra)*
Gray birch *(Betula populifolia)*
European white birch *(Betula pendula)*
Sycamore *(Platanus occidentalis)*
Ironwood, hop hornbeam *(Ostrya virginiana)*

Tapping in the Tropics

Some palm trees are another source of sweet sap—but instead of tapping the trunk, the flowering stem is cut and tapped. This requires reaching the leafy tops of the tree, which is not for the faint of heart.

DIY

Tapping the Trees

Accessing the sap that's naturally running through the trees requires breaching the tree's protective layer.

Tapping a spile into a tree trunk opens access to the sap.

Think of the sap as the tree's lifeblood: Just as a lab takes a small sample of your blood for medical purposes, you can "draw" sap from the tree. Doing so doesn't damage the tree, so long as you follow the basic guidelines outlined in the chart.

You'll Need:
Battery-operated drill with a ⅜-inch or 7/16-inch bit
Spiles and hooks, one for each hole
Hammer
Buckets or containers with lids for catching the sap

1. Drill a hole in the trunk of the tree roughly 2 to 3 feet above ground level. Do this only when temperatures are above freezing to prevent damage to the tree. Drill at a slight upward angle, making a hole measuring between 2 and 2½ inches deep. If the tree has been tapped previously, choose a spot at least 6 inches away from the previous taphole horizontally and 24 inches vertically. This assures that you'll be accessing good sapwood. If the tree is large enough for more than one tap, try to spiral them evenly around the circumference of the tree.
2. Insert the spile into the taphole, tapping it gently with the hammer to set it in place. Once set, it should be sturdy enough that you can slip a hook over the spile and hang a bucket in place to catch the sap. A lid or cover for the bucket will prevent bugs, debris, and rainwater from getting into the sap.
3. If your spile does not have a hook, you can pound a separate hanger for your bucket. Alternatively, connect plastic tubing to the spile and snake it down to a container on the ground.
4. Collect sap daily and transfer to a large storage container. Keep it as cool as possible until you've gathered enough to start processing it into syrup. The sooner you can process the sap, the better quality your end product will be.
5. Clean all your equipment well at the end of each maple syrup season.

Number of Taps per Tree, Based on Circumference

To make certain that you don't overtap a tree, experts suggest limiting how many taps you use. Although this isn't an exact science, the following suggestions are a good guideline to follow. It's a good idea to err on the side of caution, though. When in doubt, leave it out.

Circumference of Tree	Number of Taps
Less than 30 inches	Zero
31 to 53 inches	One
57 to 75 inches	Two
76 inches or greater	Three

As sap flows, it drips into a bucket hanging from the spile.

Making Maple Candy

To make an easy maple candy, pack clean snow into a baking dish (or you can do it outside). Pour boiling maple syrup onto the hard snow and allow to cool to a taffy-like consistency.

DIY

Making Maple Syrup

Processing sap into syrup is a satisfying endeavor that will put a natural sweetener on your shelf for substantially less than you'd pay at a gourmet market. Of course, it does require an investment of time. But who could complain about working over a warm fire during chilly days, breathing in the sweet, steamy aroma of syrup in the works?

Sap, as it comes out of the tree, is a thin liquid. Transforming it into a thicker syrup requires cooking it down into a thicker, sweeter product. The process of evaporating water from the sap creates a lot of steam for an extended period of time. This can be damaging to interior walls, and is why you often see this process taking place out of doors over an open fire. People who make maple syrup annually often use a rectangular metal syrup pan that will hold a large amount of liquid—and provide a larger area of evaporation.

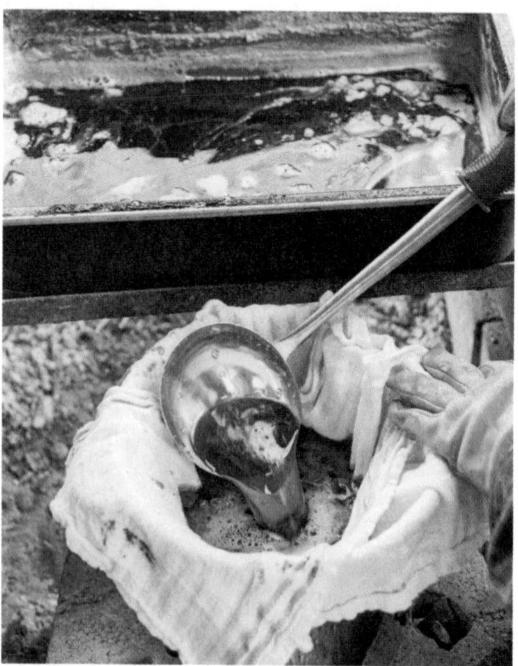

Straining the finished syrup removes crystals and other bits.

It takes a lot of time and effort to make maple syrup. Rather than processing each batch as you harvest sap, collect it over a number of days and boil down syrup once you have several gallons at the ready. You'll need some big cooking containers. A 21.5-quart canning pot is a good bet, and using multiple pots if you have a means of heating them can hasten the process. Even so, be sure to set aside a couple of days to complete the process:

1. Bring sap to a boil in your pot or pan. Do not fill all the way to the brim or your pot could boil over. (Use a candy thermometer to make note of the boiling temperature; you'll need this information later.)
2. As the liquid evaporates, add more sap little by little, making sure you don't add enough to halt the boiling process.
3. Continue adding sap in this manner until it is all condensed into boiling containers.
4. Cook until you notice the sap begin to darken. This means you're nearing the end of the process. (If the batch is small enough, you can transfer it to a smaller container and move it inside at this point.)
5. Filter the syrup to remove crystals or unwanted material that drifted in during your boil. Line a funnel with a piece of flannel material and allow the syrup to strain through slowly. Don't force the syrup through, or you'll just push smaller crystals into the finished product.
6. You're aiming for 66 to 67 percent sugar content with your syrup; less than that, and it can tend to

Grades and Flavors

Natural maple syrup isn't as thick as maple-flavored, high-fructose corn syrup in your supermarket's breakfast aisle, nor is it usually as sweet. Maple syrup comes in four different grades:

U.S. Grade A "Golden" has a delicate flavor with a hint of maple flavor.

U.S. Grade A "Amber" has a rich flavor.

U.S. Grade A "Dark" has a robust maple flavor and is a favorite for topping pancakes.

U.S. Grade A "Very Dark" has a strong taste that's been likened to molasses.

Maple syrup comes in a range of grades and flavors visible in the hue of the finished syrup.

sour. To achieve this, monitor the temperature of the syrup with a candy thermometer. When it reaches 7°F above boiling temperature (as noted earlier), it's done.

7. Strain the hot syrup into sterile jars, and process in a water bath canner for 10 minutes (see page 24). Store in a cool, dry place. Once opened, syrup will keep in the refrigerator for up to a year.

A Cool, Refreshing Drink

Although we mostly think of maple sap as the start of maple syrup, the sap itself makes a nice, slightly sweet beverage. Maple water isn't sticky like you might imagine. It's packed with minerals and nutrients, too, making for a healthy, all-natural drink.

AFTERWORD

My Aunt Roberta always had a project going. Whether making a set of curtains with her sewing machine or hand-stitching quilt squares while visiting with company, she was always creating something. She was a skilled cake decorator (she made my wedding cake), an avid gardener, and a seamstress.

She worked hard at her various projects, laboring to get them just right. Making things from scratch isn't always easy—she'd be the first to tell you that—but handcrafting items and cooking food for our loved ones is more than just one more thing to labor over. When we've finished our daily obligations, creating something with our own hands offers a sense of fulfillment that is unmatched.

Sure, preparing yet another busy weeknight dinner can start to feel like drudge work. But setting aside time to make a batch of raspberry jam with fresh fruit from your garden? That's a different sort of cooking project that will delight you and your family not just upon completion, but every time you open another jar. Baking a crusty loaf of bread and slathering it with butter (or maybe some of that raspberry jam) when it's fresh out of the oven is pure satisfaction that store-bought bread can't quite match.

In the fast-track, busy, busy lives so many of us lead, a certain sense of calm comes when we stop the mad rush for a moment or two and use our hands to create. Taking time to be creative can overflow into other parts of our lives, building our confidence and perhaps even improving how we approach other difficult tasks.

Like you, my life is a busy whirlwind. I struggle to fit yoga classes between my work as a small business owner, author, mother, and wife. The four o'clock "What's for dinner tonight?" scramble happens more often than I'd like to admit. As I write this last section, my bed is unmade, the sink's full of dirty dishes, and my couch is more laundry station than furniture. But in the midst of this whirlwind of life, I'm reminded how important it is to break the monotony of the days to nourish my soul.

I hope the projects in these pages have inspired you to strive for the simple lifestyle you dream of. And, hey: Start small. Head outside and take a moment to notice the trees as they rustle in the breeze. Pull out that box of fabric scraps and plan your next project. Mix up a batch of sourdough starter. These are not complicated activities, but allowing ourselves time to tackle new projects helps us remain rooted to the idea of a life that includes more traditional skills, more hand-making, and less consumerism. Enjoy the journey, friends!

KRIS BORDESSA

PS: I'd love to hear about your efforts! Write to me at kris@attainable-sustainable.net.

Medicinal herbs can be dried and saved for later use.

KNOW YOUR CLIMATE ZONE

Different plants thrive in different climates. This map breaks the United States into zones based on the average annual minimum winter temperature. Knowing your climate zone will help you determine which plants are likely to thrive in your garden—and which ones may not survive. Reference guides like *The New Sunset Western Garden Book* and the *American Horticultural Society Encyclopedia of Plants and Flowers* provide detailed information about individual plants, including the recommended climate zone for growing them. This information is a boon to gardeners, but it's also not cut in stone. Every area has microclimates, where the temperature is higher (or lower) than the average and may allow you to grow some plants that are listed slightly out of your designated zone.

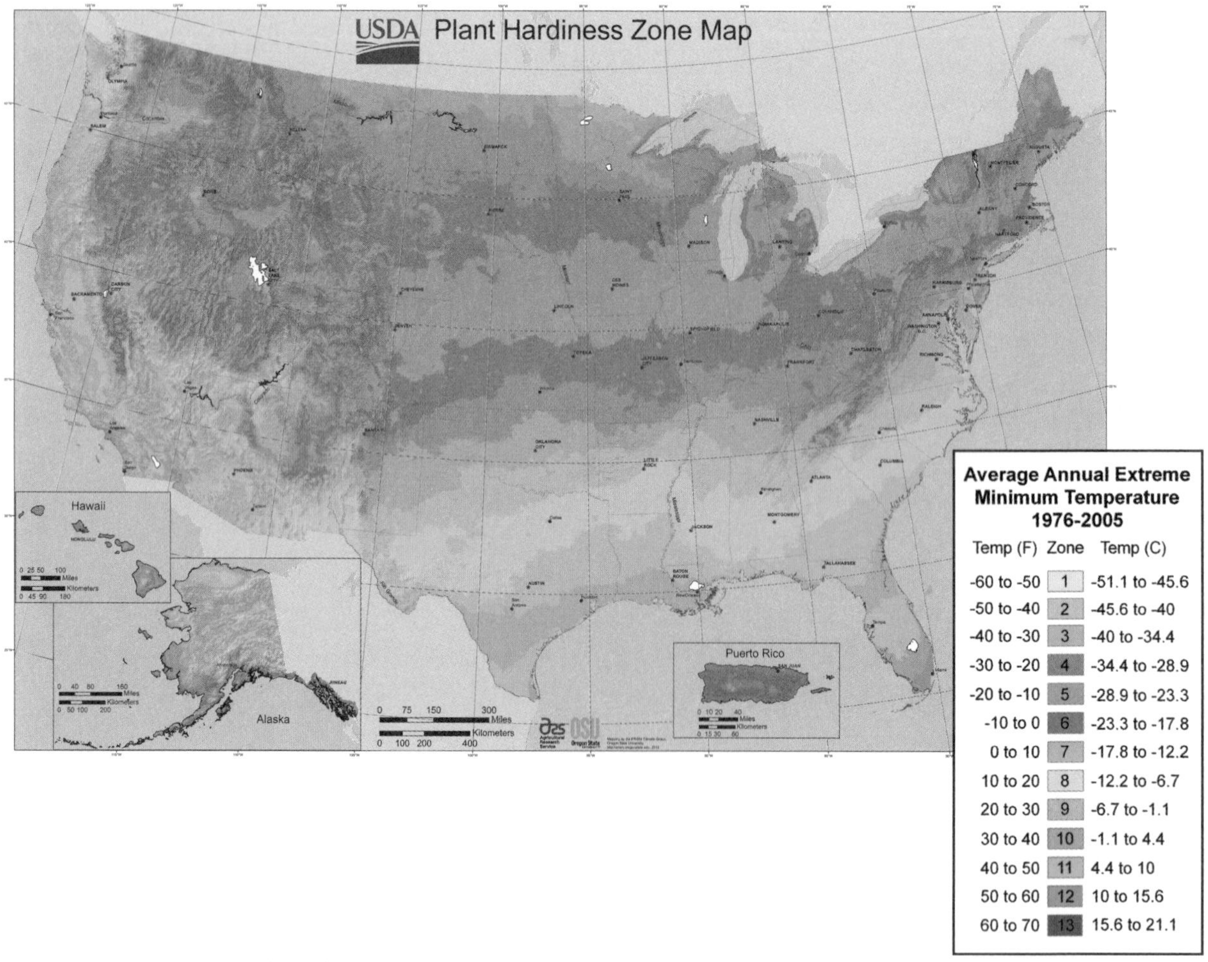

TOOLS EVERY HOMESTEADER SHOULD HAVE

I rely on some tools regularly to be as efficient as possible. Sure, I could get by without some of this equipment: I could knead bread by hand, but a stand mixer makes quick work of it. Having the necessary tools or a simple shortcut readily available makes it easier to adopt a do-it-yourself attitude.

In the Kitchen:

- Ball canning jars with both metal and plastic lids
- Cast-iron cookware (mine is from Lodge)
- Wooden spoon with a sturdy handle
- A good garlic press (my Pampered Chef model is by far the best I've owned)
- Slow cooker
- Instant Pot electric pressure cooker
- Stand mixer with a dough hook for kneading bread. I like my KitchenAid because I can add attachments for grating, slicing, or grinding.
- Canning equipment, including a big canning pot, jar tongs, and a canning funnel
- Cheesecloth may not see daily use, but when you need it, you need it, so I try to keep some on hand.

In the Garden Shed:

- Wheelbarrow or garden cart
- Saw tooth sickle
- Headlamp for nighttime slug hunting
- Diatomaceous earth is my go-to for natural pest control
- Tennis racket (surprise!) for whacking cabbage moths out of the air
- A trug or basket for gathering the harvest
- Jute twine

In the Cupboards:

- Sewing machine
- A good pair of fabric scissors
- Dr. Bronner's liquid castile soap and Sal Suds, a laundry booster with plant-based surfactants
- Shampoo/cosmetic brands rated highly by Environmental Working Group *(ewg.org)*, like Avalon Organics, Beautycounter, and Attitude
- Essential oils

ABOUT THE AUTHOR

KRIS BORDESSA has been working diligently to live a greener, more self-reliant lifestyle for much of her adult life. Along with her husband and two sons, she adopted Hawaii as her home more than a dozen years ago. Although she struggles to grow tomatoes and zucchini in the tropical climate, the banana and avocado crops (almost) make up for it. When she's not digging in the garden, she's likely having an animated conversation with the chickens, ducks, rabbits, and cats that make up her menagerie. She's the founder of *attainable-sustainable.net*, a freelance writer, author, and an obsessive collector of vegetable seeds.

ACKNOWLEDGMENTS

My friend Kathy inspired me to start Attainable Sustainable with a simple conversation about adopting small changes and learning new skills. Years later, in late 2016, my phone rang. Caller ID said "Washington, D.C." Perfect, I thought! I've got some things to say to Washington, D.C. Instead of a staffer wishing to hear my thoughts on the state of the union, it was a team of editors from National Geographic Books. From that initial phone call through the ensuing years (!) of making this book happen, Hilary, Moriah, and Michelle were an absolute pleasure to work with. Much aloha to you all.

The continued support of my SAH gals has helped me maintain my sanity throughout the book writing process—special shout-out to Devon, Colleen, Jan, and Connie who freely offered their eyeballs and their expertise to check my accuracy. Quinn had my back while I was deep in writing and editing; for that I am grateful.

Mahalo nui to Jane, Toni, Debbi (no e), and the Monday morning yoga crew for being some of my biggest cheerleaders, as well as for taking a few of my green living initiatives to heart.

I have such gratitude for the wonderful online Attainable Sustainable community—you all rock, and this book wouldn't be in your hands without your continued support.

Big hugs to my three guys—Joe, Brad, and Evan—who support me through thick and thin, provide ungilded (and sometimes unrequested) feedback on my many, many ideas, and patiently wait while I take *one more photo* of dinner before they can dig in, all with only occasional eye rolling.

I was lucky enough to spend several days at the National Geographic offices; thanks to all of you who welcomed me kindly, and especially to the photo team for letting me watch them in action and pester them with questions. Thank you to all the contributors at National Geographic Partners, including creative director Melissa Farris, photo editors Jill Foley and Moira Haney, photo director Susan Blair, and publisher Lisa Thomas. Special thanks goes to Jill, who worked so diligently to communicate with me to get each shot right. Carol Norton is the mastermind behind the gorgeous design. The photographers who brought these crafts and recipes to life were Laura Chase de Formigny (who said nice things about my biscuits), Melissa Goodwin, Rebecca Hale, and Mark Thiessen, with the expert assistance of stylists Linda Russell, Giulietta Pinna, Nichole Bryant, Diana Jeffra, Sebastian Zijp, and Sarah Jones Decker, as well as lighting from tech Peter Grill. Mairead Hunter Herbers contributed handmade soap. The gracious hand models were Rahsaan Jackson, Joe Chidley, Latasha Lewis, Kris Moon, Sebastian Zijp, Sarah Jones Decker, Linda Russell, Moriah Petty, Mark Thiessen, Rebecca Hale, Jill Foley, and Moira Haney. Erika Lenkert thoroughly double-checked the recipes for consistency.

The following books and websites are but a small sampling of the vast amount of information available on topics covered in this book. If your interest in a specific topic or activity is piqued, you'll find more information to explore here.

For live links to these resources and more, please visit *attainable-sustainable.net/resources.*

EAT

Carroll, Rikki. *Home Cheese Making.* Storey Publishing, 2010.

Katz, Sandor Ellix. *Wild Fermentation: The Flavor, Nutrition, and Craft of Live-Culture Foods.* Chelsea Green Publishing, 2016.

Kilcher, Eve, and Eivin Kilcher. *Homestead Kitchen: Stories and Recipes from Our Hearth to Yours.* Pam Krauss/Avery, 2016.

Kramis, Sharon. *The Dutch Oven Cookbook: Recipes for the Best Pot in Your Kitchen.* Sasquatch Books, 2014.

MacCharles, Joel, and Dana Harrison. *Batch: Over 200 Recipes, Tips and Techniques for a Well Preserved Kitchen.* Appetite by Random House, 2016.

McClellan, Marisa. *Food in Jars: Preserving in Small Batches Year-Round.* Running Press Adult, 2012.

The Modern Dutch Oven Cookbook: Fresh Ideas for Braises, Stews, Pot Roasts, and Other One-Pot Meals. Rockridge Press, 2015.

Norris, Melissa K. *Hand Made: The Modern Woman's Guide to Made-From-Scratch Living.* Harvest House Publishers, 2017.

Reinhart, Peter. *The Bread Baker's Apprentice, 15th Anniversary Edition: Mastering the Art of Extraordinary Bread.* Random House, 2016.

Ruhlman, Michael, and Brian Polcyn. *Charcuterie: The Craft of Salting, Smoking, and Curing.* W. W. Norton and Company, 2013.

Simmons, Marcia, and Jonas Halpren. *DIY Cocktails: A Simple Guide to Creating Your Own Signature Drinks.* Adams Media, 2011.

Stonger, Shannon. *Traditionally Fermented Foods: Innovative Recipes and Old-Fashioned Techniques for Sustainable Eating.* Page Street Publishing, 2017.

Wells, Shelle. *Prepper's Dehydrator Handbook: Long-Term Food Storage Techniques for Nutritious, Delicious, Lifesaving Meals.* Ulysses Press, 2018.

Web resources

Cultures for Health: *culturesforhealth.com*

National Center for Home Food Preservation (the USDA Complete Guide to Home Canning): *nchfp.uga.edu/publications/publications_usda.html*

Non-GMO Project: *www.nongmoproject.org*

Slow Food: *www.slowfood.com*

MAKE

Brandvig, Jera. *Quilt As-You-Go Made Vintage: 51 Blocks, 9 Projects, 3 Joining Methods.* Stash Books, 2017.

Burgess, Rebecca. *Harvesting Color: How to Find Plants and Make Natural Dyes.* Artisan, 2011.

Ekarius, Carol, and Deborah Robson. *The Fleece & Fiber Sourcebook: More Than 200 Fibers, from Animal to Spun Yarn.* Storey Publishing, 2011.

Hird, Laurie Aaron. *The Farmer's Wife 1930s Sampler Quilt: Inspiring Letters from Farm Women of the Great Depression and 99 Quilt Blocks That Honor Them.* Fons & Porter, 2015.

Katz, Emily. *Modern Macramé: 33 Stylish Projects for Your Handmade Home.* Ten Speed Press, 2018.

Lane, Ruth. *The Complete Photo Guide to Felting.* Quarry Books, 2012.

Mallow, Judy. *Pine Needle Basketry: From Forest Floor to Finished Project.* Lark Crafts, 2010.

Oppenheimer, Betty. *The Candlemaker's Companion: A Complete Guide to Rolling, Pouring, Dipping, and Decorating Your Own Candles.* Storey Publishing, 2012.

Wada, Yoshiko Iwamoto, Mary Kellogg Rice, and Jane Barton. *Shibori: The Inventive Art of Japanese Shaped Resist Dyeing.* Kodansha USA, 1999.

Yaker, Rebecca, and Patricia Hoskins. *One-Yard Wonders: 101 Sewing Projects; Look How Much You Can Make with Just One Yard of Fabric.* Storey Publishing, 2009.

FURTHER READING

CLEAN

Aron, Jules. *Fresh & Pure: Organically Crafted Beauty Balms & Cleansers.* The Countryman Press, 2018.

Berry, Jan. *101 Easy Homemade Products for Your Skin, Health & Home: A Nerdy Farm Wife's All-Natural DIY Projects Using Commonly Found Herbs, Flowers & Other Plants.* Page Street Publishing, 2016.

——. *Simple & Natural Soapmaking: Create 100% Pure and Beautiful Soaps with The Nerdy Farm Wife's Easy Recipes and Techniques.* Page Street Publishing, 2017.

Codekas, Colleen. *Healing Herbal Infusions: Simple and Effective Home Remedies for Colds, Muscle Pain, Upset Stomach, Stress, Skin Issues and More.* Page Street Publishing, 2018.

Cottis, Halle. *Natural Solutions for Cleaning & Wellness: Health Remedies and Green Cleaning Solutions Without Toxins or Chemicals.* Page Street Publishing, 2017.

Dalziel, Christine J. *The Beeswax Workshop: How to Make Your Own Natural Candles, Cosmetics, Cleaners, Soaps, Healing Balms and More.* Ulysses Press, 2016.

Fewell, Amy. *The Homesteader's Herbal Companion: The Ultimate Guide to Growing, Preserving, and Using Herbs.* Lyons Press, 2018.

Gladstar, Rosemary. *Medicinal Herbs: A Beginner's Guide: 33 Healing Herbs to Know, Grow, and Use.* Storey Publishing, 2012.

Shealy, C. Norman. *The Illustrated Encyclopedia of Healing Remedies.* Harper Element, 2009.

Web resources

Bulk Apothecary: *www.bulkapothecary.com*

Environmental Working Group: *www.ewg.org/skindeep*

The Herbal Academy: *theherbalacademy.com*

Majestic Mountain Sage lye calculator: *www.thesage.com/calcs/LyeCalc.html*

GROW

Bartholomew, Mel. *All New Square Foot Gardening: The Revolutionary Way to Grow More in Less Space.* Cool Springs Press, 2013.

Bradley, Fern Marshall, Barbara W. Ellis, and Deborah L. Martin, eds. *The Organic Gardener's Handbook of Natural Pest and Disease Control: A Complete Guide to Maintaining a Healthy Garden and Yard the Earth-Friendly Way.* Rodale Books, 2010.

Creasy, Rosalind. *Edible Landscaping.* Counterpoint, 2010.

Deppe, Carol. *The Resilient Gardener: Food Production and Self-Reliance in Uncertain Times.* Chelsea Green Publishing, 2011.

Hemenway, Toby. *Gaia's Garden: A Guide to Home-Scale Permaculture,* 2nd edition. Chelsea Green Publishing, 2009.

Jeavons, John. *How to Grow More Vegetables Than You Ever Thought Possible on Less Land Than You Can Imagine.* Ten Speed Press, 1991.

Karsten, Joel. *Straw Bale Gardens Complete: Breakthrough Vegetable Gardening Method.* Cool Springs Press, 2015.

Riotte, Louise. *Carrots Love Tomatoes: Secrets of Companion Planting for Successful Gardening.* Storey Publishing, 1998.

Stout, Ruth. *Gardening Without Work: For the Aging, the Busy & the Indolent.* Norton Creek Press, 2016.

Stross, Amy. *The Suburban Micro-Farm: Modern Solutions for Busy People.* Twisted Creek Press, 2018.

Toensmeier, Eric. *Perennial Vegetables: From Artichoke to Zuiki Taro, a Gardener's Guide to Over 100 Delicious, Easy-to-Grow Edibles.* Chelsea Green Publishing, 2007.

Web resources

Baker Creek Heirloom Seeds: *www.rareseeds.com*

Cooperative extension: *articles.extension.org*

Johnny's Selected Seeds: *www.johnnyseeds.com*

Seeds of Change: *www.seedsofchange.com/seeds*

FARM

Damerow, Gail. *The Backyard Homestead Guide to Raising Farm Animals*. Storey Publishing, 2011.

Edey, Anna. *Solviva: How to Grow $500,000 on One Acre, and Peace on Earth*. Trailblazer Press, 1998.

Elliot, Shaye. *Welcome to the Farm: How-To Wisdom from The Elliot Homestead*. Lyons Press, 2017.

Garman, Janet. *50 Do-It-Yourself Projects for Keeping Chickens*. Skyhorse Publishing, 2018.

Hemenway, Toby. *Gaia's Garden: A Guide to Home-Scale Permaculture*. Chelsea Green Publishing, 2009.

Jones, Richard. *The Beekeeper's Bible: Bees, Honey, Recipes & Other Home Uses*. Stewart, Tabori and Chang, 2011.

Mollison, Bill. *Introduction to Permaculture*. Tagari, 2002.

Page, Teri. *Family Homesteading: The Ultimate Guide to Self-Sufficiency for the Whole Family*. Skyhorse Publishing, 2018.

Stonger, Stewart, and Shannon Stonger. *The Doable Off-Grid Homestead*. Page Street Publishing, 2018

Ussery, Harvey. *The Small-Scale Poultry Flock: An All-Natural Approach to Raising Chickens and Other Fowl for Home and Market Growers*. Chelsea Green Publishing, 2011.

Web resources

The Livestock Conservancy: *livestockconservancy.org*

Permies: *permies.com*

TREK

Brill, Steve. *Identifying and Harvesting Edible and Medicinal Plants in Wild (and Not So Wild) Places*. William Morrow Paperbacks, 1994.

Chin, Ava. *Eating Wildly: Foraging for Life, Love and the Perfect Meal*. Simon and Schuster, 2014.

Gooley, Tristan. *The Lost Art of Reading Nature's Signs*. The Experiment, 2015.

——. *The Natural Navigator: The Rediscovered Art of Letting Nature Be Your Guide*. The Experiment, 2012.

Shaw, Hank. *Hunt, Gather, Cook: Finding the Forgotten Feast*. Rodale Books, 2011.

The Stars: The Definitive Visual Guide to the Cosmos. DK, 2016.

Thayer, Samuel. *The Forager's Harvest: A Guide to Identifying, Harvesting, and Preparing Edible Wild Plants*. Forager's Harvest Press, 2006.

Young, Devon. *The Backyard Herbal Apothecary: Effective Medicinal Remedies Using Commonly Found Herbs & Plants*. Page Street Publishing, 2019.

Web resources

Animated Knots: *www.animatedknots.com*

Edible Wild Food: *www.ediblewildfood.com*

National Audubon Society: *www.audubon.org*

The Natural Navigator: *www.naturalnavigator.com*

Nature Tracking: *www.naturetracking.com*

The Seaweed Site: *www.seaweed.ie/descriptions*

USDA Plants Database (plant ID): *plants.usda.gov*

Wildflower Guide: *www.wildernesscollege.com/plant-identification.html*

All cover photos by Laura Chase de Formigny except back cover (LO LE) by Melissa Goodwin and back cover (LO RT) by Rebecca Hale, NG Staff.

2-3, Melanie DeFazio/Stocksy; 4, Melissa Goodwin; 6, Laura Chase de Formigny; 8, Laura Chase de Formigny; 9, Rebecca Hale, NG Staff; 11, Vitalii Borovyk/easyfotostock/age fotostock; 12-13, Elena Grigarchuk/Getty Images; 14, Laura Chase de Formigny; 16, karakedi35/Shutterstock; 17, StockFood/Hans Gerlach; 19, Laura Chase de Formigny; 20, Laura Chase de Formigny; 22, Harald Walker/Stocksy; 23, Helen Rushbrook/Stocksy; 24, Ron Bailey/Getty Images; 25, Juli Leonard/Raleigh News & Observer/MCT/Alamy Live News; 26, Lew Robertson/Getty Images; 28, Jiang Hongyan/Shutterstock; 29, Darren Muir/Stocksy; 30, M. Schuppich/Shutterstock; 31 (ALL), Mark Thiessen, NG Staff; 32, timquo/Shutterstock; 33, Laura Chase de Formigny; 35 (UP), Laura Chase de Formigny; 35 (LO), Viktar Malyshchyts/Shutterstock; 37, StockFood/Colin Erricson; 39, Laura Chase de Formigny; 41 (UP), Natalie Jeffcott/Stocksy; 41 (LO), princessdlaf/Getty Images; 43, Laura Chase de Formigny; 44-5, Rebecca Hale, NG Staff; 46 (UP), Volosina/Shutterstock; 46 (LO), StockFood/Sarah Hogan; 47, Darren Muir/Stocksy; 48, Brian McEntire/Shutterstock; 49, Laura Chase de Formigny; 50, Ross Woodhall/Getty Images; 51, Lili Blankenship/Shutterstock; 52, Alberto Bogo/Stocksy; 53, Catherine Hoggins/Alamy Stock Photo; 54, Darren Muir/Stocksy; 55, Mahathir Mohd Yasin/Shutterstock; 56, Brett Stevens/Getty Images; 57, Neyssa/LatinaMomMeals; 58, Neyssa/LatinaMomMeals; 59 (ALL), Mark Thiessen, NG Staff; 61, Laura Chase de Formigny; 62, Maks Narodenko/Shutterstock; 63, Laura Chase de Formigny; 64, Kirsty Begg/Stocksy; 65, Hero Images/Getty Images; 67, Laura Chase de Formigny; 68, Kkgas/Stocksy; 70-71, Pixelchrome Inc/Getty Images; 72, Laura Chase de Formigny; 74, Alanna Dumonceaux/Design Pics/Getty Images; 75 (UP), Lilian Rose/Alamy Stock Photo; 75 (LO), Clive Streeter/Getty Images; 76, Rebecca Hale, NG Staff; 77 (ALL), Rebecca Hale, NG Staff; 78, Eva Kosmas Flores; 79, Polly Thomas/Alamy Stock Photo; 80, Nicole Mlakar/Stocksy; 81, Hero Images/Getty Images; 82-3, Laura Chase de Formigny; 84, LuisPortugal/Getty Images; 85, Laura Chase de Formigny; 86, Laura Chase de Formigny; 87, Laura Chase de Formigny; 88, Tavia/Getty Images; 89 (ALL), Mark Thiessen, NG Staff; 90, Erika Ray/Offset; 91, JGI/Jamie Grill/Getty Images; 92, Laura Chase de Formigny; 93, Laura Chase de Formigny; 95 (ALL), Rebecca Hale, NG Staff; 96, Kris Bordessa; 97, Laura Chase de Formigny; 98 (BOTH), Laura Chase de Formigny; 99 (UP), Satit Sewtiw/Shutterstock; 99 (CTR and LO), Laura Chase de Formigny; 100, Laura Chase de Formigny; 101, Carey Shaw/Stocksy; 102, Rebecca Hale, NG Staff; 103 (ALL), Rebecca Hale, NG Staff; 104, Jake Fitzjones/Getty Images; 105, John Burke/Getty Images; 106, Katarina Radovic/Stocksy; 107, Laika One/Stocksy; 108-109, Trinette Reed/Stocksy; 110, Laura Chase de Formigny; 112, Eliza317/Getty Images; 113, Laura Chase de Formigny; 114, Martí Sans/Stocksy; 115, Carlos Huang/Shutterstock; 116, Lumina/Stocksy; 119, Laura Chase de Formigny; 120, Laura Chase de Formigny; 121 (ALL), Mark Thiessen, NG Staff; 123, Laura Chase de Formigny; 124, Laura Chase de Formigny; 126-7, Laura Chase de Formigny; 128, SaGa Studio/Shutterstock; 129, Harald Walker/Stocksy; 130, Tim UR/Shutterstock; 131 (UP), Igor Marusichenko/Shutterstock; 131 (LO), Laura Chase de Formigny; 133 (ALL), Mark Thiessen, NG Staff; 134, Laura Chase de Formigny; 135, Laura Chase de Formigny; 137, Laura Chase de Formigny; 138, Laura Chase de Formigny; 140, Laura Chase de Formigny; 141, Laura Chase de Formigny; 142 (UP), asharkyu/Shutterstock; 142 (LO), Imageman/Shutterstock; 143, EzumeImages/Getty Images; 144, Kkgas/Stocksy; 145, Laura Chase de Formigny; 147, Le Do/Shutterstock; 148-9, Trinette Reed/Stocksy; 150, J.R. Photography/Stocksy; 152, Helen Rushbrook/Stocksy; 153, yunava1/Getty Images; 154, Melanie DeFazio/Stocksy; 155, Duet Postscriptum/Stocksy; 156 (UP), Billion Photos/Shutterstock; 156 (LO), Joshua McCullough/Getty Images; 157, Cavan Images/Getty Images; 158-9, Laura Chase de Formigny; 160, Kris Bordessa; 161, schulzie/Getty Images; 162, Jiang Hongyan/Shutterstock; 163, Nadine Greeff/Stocksy; 164, tchara/Shutterstock; 165 (UP), Elena Zhukovskaya/Shutterstock; 165 (LO), Flower Studio/Shutterstock; 166, Kris Bordessa; 167, Kris Bordessa; 168, Rowena Naylor/Stocksy; 169, Johner Images/Getty Images; 170, Marco Govel/Stocksy; 171 (UP), Valentyn Volkov/Shutterstock; 171 (LO), Bisual Studio/Stocksy; 173, Laura Chase de Formigny; 175, living4media/Thomas Engelhardt; 176, Liliya Rodnikova/Stocksy; 177, Harald Walker/Stocksy; 178, Pete Broyles/Shutterstock; 179, Alistair Berg/Getty Images; 180, Charles Gullung/Offset; 181, Westend61/Konstantin Trubavin/Getty Images; 182 (ALL), Mark Thiessen, NG Staff; 185, Maarigard/Getty Images; 187 (ALL), Mark Thiessen, NG Staff; 189, Amanda Large/Stocksy; 190, Ann E Parry/Alamy Stock Photo; 191 (UP), Volosina/Shutterstock; 191 (LO), CatherineLProd/Shutterstock; 192, Jayme Burrows/Stocksy; 193, Jamie Hooper/Shutterstock; 194, Rowena Naylor/Stocksy; 195 (UP), living4media/Hans Gerlach; 195 (LO), living4media/TT News Agency/Peter Ericsson; 197, Laura Chase de Formigny; 198, Mint Images/Alamy Stock Photo; 199, Sara Winsnes/Johnér/Offset; 200, living4media/Foodcollection; 201, Kris Bordessa; 202, Christian Ferm/Folio/Getty Images; 203, living4media/Sibylle Pietrek; 204, scottledbetterstudio/Shutterstock; 205, Zoonar/j.wnuk/Getty Images; 206, Donald Specker/Animals Animals/age fotostock; 207, Ed-Ni-Photo/Getty Images; 208, Derek Harris/Alamy Stock Photo; 209 (UP), Muhammad Naaim/Shutterstock; 209 (LO), irin-k/Shutterstock; 210 (UP), Joseph De Sciose/age fotostock; 210 (LO), IrinaK/Shutterstock; 211, Ligak/Shutterstock; 212-13, Melanie DeFazio/Stocksy; 214, Urs Siedentop & Co/Stocksy; 216, Dionisvera/Shutterstock; 217, living4media/ETSA; 218, living4media/Friedrich Strauss; 219, StockFood/Rua Castilho; 220, markara/Shutterstock; 221, Zoonar/Peter Himmelhuber/Alamy Stock Photo; 222, itsabreeze photography/Getty Images; 223 (UP), typo-graphics/Getty Images; 223 (LO), Dave King/Getty Images; 224 (UP), David Hansom/Getty Images; 224 (LO), Paul Sutherland/National Geographic Image Collection; 225, AntiMartina/Getty Images; 226 (UP), Dani Vincek/Shutterstock; 226 (LO), Africa Studio/Shutterstock; 227 (UP), Mauro Grigollo/Stocksy; 227 (LO), Paul Tessier/Stocksy; 228, Isabel Subtil/Offset; 229, Laura Chase de Formigny; 231 (ALL), Mark Thiessen, NG Staff; 232, Evan Lorne/Shutterstock; 233, living4media/NouN; 234, Dave Bevan/Garden World Images Ltd./age fotostock; 235 (UP), hsagencia/Shutterstock; 235 (LO), Kris Bordessa; 236-7, Laura Chase de Formigny; 238, Aubrie LeGault/Stocksy; 239, Justine Di Fede/Stocksy; 240, Bonninstudio/Stocksy; 241, Raymond Forbes LLC/Stocksy; 242, Jennifer Esperanza/Getty Images; 243, Leon Werdinger/Alamy Stock Photo; 245 (ALL), Mark Thiessen, NG Staff; 246 (UP), Deirdre Malfatto/Stocksy; 246 (LO), koosen/Shutterstock; 247, Galina Mikhalishina/Shutterstock; 248, Lizard/Shutterstock; 249, Borislav Zhuykov/Stocksy; 250, Sergey Lavrentev/Shutterstock; 251, Stephen Morris/Stocksy; 252, Laura Chase de Formigny; 253, Jack Sorokin/Stocksy; 254-5, Melissa Goodwin; 256, Trinette Reed/Stocksy; 258, Hong Vo/Shutterstock; 259, Nathan Yan/Stocksy; 260, forest badger/Shutterstock; 261 (UP), Klaus Vedfelt/Getty Images; 261 (LO), Gallinago_media/Shutterstock; 262, Melissa Goodwin; 263, Melissa Goodwin; 264, Melissa Goodwin; 265, Laura Chase de Formigny; 267, Laura Chase de Formigny; 268, Melissa Goodwin; 269, Melissa Goodwin; 270 (BOTH), Melissa Goodwin; 271, Melissa Goodwin; 272-3, Rebecca Hale, NG Staff; 274, 4kodiak/Getty Images; 275, StockFood/Fotos mit Geschmack; 277 (ALL), Melissa Goodwin; 278, Peter Mulligan/Getty Images; 279, Thinglass/Shutterstock; 281, Rebecca Hale, NG Staff; 282, David Liittschwager/National Geographic Image Collection; 283 (UP), Babak Tafreshi/National Geographic Image Collection; 283 (LO), Steven R Smith/Shutterstock; 285, Jared Travnicek; 287, Hero Images/Getty Images; 288, Jared Travnicek; 289 (UP), Darlyne A. Murawski/National Geographic Image Collection; 289 (RT), Organica/Alamy Stock Photo; 289 (LO), Dwight Smith/Shutterstock; 291, Paul Schlemmer/Stocksy; 292 (UP LE), Anastasiia Malinich/Shutterstock; 292 (LO LE), domnitsky/Shutterstock; 292 (UP RT), spline_x/Shutterstock; 292 (CTR RT), Alfio Scisetti/Shutterstock; 292 (LO RT), Alfio Scisetti/Shutterstock; 293 (UP), StockFood/Syl Loves; 293 (LO), NinaM/Shutterstock; 294, Brent Hofacker/Shutterstock; 295, GARO/PHANIE/Alamy Stock Photo; 296, Kent Kobersteen/National Geographic Image Collection; 297, Sabine Lscher/Getty Images; 298 (ALL), Mark Thiessen, NG Staff; 299, Lumina/Stocksy; 301 (UP), Deirdre Malfatto/Stocksy; 301 (LO), flariv/Getty Images; 302, EAGiven/Getty Images; 303, Raymond Forbes LLC/Stocksy; 304, Laura Chase de Formigny; 307, Graham Taylor Photography/Shutterstock; 308, Rebecca Hale, NG Staff. Design ornaments from Chalkboard Lettering Project Creation Kit © Alexander Nedviga, www.youworkforthem.com.

Boldface indicates illustrations.

T

U

Since 1888, the National Geographic Society has funded more than 13,000 research, exploration, and preservation projects around the world. National Geographic Partners distributes a portion of the funds it receives from your purchase to National Geographic Society to support programs including the conservation of animals and their habitats.

National Geographic Partners
1145 17th Street NW
Washington, DC 20036-4688 USA

Get closer to National Geographic explorers and photographers, and connect with our global community. Join us today at nationalgeographic.com/join

For rights or permissions inquiries, please contact National Geographic Books Subsidiary Rights: bookrights@natgeo.com

Library of Congress Cataloging-in-Publication Data
Names: Bordessa, Kris, author.
Title: Attainable sustainable : the lost art of self-reliant living / Kris Bordessa.
Description: Washington, DC : National Geographic, 2020. | Includes bibliographical references and index. | Summary: "Based on the blog of the same name, Attainable Sustainable shows readers how to live a simpler, more self-reliant life. It includes instructions not only for growing and cooking food but also for creating artisanal items for the home as well as navigating the great outdoors"-- Provided by publisher.
Identifiers: LCCN 2019030815 | ISBN 9781426220548 (hardcover)
Subjects: LCSH: Sustainability. | Sustainable living. | Self-reliant living.
Classification: LCC GE196 .B67 2020 | DDC 640--dc23
LC record available at https://lccn.loc.gov/2019030815

Printed in the United States of America
20/VP-PCML/3

FOR THE FIELD
OR AT HOME
NATIONAL GEOGRAPHIC
BACKYARD GUIDE TO THE BIRDS OF NORTH AMERICA
SECOND EDITION
NATIONAL GEOGRAPHIC
Backyard Guide to Insects & Spiders of North America
ARTHUR V. EVANS
NATIONAL GEOGRAPHIC
BACKYARD GUIDE TO THE NIGHT SKY
SECOND EDITION
ANDREW FAZEKAS